39·24

CW00503933

Technical education and the state

Hilary Barnard

TECHNICAL EDUCATION AND THE STATE SINCE 1850:
Historical and contemporary perspectives

edited by
Penny Summerfield and Eric J. Evans

Manchester University Press
Manchester and New York

Distributed exclusively in the USA and Canada by St. Martin's Press

Published by Manchester University Press
Oxford Road, Manchester M13 9PL, UK
and Room 400, 175 Fifth Avenue,
New York, NY 10010, USA

Distributed exclusively in the USA and Canada
by St. Martin's Press, Inc.,
175 Fifth Avenue, New York, NY 10010, USA

British Library cataloguing in publication data
Technical education and the state since 1850.
1. Great Britain. Technical education, history
I. Summerfield, Penny II. Evans, Eric J. (Eric John),
1945–
607.41

Library of Congress cataloging in publication data
Technical education and the state since 1850 : historical and
  contemporary perspectives / edited by Penny Summerfield and Eric J. Evans.
    p.   cm.
  ISBN 0–7190–2967–8
    1. Technical education—Government policy—Great Britain—History.
  I. Summerfield, Penny.   II. Evans, Eric J.
  T107.T4   1990
  607′.1141—dc20   90–6000

Typeset by
Northern Phototypesetting Co Ltd, Bolton

Printed in Great Britain
by Billings of Worcester

Contents

Contributors

Bill Bailey works in the Faculty of Post-Compulsory Teacher Education at Thames Polytechnic where he is Deputy Head of the School of Pre-Service Teacher Education. He has published articles on the development of English technical and further education.

Ian Bliss is Senior Lecturer in Education at St Martin's College, Lancaster and has a particular interest in inter-cultural issues.

Martin Davis was formerly Senior Lecturer in History and Politics at Coventry Polytechnic.

Eric Evans is Professor of Social History at Lancaster University. He has published widely on eighteenth and nineteenth-century British political and social history, including '*The Forging of the Modern State: Early Industrial Britain*' (Longman, 1983). He also works in the field of school examinations and curriculum development.

Oliver Fulton is Head of the Department of Educational Research and a member of the Institute for Research and Development in Post-Compulsory Education at the University of Lancaster. His earlier academic posts were at the Universities of California (Berkeley) and Edinburgh. He has published extensively on education policy, especially in higher education.

Jim Garbett is Dean of Undergraduate Teacher Education at St Martin's College, Lancaster, and has interests in the ways that children in continental Europe are brought up and schooled.

Sarah King studied History at the University of Cambridge and went on to train as a teacher. She then undertook research for an MA degree at the University of Sussex, part of which was subsequently published as 'Feminists in teaching; the National Union of Women Teachers 1920–1940' in M. Lawn and G. Grace eds., *Teachers: The Culture and Politics of Work* (Falmer Press, London, 1987). For the past three years Sarah has been a Research Assistant in the School of Humanities, Thames Polytechnic. She is currently completing her PhD thesis and has just started training to become a solicitor.

Keith McClelland teaches part-time for Reading University and the Open University. He is the author of several articles on nineteenth-century British working-class history and co-editor of *E. P. Thompson: Critical Perspectives* (Polity Press, Cambridge, 1990).

Murray Saunders is a Senior Fellow of Lancaster University, and Director of the Institute for Research and Development in Post-Compulsory Education. He has published widely in the fields of technical education, work experience and school/industry links.

Penny Summerfield is Senior Lecturer in the Social History of Education at Lancaster University. She is author of *Women Workers in the Second World War* (Croom Helm, London, 1984; 2nd ed. Routledge, London, 1989) and co-author of *Out of the Cage. Women's Experiences in Two World Wars* (Pandora Press, London, 1987). She has also published articles on war and social change and on gender, class and schooling in the twentieth century. Her current project, funded by the ESRC, is on gender, training and employment 1939–1950.

David Thoms is Head of the Department of Humanities, Leicester Polytechnic. He has published widely in the field of education and business history.

Mel Vlaeminke is a Part-time Lecturer in the School of Education, University of Leicester. She taught in comprehensive schools for ten years before moving to Leicester to research the higher-grade schools. Her interests are in the history of education, equal opportunities and the pastoral curriculum.

Preface

This book grew out of a conference on Education and the Labour Market, held with Economic and Social Research Council funding at Lancaster University in April 1987. Many aspects of the labour market and many different types of education, from the mid nineteenth century to the present day, were discussed at that conference.[1] But recurring themes were the relationship of the state to the provision of technical education, and official and non-official expectations as to the kinds of employment to which such education should have, and in practice has, led. The useful interplay between the historical and sociological approaches which contributors brought to bear on these topics, and the importance which was attached to them by conference participants and others, led to the decision to compile this collection of essays. Some originated as papers given at the conference; others were added later to cover the ground historically and give the volume coherence. Though these essays represent only a fraction of the papers given at the conference, some of which have since been published separately,[2] all benefited from the discussions held during that wet April and we should like to take this opportunity of thanking all the participants and also the ESRC for its support.

Penny Summerfield
Eric Evans
Lancaster, August 1989

Notes

1 For a résumé of the conference proceedings see P. Summerfield, 'Education and the labour market', *History Workshop*, Issue 25, Spring 1988.
2 E.g. H. Hendrick, *Images of Youth. Age, Class and the Male Youth Problem 1880–1920*, Oxford, Clarendon Press, forthcoming 1990, ch. 8; P. Horn, 'The education and employment of working-class girls 1870–1914', *History of Education*, 17, 1, 1988; M. Rose, 'Social policy and business: parish apprentices and the early factory system 1750–1834', *Business History*, vol. 31, October 1989; P. Summerfield (ed.), *Women, Education and the Professions*, History of Education Society, Occasional Publication No. 8, 1987, essays by Janet Howarth, Helen Corr, Meta Zimmeck and Penny Summerfield.

Introduction: Technical education, the state and the labour market

Penny Summerfield and Eric Evans

Since 1851 technical education has been regarded by some as vitally important for economic success. In particular it has been urged that Britain's patchy economic performance since the Second World War has been the result of the inadequacies of British technical education, which is seen as languishing for want of status, funding and guidance. 'The state' (of which more shortly) is frequently held responsible for failing to give technical education the support it has needed over the last century.[1] A more meta-historical approach to the apparent lack of commitment to technical education in Britain compared with other countries, notably Germany, has also been developed. Most recently and influentially these failings have been explained by Wiener as the product of a British culture antipathetical both ' cience, particularly applied science, and to entreprenurial activity. Engineering, he argued, was considered 'not a suitable career' for the sons of manufacturers aspiring to the status of gentleman and he cited lively correspondence from the *New Statesman* as recently as 1976 which testified to the continuing low perceived status in Britain of applied science in general, and engineering in particular, compared with the rest of Europe.[2] Correlli Barnett explained British inadequacies as the result of British leaders' anachronistic commitment to a military–political role as a world power.[3]

Such grandiose explanations are not necessarily helpful. A closer scrutiny of the history of technical education in this country may provide more clues both about the role that it has played in economic and social development and its limitations. This close scrutiny is the purpose of this book. Contributors examine aspects of the development of technical education as it occurred at different times and in various institutional and non-institutional forms since the 1850s.

In order to set these contributions in context three themes will be explored briefly here. The first concerns problems of definition. How technical education has been understood has been a key aspect of the debate about its role in the education system and in society. Secondly, and importantly given the burden of responsibility so often placed upon it, is the issue of the role of the state. This raises a number of questions, for example what is meant by 'the state', why one might expect it to intervene, and what the relationship has been between central and local government in the development of technical education. The third theme concerns the labour market. How have employers responded to the products of technical education, and to what extent can they be held responsible for its development and shortcomings?

Definitions of technical education[4]

C. T. Millis stated in *Technical Education* in 1925 that the objectives of technical education were 'to provide instruction in the principles of art and science applicable to industry and in the application of special branches of art and science to specific industries and employment'.[5] He was drawing on definitions offered since the 1870s. His definition could be said to embrace both technical and technological education, terms about which there has been considerable confusion, reflected for example in their interchangeability in the title of the Board of Education's 'T' branch established in 1901. But his statement did not tackle the most fundamental definitional problem concerning technical education in that period, that is, the relative importance within it of theory and practice. The implications of this relationship are far-reaching: if technical education was mainly theoretical it could be subsumed into a redefined 'liberal education', as T. H. Huxley would have liked in 1877, when he wrote that technical education was 'simply a good education, with more attention to physical science, to drawing, and to modern languages than is common, and there is nothing specially technical about it'.[6] Concurrence with this view came from Bernhard Samuelson, another Victorian campaigner for technical education, who in 1890 provided James Bryce with a definition almost identical to that which the Bryce Commission later used for secondary education. Technical education, said Samuelson, was 'everything which prepares a man or a woman for the walk of life which he or she intends to pursue'.[7] 'Walks of life' could obviously be more or less lofty. But the idea that technical education should be occupational preparation of the most general kind was applied to both the higher and the lower ranks of industry. Managers would benefit from such education, wrote Alfred Marshall in 1890, and the Bryce Commission urged that at the other end of the scale the appropriate preparation for intending apprentices was a general technical education.[9]

Samuelson's even-handedness towards the sexes was relatively unusual. The more practically oriented definitions of technical education obliterated women. Such definitions throw into sharper relief the problems of how to conceptualise the teaching of technical subjects, whether as 'training' or 'education', and what the most appropriate learning environment might be: the workshop (assumed to be a male enclave) or the classroom. There was agreement that the workshop was 'the only real school for handicraft'.[9] It was a contention with which employers and trade unionists largely concurred, both wishing for their own reasons to maintain control of the transmission of skills, as Keith McClelland demonstrates in his study of engineering and shipbuilding apprenticeships in the period 1850–1914 (see Chapter 1). Thomas, in Chapter 2, however, gives an example of institutionalised technical education which was popular with employers, parents and pupils in Coventry between 1900 and 1939. The conditions of success in Coventry appear to have been that such education was practically oriented, and that it supplied trained workers to new industries endeavouring to attract a new workforce but with no tradition of workshop apprenticeships.

'Education' in the scientific and artistic principles on which an industrial undertaking depended could occur in isolation from 'training' in 'the actual carrying out of the different trades'.[10] But if technical education lacked a practical element it was open to the accusation of irrelevance. It was increasingly urged in the 1880s that even theoretical technical education should contain some practical component, if no more than the general 'training of hand and eye'.[11] Under the Technical Instruction Act of 1889, passed to enable the newly formed local authorities to supply or aid technical instruction from the rates, technical education meant in practice a combination of the teaching of general principles with some manual instruction. This was the case even though the terms of the Act ruled out the teaching of a trade as such, as it did in the plans for the London polytechnics founded from 1891 using money from the City Parochial Charities, unless that trade could not be learnt in the workshop or place of business.

The optimum balance between the teaching of general principles and practical trade-specific skills was a matter of contention. It continued to be so throughout the twentieth century, for example in the context of the debates about technical education for adolescents in the period 1905–45 which Bailey discusses in Chapter 5. But the idea was that the instruction developed by the City and Guilds of London

3

Institute established in 1881, under the 1889 Act, and in the technical colleges and polytechnics, would in general supplement practical experience in employment. The kinds of employment envisaged were mainly in trade and industry, but as Millis pointed out in 1925, there was no logical reason why the concept of technical education, understood as the teaching of the principles of art and science applicable to industry, could not be applied to education for the professions and services.[12] The dividing line between technical and vocational education was and remains a hazy one.

However, any association of 'higher' education (embracing in the period to 1944 both secondary and university education) with technical education was, in practice, hotly resisted by the architects of the reformed system of secondary education from 1902. Both Vlaeminke and Bailey stress this in Chapters 3 and 5. The university sector remained sceptical about the link also, throughout the period up to and including the late 1950s, as Davis demonstrates in Chapter 6. The reasons for resistance suggested in this book are consistent with Wiener's interpretation of the relation between British culture and education. They concern both status and class. The secondary schools and universities were seen by those running them as offering varieties of cultural preparation for a very different place in the occupational, and hence class, structure from those to which the recipients of technical education were expected to aspire. The practical component in technical education confirmed its low status character.

This attitude survived the 1944 Education Act in spite of the plans for the 'tripartite' reorganisation of secondary education into grammar, modern and technical schools advocated before and after its passing, and the statutory duty placed on local authorities to provide further education, intended to embrace the plethora of technical colleges and similar institutions, which had grown up since the nineteenth century. There was no guidance on organisation in the Act itself and no attempt to define technical education in the clauses dealing with either the secondary or the further education sectors. Indeed, due to the difficulty of definition and consequent possibility of excluding some subjects from eligibility for grants, mention of 'technical, commercial and art subjects' was removed from the clause of the education bill which explained that local authorities could fulfil their duties with respect to further education by providing 'full-time and part-time education for persons over compulsory school age'.[13] As Bailey argues, technical education played a minor role in secondary reorganisation partly because its lobbyists (the Technical Branch of the Ministry of Education and the professional technical associations) favoured technical colleges (now incorporated in the further education sector) above schools, and partly because the Secondary Branch of the Ministry was, in accordance with tradition, unenthusiastic about incorporating technical education into secondary schooling.

However, by the late 1970s, with comprehensive schooling largely in place, it became impossible to maintain the schizophrenia of the selective system. Post-war grammar schools had denied that they had any technical or vocational orientation while at the same time acting as feeders to the professions, management and clerical work; secondary modern schools claimed to feed the lower ranks of clerical work and all types of manual employment while being denied resources to undertake effective technical education. Comprehensive secondary education prepared the ground for the acceptance of efforts by government in the late 1970s and the 1980s to make secondary education more 'relevant' to employment. The problem of definition nevertheless remained. In the early stages of the Technical and Vocational Education Initiative (TVEI), as Saunders shows in Chapter 8, technical and vocational education was understood to imply a specific curriculum content – 'technical' subjects like Information Technology, Electronics and 'Craft, Design and Technology', and 'vocational' ones like business education, food technology, community care and horticulture. But gradually during the 1980s the understanding of TVEI shifted to a curricular orientation which permitted variety of content, characterised by a commitment to learning experiences 'beyond the classroom', that is, in places of work.

Girls were written into the TVEI scheme as a result of a deliberate attempt to make the initiative work for equal opportunities, with the aim of increasing the technical competence of the labour supply without regard to gender.[14] Their place in technical education had been constrained since the demise of the higher grade schools in 1900. Vlaeminke argues in Chapter 3 that girls as well as boys left higher grade schools well qualified in science and mathematics and that parents and girls themselves resisted the provision of a distinctively 'feminine' curriculum. This is not to suggest that manual instruction in wood- and metal-work was available to girls; such a crossing of gender boundaries with its occupational implications would have been inconceivable in the nineteenth century. But the unpopularity of needlework and the other domestic subjects provided in their stead, and the female demand for maths and science, signal a struggle against some of the

5

kinds of gender stereotyping which limited girls' chances in the labour market.

However, the definition of appropriate technical and vocational education for girls hardened in the central schools (by which higher grade schools were replaced). These provided a substitute for 'genuine' secondary education for some working and lower middle class children in the period 1911–44. As King discusses in Chapter 4, the Board of Education effectively wrote girls out of industrial training using a definition of labour-market demands that was possibly even more narrow than the reality. Technical subjects for girls were limited to the various branches of domestic economy and needlework. Within this confined space girls experienced the same problems in relation to employment as boys. School training was not as practical as an apprenticeship, nor did it provide entry to a trade. On the other hand vocational training in clerical work, where apprenticeships did not exist, could advantage central school girls by providing them with occupationally useful skills which 'genuine' secondary schools not only did not teach, but also looked down upon because they led to relatively low status (non-professional) occupations.

Like secondary schools, universities have since the 1960s slowly and somewhat painfully accommodated themselves to the view that they have a role in relation to employment. They have not, however, readily embraced the terms 'technical' and 'vocational'. Since the recommendation of the Robbins Committee in 1963 that the Colleges of Advanced Technology should be admitted to university status, universities have haltingly accepted that their role is to prepare students for jobs, not only as doctors and teachers (occupations for which there has been a long higher education tradition), but in fields ranging from Technology and Information Technology to Social Work. Fulton (Chapter 7) demonstrates the difficulties involved in determining what kind of preparation might be appropriate and how close the relationship between university education and employment should be. Fulton's focus is on policymakers, and it is to the role of the state that we must now turn our attention.

Technical education and the state

Informed concern with the quality of technical education available in Britain dates from the period of the so-called 'Great Depression' in the last quarter of the nineteenth century. As has been convincingly demonstrated, 'Depression' is a misleading term, since British economic performance between 1870 and 1914 was, on the whole, effective. The 'Depression', real enough in arable agriculture, was, in the industrial sector, more in the minds of businessmen finding it increasingly difficult to fight off competition from the USA and Germany.[15]

Business perceptions, however, were vitally important. Examples of state-directed education geared directly to the production of highly qualified technologists were widely used to explain Britain's backwardness and alleged ineffectiveness in foreign competition. In Germany, for example, substantial state funding of *Technische Hochschulen* had seen these establishments achieve broad comparability with universities by 1900. Martin Wiener suggests that the educational system in Britain was vital in the nurturing of 'a national elite' whose culture and beliefs were anti-competitive. The standards of this elite, steeped by a 'liberal education' in the classics and the humanities, Wiener argues, 'did little to support, and much to discourage, economic dynamism'. Britain by the end of Victoria's reign had surrendered that 'capacity for innovation and assertion' which was vital to commercial success.[16]

Simple cause-and-effect explanations of this kind inevitably oversimplify. Inadequate provision for technical education could at most have been only one factor in the complex story of Britain's industrial decline. It is also striking that, at the very time when the damaging connection between poor economic performance and inadequate educational provision was being made, scientific subjects were making important strides in both public school and university curricula. In 1900, 27 per cent of Cambridge undergraduates passing Part 1 of the Tripos were reading Natural Sciences. More graduates were going into business by 1914 than ever before.[17]

Wiener is surely right to stress, however, that the prevailing ethic in British education for most of the period under study was anti-practical. Education was conceived hierarchically and in terms of provision appropriate for the different classes. The ethos, if not the specific recommendations, of the Taunton Commission, which reported in 1868, still prevailed at the end of the nineteenth century. The Commissioners proposed to divide schools into three categories, intending those from the smaller business and shopkeeping classes to leave school at sixteen and go into commerce or industry. Only the landowning and higher business classes were expected to pursue higher education. Irrespective of the higher education curriculum, as Harold Perkin has recently shown, the orientation of the university-trained mind was towards public service, where 'practical' or technical skills were of limited value and no kudos. 'In contemporary terms', he argues, 'this meant service of the public in politics, the home Civil Service, administration of the empire, and the liberal professions.' Here, 'service to the community should come before the pursuit of profit'.[19]

Even had the ethic been otherwise, mighty obstacles would still have stood in the way of the formulation of a national policy for technical education. Most forms of social policy developed locally, within a broadly permissive national framework, and were subordinate in importance to charitable activity and individual initiative. The commitment to voluntary and local effort derived not only from the concern for economy but also from the belief, fervently held by most MPs before 1900, that social questions were best tackled locally. The Municipal Corporations Act of 1835 had provided an appropriate administrative framework within which this ideology could flourish. The natural fears of backbench MPs that the state could emerge as an overbearing and bureaucratic regulator harmonised with the perceptions of dominant political leaders like Gladstone that government should be both cheap and efficient.

Nineteenth-century educational reform was based on the principle that the state might subsidise, but would not direct, provision. Until 1870, it provided grants in aid of going concerns – the Church schools – and after the Elementary Education Act of 1870 also permitted local rates to be raised to support Board schools. It did, of course, reserve the right to determine the conditions under which its support was provided and it appointed Inspectors to ensure that state money was not wasted. State support for education was not directed towards maximising the educational potential of working class children. As Robert Lowe sternly noted when pushing through the Revised Code governing grants paid to elementary schools in 1862: 'We do not profess to give these children an education that will raise them above their station and business in life; that is not our object, but to give them an education that may fit them for that business.'[19]

The same principle informed the Science and Art Department grants paid from 1852 in respect of specific technical courses, on the basis of examination results. The state was providing a framework within which voluntary effort might be supplemented in the case of elementary education, or both supplemented and aided in the case of technical education, by local authorities. Local taxation to fund local policies was the key in both cases; rates fed the development of elementary education after 1870, and rates, plus a local tax on the sale of beer and spirits, made public funds available for both local technical colleges and technical and scientific classes within schools after the Technical Instruction Act of 1889.

Such an approach necessitated a wide variety of provision. Its main potential advantage was the freedom to develop imaginatively to suit local needs. This apparently happened in the case of Coventry in the period 1900–39 as Thoms argues in Chapter 2. Its disadvantages included a lack of consistency in standards (though central government inspection linked to grant giving provided some regulation), and the likelihood that, while in some localities much would be accomplished, in others nothing would be done, or that education would be overwhelmed by competing demands for other types of provision (housing, lighting, drainage, social security, etc.). There were signs that the latter posed problems for technical education even in Coventry with its relatively good record of provision, and also in other large industrial cities such as Leeds.[20] The *laissez-faire* approach naturally conflicted with government belief that 'something should be done' and that government should offer leadership as to what.

Nowhere was this clearer than in the case of secondary education, with major implications for technical provision. The secondary sector followed, rather than led, elementary and technical education into the rate-aided local-authority-controlled framework in 1902, but it profoundly influenced the shape of education in these other sectors. In the initial phase of secondary reform from 1869, the state did no more than arrange for the 'modernisation' of the statutes governing the charities on which secondary schools had been founded to enable those schools to serve local communities more effectively. But such an objective conflicted with the intention of some schools to serve, not the locality, but the nation. By the end of the nineteenth century the concept of the national interest in a particular form of secondary education was becoming dominant. This was a 'liberal education' dominated by the classics and bolstered by other literary subjects and non-applied sciences. This concept, as we have seen, was considered by many to be the antithesis of what was understood by a 'technical education'. The vision of the early twentieth-century policy-makers required a more directive role for the development of such secondary schools in every locality than had been followed by their nineteenth-century forebears (Kay-Shuttleworth not excluded) in any area of education.

Analyses of the impact of such directiveness on elementary and technical education are provided by Vlaeminke and Bailey, in

9

Chapters 3 and 5. The argument briefly is that, in order to protect the version of secondary education favoured by the Board of Education, local initiatives to develop higher elementary or higher grade schools with largely technical and vocational curricula were stifled. Such technical and vocational initiatives were popular locally but they threatened 'genuine' secondary education, by deflecting the 'appropriate' recipients of such education (members of the various ranks of the middle class) and by offering the working classes an education above their station. The dominant educational administrator of the Edwardian age, Sir Robert Morant, could see merit in plucking from the elementary system 'individual children who show promise of exceptional capacity' in order to 'develop their special gifts'.[21] But this was a secondary objective to forming and strengthening the character of the mass of elementary pupils in ways which would have won the approval of Robert Lowe half a century earlier, and the tiny minority of the brightest and best were to be steered, via scholarships, into secondary education and perhaps on to university, and certainly not into local technical colleges.

The stifling process confined technical education within narrower bounds than the generous ones proposed by Huxley and Samuelson. Under the Higher Elementary School Minute of 1900 the curriculum was to be theoretical but not so abstract as to overlap with, and thus challenge, what was done in secondary schools. Yet its practical and applied component was limited by the contention we have already reviewed, that technical education should be about principles rather than the acquisition of skills. This was underpinned by the general reluctance of employers and trade unionists to support trade schools over apprenticeships, and by other constraints such as the problems for local authorities of providing adequate equipment for the teaching of actual industrial processes. Secondary schools, on the other hand, were not to 'descend' to the kinds of applied and vocational subjects dealt with in technical schools, in their various guises. Between 1900 and 1980 these have included the higher elementary schools discussed by Vlaeminke, the technical colleges for adults (offering, from the 1920s, nationally recognised certification in the form of Ordinary and Higher National Certificates and Diplomas), the junior technical schools mainly for boys discussed by Bailey (Chapter 5), the central schools described by King (Chapter 4), and after 1944 the secondary modern schools which inherited the mantle dropped by the central schools but with even lower status, since they were increasingly seen as sponges soaking up the grammar school 'rejects', despite providing secondary education for 70–80 per cent of the population.

How are we to understand why a *laissez-faire* state reneged on the principle of self-help so positively demonstrated by the higher grade schools of the late nineteenth century? Its behaviour does not appear to fit prevailing models of the state in modern industrial societies. In such societies, educational policy should serve to supply private employers and the government with the kinds of workers they need: in the ranks of the salaried these would be managers and foremen on the one hand, and civil servants and professionals on the other; at the manual level, they would be adaptable, docile and hardworking wage labourers. Education would also have to produce women who would be both compliant servicers of men and reproducers of children, and potential paid workers. Crudely, this is what the German and French educational systems were designed to do. By contrast, the British system of 'liberal education' emphasised the ethic of service for senior government employees and other professionals and assumed that this ethic was also what industry required for its owners and managers. Vocational training was otiose, if not actually demeaning.

This was the case even after the Second World War had demonstrated Britain's shortage of technologists, and a higher technological qualification was urged by the Percy and Barlow Committees of 1945 and 1946. As Davis shows in Chapter 6, industrialists were not consulted about the best way to supply them or the numbers required. There was a yawning gulf of misunderstanding between the civil servants who might have enquired as to the nature and demands of technology, and industrialists who could have expressed an informed view. In this void, the achievement of a higher technological qualification foundered on the rival interests of the universities, technical colleges and professional engineering associations.

Technical education was not to be given a national direction. By the late 1950s official faith returned to the ability of local authorities to supply the kinds of technical training required in local technical colleges. In the words of Burgess and Pratt, 'if the colleges were to respond to local industrial demand, they had to meet those demands locally'.[22] The Ministry of Education agreed to let the market dictate what they offered, which meant, in the post-war context, increasingly advanced work. Hence the locally devised, though nationally accredited, Diploma in Technology of 1955. However, the Ministry of Education was not consistently *laissez-faire* in its approach. The national interest was deemed to dictate the emergence of a hierarchy of institutions, topped by a chosen few doing the most advanced work.

Colleges of Advanced Technology (CATs) were thus removed from local authority control in 1962 and, as we have seen, granted full university status in 1966.

In spite of this development, the government was committed to a division between a national system of essentially autonomous universities and a locally-controlled set of technical colleges. The technical colleges remained theoretically responsive to local social and industrial needs, providing a wide range of courses from the most elementary to the most advanced, to both full- and part-time students. The high level of demand for increasingly advanced work in such colleges, and the absence of evidence of unfilled demand for university places in science and technology contributed to the creation by the government in 1966 of thirty polytechnics from existing technical colleges. The locally controlled polytechnics have since the 1960s made increasingly strong claims for parity with the universities. After much debate about their anomalous position as locally controlled institutions granting degrees they finally, in April 1989, followed the trail blazed by the CATs twenty-seven years earlier, and left LEA control.

Only very recently has the government made efforts to circumvent the interests of rival educational institutions and professional bodies in order to achieve a closer national *rapprochement* between education and employers. The political process involved in the case of the Technical and Vocational Education Initiative directed at secondary schools is analysed by Saunders (see Chapter 8), while in Chapter 7 Fulton discusses latest attempts to change the orientation of universities through, for example, the Enterprise in Higher Education scheme and the replacement of the more academic University Grants Council by the more employer-dominated University Funding Council. Other examples of similar steps include new funding arrangements by 'Work Related Non-Advanced Further Education' introduced in 1985/6 to involve employers in the development of FE syllabi and obtain their commitment to employing the products of these courses,[23] and the inclusion of employers on the governing bodies of FE colleges, schools and institutions of higher education under the 1988 Education Act.

Why such efforts to address the 'needs of industry' and to draw both employers into education and education into the workplace are of such recent origin is something of a puzzle. It is as if Britain, the nineteenth-century workshop of the world, created a state committed to reproducing itself rather than to regenerating the higher ranks of industry and business on which its wealth in fact depended. But nineteenth-century

Britain, compared with other European countries, developed relatively representative structures of government, especially at local level. One way of seeing the political process within a representative system is as the interaction of a collection of interest groups attempting to influence government policy in competition with each other. While technical education had its advocates, they were on the whole small groups of individuals, some of whom were industrialists (such as Samuelson), but many of whom were scientists or professionals (like Huxley and the professional societies of technologists working in industry and commerce, such as the various Engineering Institutes). Employers as such did not form a powerful interest group prepared to urge state-directed technical education. For clues as to why that was so we must address the question of the relation between technical education and the labour market.

Technical education and the labour market

It has been widely felt that employers have turned their backs on technical education because they refuse to accept its advantages. This apparently irrational behaviour requires explanation. One interpretation is that employers have long distrusted booklearning, preferring practical experience. The industrial revolution, so the argument goes, was based on a combination of the experience of practical men and the enthusiasm and capital of gentlemen amateurs.[24] Thus a tradition developed in which there was no space for the trained professional. As D. S. Landes has written: 'even when employers did come to recognize the need for trained technical personnel, they yielded grudgingly. The underpaid "scientists" were put in sheds, reclaimed workrooms, and other improvised quarters that hardly permitted controlled conditions and accurate tests. Their work was one cut above the rule-of-thumb techniques of the skilled workman; it was far below that of the German laboratory researcher.'[25] Ambitious school leavers and university graduates, the argument continues, looked towards other occupations, reinforcing the low status and backwardness of British industry and commerce. In contrast, in an effort to catch up with British economic development, the German state in the late nineteenth century systematised its scientific and technical training and German employers, small as well as large, offered key positions to the graduates of its *Hochschulen* and universities.

This picture of nineteenth-century British employers is one of a demand for proficiency rather than principles. Since for the reasons we have reviewed, technical schools and colleges emphasised the latter, employers could, according to this interpretation, be expected to reject their products. Evidence abounds of the continuity of such attitudes in the twentieth century. In 1909, for example, the Board of Education reported 'a strong preference for the man trained from an early age in the works, and a prejudice against the so-called "college-trained man" '.[26] In the 1950s industrialists complained that the university product 'was too academic, too remote from industrial reality, barely interested in production and seeing his future in a university or research establishment rather than industry'.[27] Such an attitude may have been reinforced by employers' interest in keeping down the salaries of their managers and technicians. Additionally, unions as well as employers preferred apprenticeships as routes of entry to industrial jobs since this system of training offered opportunities for control over the size of the skilled workforce and the economic value of the skills transmitted. Another perennial which found expression from the 1870s to the 1950s was the fear that training and job mobility would lead to the disclosure or devaluing of trade secrets.[28]

Underlying the implied criticism of these employer attitudes is the assumption that in order to improve economic performance employers ought to want to employ technically trained individuals (almost always assumed to be men, such is the gender division of labour). As Fulton shows in Chapter 7, the arguments urged in the higher education sphere since 1960 have been based on claims that more and better-qualified scientific and technical manpower would represent a raising of 'human capital' to the general benefit of society as well as to the specific advantage of individual employers.

Taking a longer time perspective, it might be useful to ask whether the changing occupational structure suggests that employers should have been demanding and making use of technically trained personnel. Guy Routh shows that the main trends in the labour market between 1911 and 1971 have been away from manual jobs and towards jobs in the professional, managerial and clerical categories. Foremen and skilled, semi-skilled and unskilled workers together still constitute the majority of paid employees, but the proportion declined over the sixty years from 81 to 63 per cent of all those in paid employment. In 1985 it stood at about 52 per cent of the male labour force while only 35 per cent of employed women come into these categories. The distribution within them has been uneven: between 1911 and 1971 the proportion of foremen increased, that of skilled and semi-skilled workers fell, and that of unskilled workers rose. But the most dramatic rise in the occupational structure has been in the proportion of clerks, from 5 to 15 per cent of all those in paid employment. The numbers and proportions of professionals have also risen dramatically, from 4 to 11 per cent. Those of employers and managers have risen relatively slightly, from 10 to 12·5 per cent.[29]

These figures do not in themselves present an *a priori* case for more technical education defined as education in the principles of art and science applicable to industry, except in so far as the growing proportions of employers, managers and foremen might need to be aware of such principles and the diminishing proportion of skilled and semi-skilled workers might need more training in them because of the greater complexity of their work in an increasingly technological (and labour saving) society. The argument really hinges on the content of the job, rather than what will often be arbitrary and fixed occupational categories. One of the most powerful arguments against institutionalised technical and vocational preparation and in favour of on-the-job training is that an immense variety of specific jobs exists and they change rapidly. As Fulton observes in the context of his discussion of higher education since 1960, 'there is . . . no course less vocationally relevant than one that trains solely for a non-existent vocation'.[30]

On the other hand, the picture painted above of employers' resistance since 1850 to the technically trained manual worker, scientist or technologist significantly distorts the history of the relationship between employers and education. Though, as we have already stated, employers have not formed a national lobby demanding the expansion of technical and vocational education, a long roll call of individual employers who have supported such education can be compiled – starting with those who generously endowed civic colleges in the nineteenth century, like the steelmasters who endowed Firth College, Sheffield in order to train metallurgists, and the City and Guilds of London Institute which founded the first two technical colleges in London in 1881.[31]

But then, as now, there was uncertainty among employers about the best sort of preparation for employment in industry and commerce. Thoms' work on Coventry (Chapter 2) provides a case of a group of employers who did have a relatively clear and unified idea of what they wanted from institutionalised technical education, in the context of rapidly expanding automobile and electrical goods industries. But they were not typical, and at the end of the period did not form an effective pressure group to ensure that the town council would not prioritise other demands on its spending, or that central government would help the council to meet the demand for technical education. There is much evidence to suggest that employers nationally have favoured 'a good general education' as the appropriate preparation for work in their enterprises, whether within the elementary sphere for manual workers or within higher education for others. General education should perhaps widen its scope beyond the prevailing literary bias, as employers urged the Prime Minister's Committee on Natural Science in 1918, and embrace the 'scientific principles on which industrial processes are based'.[32] But employers, it has been argued, could organise any specific training that was required.[33] If, as Fulton suggests, manpower planning is a mug's game, this is a rational response. We are back to Huxley's at first sight unhelpful definition of technical education as 'simply a good education'.

This volume presents essays which raise some fundamental questions about the relationship between employers, the state and technical education. For example, could, or should, the British state act for employers in devising forms of education appropriate in industrial and commercial terms? The commitment to localism in education might have achieved such an outcome (as indeed it appeared to do episodically in specific cases). But the capacity for local initiatives to supply such education was limited by the prior orientation of policy-makers at a national level to a separate, high-status variety of secondary and higher education. Until the very recent past, this has precluded a technical or vocational element, in either the broad sense of an education relating closely to the world of work or even the more focused sense of the teaching of the principles and the practice of art and science applicable to industrial and other types of employment. Employers may not have acted in more united ways to press for 'technical' education simply because they have not felt sufficiently competent in matters of educational policy and practice to do so. They may also be too influenced by the kinds of education they themselves experienced. Finally, why has the British state not looked abroad, and copied the apparently successful recipes of, for example, Germany and Japan with regard to technical education? The development of technical education in Britain, in terms of institutions, values and policy, as discussed in this book, may help to answer this question, especially since, as Bliss and Garbett argue in the final chapter, educational systems cannot develop independently of the social structures and cultures in which they are embedded, and thus cannot be reoriented by simplistic assimilation of foreign models.

A theme running throughout the book is that the potential for meeting the needs of the changing British industrial and social system has depended overwhelmingly on whose needs are both articulated and listened to within the state. The essays urge, from different historical standpoints, that the absence of an effective lobby of employers demanding technical education, the tension between local autonomy and central direction, and the institutionalisation of values antipathetical to practical training in the educational structure, have been crucial in limiting the provision of technical education. In short, Wiener's cultural and attitudinal explanation of the low status of technical education in Britain is only part of the story.

Notes

1 E.g. M. Sanderson, *Educational Opportunity and Social Change in England*, Faber, London, 1987; G. W. Roderick and M. D. Stephens, *Education and Industry in the Nineteenth Century: the English Disease?*, Longman, London, 1978.

2 M. Wiener, *English Culture and the Decline of the Industrial Spirit 1850–1980*, Cambridge University Press, Cambridge, 1981, pp. 132–5.

3 Correlli Barnett, *The Audit of War: The Illusion and Reality of Britain as a Great Nation*, London, Macmillan, 1986.

4 For a useful introduction see P. W. Musgrave, *Sociology, History and Education: a Reader*, Methuen, London, 1970, chapter 5.

5 C. T. Millis, *Technical Education: Its Development and Aims*, Edward Arnold, London, 1925, p. 2.

6 T. H. Huxley, *Collected Essays*, Vol. III, London, 1893, pp. 411–12.

7 Royal Commission on Secondary Education (Bryce Commission), Vol. 1, 1895, Questions 6243–8 for Samuelson's definition and pp. 135–6 for the Commission's definition: '[Secondary education] is the education of the boy or girl not simply as a human being who needs to be instructed in the mere rudiments of knowlege, but it is a process of intellectual training and personal discipline conducted with special regard to the profession or trade to be followed.'

8 A. Marshall, *Principles of Economics: An Introductory Volume*, Macmillan, London, 1890, p. 209; Bryce Commission, Vol. 1, 1895, pp. 133–4.

9 Huxley, *Collected Essays*, pp. 411–12.

10 Report of a committee formed to investigate how certain Livery Companies of the City of London could assist Technical Education, 1877, quoted by Millis, *Technical Education*, p. 56.

11 E.g. Royal Commission into the Elementary Education Act (England and Wales) (Cross Commission), *Final Report*, 1888, p. 146.

12 Millis, *Technical Education*, p. 2.

13 P. F. R. Venables, *Technical Education: Its Aims, Organisation and Future Development*, Bell, London, 1956, p. 3.

14 Val Millman and Gaby Weiner, 'Engendering equal opportunities: the case of TVEI' in D. Gleeson (ed.). *TVEI and Secondary Education: a Critical Appraisal*, Open University Press, Milton Keynes, 1987, pp. 167–8.

15 S. B. Saul, *The Myth of the Great Depression*, Macmillan, London, 1969; W. Beckerman (ed.), *Slow Growth in Britain: Causes and Consequences*, Blackwell, Oxford, 1979.

16 M. Wiener, *English Culture*, p. 158.

17 E. Royle, *Modern Britain: A Social History, 1750–1985*, Arnold, London, 1987, p. 372.

18 H. J. Perkin, *The Rise of Professional Society: England since 1880*, Routledge, London, 1989, pp. 370, 374.

19 *Hansard*, 3rd ser., clxv, col. 238, 13 February 1862.

20 E. W. Jenkins, 'Junior Technical Schools 1905–45: the case of Leeds', *History of Education*, 16, 2, 1987. See also Bill Bailey, 'The development of technical education 1934–1939', *History of Education*, 16, 1, 1987.

21 Perkin, *Rise of Professional Society*, p. 165.

22 T. Burgess and J. Pratt, *Technical Education in the United Kingdom*, Organisation for Economic Co-operation and Development, n.d. [1971], p. 26.

23 Department of Employment/Department of Education and Science, *Training for Jobs*, cmnd. 9135, HMSO, London, 1984; Further Education Unit, *Work-Related Non-Advanced Further Education*, FEU, London, 1987.

24 D. C. Coleman, 'Gentlemen and players', *Economic History Review*, 26, 1, 1973.

25 D. S. Landes, *The Unbound Prometheus: Technological Changes and Industrial Development in Western Europe from 1750 to the Present*, Cambridge University Press, Cambridge, 1969, p. 346.

26 Board of Education, *Report* (1908–9), p. 90.

27 Burgess and Pratt, *Technical Education*, p. 25.

28 See Musgrave, *Sociology, History and Education*, p. 155.

29 G. Routh, *Occupation and Pay in Great Britain 1906–79*, Macmillan, London, 1980, pp. 5–8. See also *Social Trends*, 17, 1987, p. 75.

30 See p. 157.

31 Roderick and Stephens, *Education and Industry*, chapters 4, 5 and 6.

32 Parliamentary Papers, *Report of the committee appointed to enquire into the position of Natural Science in the Educational System of Great Britain*, Cd. 9011, HMSO, London, 1918, p. 40.

33 For a detailed historical discussion of such employer expectations see H. Silver, *Education as History*, Methuen, London, 1983, chapter 8, and for an analysis relating to the recent past, see O. Fulton, 'Needs, expectations and responses: new pressures on higher education', *Higher Education*, Vol. 13, No. 2, 1984. For a more general discussion of changing attitudes to the relationship between industrial employment and education since the nineteenth century, see D. Reeder, 'A recurring debate; education and industry' in G. Bernbaum (ed.), *Schooling in Decline*, Macmillan, London, 1979.

ONE

The transmission of collective knowledge: apprenticeship in engineering and shipbuilding, 1850–1914

Keith McClelland

There is widespread agreement that British capitalism continued to depend on the supply of relatively abundant reserves of skilled labour between 1850 and 1914.[1] What this chapter is concerned with is how those skills were reproduced in the engineering and shipbuilding industries, in particular through systems of apprenticeship.[2] Apprenticeship was not the only means by which knowledge of how to do a particular job was transmitted from one generation to the next. There were various ways in which someone might pick up skills, not least by simple observation and mimicking an already experienced worker. However, apprenticeship certainly remained a fundamental training route for many trades and it shared with most other means of learning the characteristic that knowledge was passed within the labour force itself; employers might, in some circumstances, choose the apprentices, but the business of training them was largely the responsibility of skilled men or supervisory workers. And though there were some attempts in the period to introduce formal systems of technical education, financed by either the state or employers, these had little impact on the training of young workers.

If there is general agreement about the indispensability of many skills to the British economy, arguments persist about how to define skilled labour, as they do also about the extent to which skills were maintained or diluted in the period.[3] Much of the argument about the nature of skill turns upon the extent to which it is technologically determined or 'socially constructed'.[4] However, without entering into this argument too far here, one can at least say that the technological determinants of skill are generally necessary but not sufficient to the effective definition of a 'skilled trade'. The assessment of a skill must certainly include recognising not only that there is a technical ability involved which is not universally shared, but also that there are varying degrees of ability and ones that combine reliance on mental as well as manual abilities. But there are further elements to be taken into account in the historical definition of skilled trades. They include the restriction of the knowledge and practice of the skill to a select group, which may be effected by restricting the means of training, such as through apprenticeship, or by excluding some people from taking up the trade on grounds of, for instance, sex, race or age. Furthermore, the persistence of the trade as skilled may rest upon the ability of the group to maintain both the technical components of the job (or central parts of it), and the conditions of the trade in both labour-processes and labour-markets, although these conditions may also result less from the ability of the workers themselves to do this and more because of the requirements of employers.

The degrees of skill varied considerably in engineering and shipbuilding, between both sectors and trades. In engineering, the most highly skilled were in marine engineering, which provided the 'best schools' for training because much of the work was essentially bespoke, fitting each ship with its own tailor-made engines.[5] But in locomotive engineering the key skilled trades – the fitters and turners – performed tasks that were increasingly specialised and routine, largely because of the relatively early adoption of a degree of standardisation and interchangeability of parts in the industry.[6] In armaments, which was in the van of the development of precision engineering, it was said as early as the 1860s that many of those working at lathes (usually the job of turners) were doing little more than attending to the machines, 'an occupation requiring more attention than mechanical skill'.[7] Similarly, levels of skill varied in shipbuilding. For instance, the platers, who were among the central constructive trades, not only exercised manual strength in beating, cutting and shaping plates but also a very considerable degree of intelligence, aptitude and discretion, even when their work lost some of its skill content with the introduction of steel from the 1880s.[8] On the other hand, riveters' work, essentially the hammering of rivets, was probably less skilled than this in so far as they relied more heavily on brute strength.[9]

Estimates of the numbers of the skilled in these industries vary. In engineering the Jefferys reckoned that they formed perhaps 70–75 per cent of adult men, although this is probably too high. It seems more likely that the fitters, turners, patternmakers, blacksmiths and others recognised as skilled were perhaps half the labour force in the industry as a whole. In shipbuilding, the platers, riveters, angle-iron smiths, shipwrights and others formed about 50–55 per cent, although this may be a little low.[10]

Whatever the exact levels and numbers of the skilled in these industries there can be no question that skills were of acknowledged importance in them. But in defining the nature of skills one must also recognise the central characteristics of the context in which they were performed. From the 1830s and 1840s engineering was re-shaped by the introduction and diffusion of new machine tools – the slide-rest lathe, planer and others – while shipbuilding was transformed from the 1850s by the increasing use of new materials – iron – and sources of power in ships – steam engines – in place of wood and sail. While the pace of change in both industries was uneven it can be generally said that what was involved in both cases was the destruction of older forms of production and the reconstitution of a new division of labour with new skills and tasks. But the range of skills was both different from and less all encompassing than hitherto. A degree of immediate on-the-job control and autonomy persisted, which in some trades like boilermaking was pretty considerable, but the more complete subordination of labour to capital and the more fragmented division of labour within both these industries meant that no *single* trade could exercise control within the whole labour-process to the extent that millwrights had been able to do in the early engineering industry or shipwrights in wooden shipbuilding.[11]

Once the divisions of labour and the position of the skilled in them were established in these industries, they remained relatively unchallenged during the period from the 1850s to the 1880s.[12] However, from about 1890 to 1914 there was a new wave of technical change, with important consequences for skills and the division of labour, although these changes were more far-reaching in engineering than in shipbuilding. In engineering the period was characterised by the introduction of the turret-lathe and other mechanical improvements, by an assault by employers on the craft regulation of the skilled unions, including on the content of skills in some key trades, and by an increasing use of apprentices as cheap labour. In shipbuilding, on the other hand, the position of the skilled was challenged much less severely and apprenticeship could be sustained to a greater degree, although here too there were attempts by employers to curtail some of the powers of the Boilermakers' Society's regulation of it. While there are aspects of these developments which are turned to below, for the moment it should be stressed that there is no question that throughout the period the maintenance of apprenticeship was seen as a vital part of the strategies of the skilled unions, such as the Amalgamated Society of Engineers or the Boilermakers, to controlling entry to the labour market, and to the transmission of skills and knowledge. What has also to be said is that apprenticeship in some form was also an important means by which employers could sustain a trained labour force.

Before elaborating on these points, once can ask what form did apprenticeship take, what was the extent of it, and who became apprentices? There were three central characteristics of strict apprenticeship. First, the trainee would serve time at the trade, usually for five years. Second, there would have been a formal agreement with an employer that the apprentice would stay with the company for the duration, an agreement which might take the form of an indenture (although this form was decreasing in importance in the second half of the century),[13] or a verbal or written contract. And, third, the apprentice learned the trade very largely from the journeymen rather than the employer (or 'master'). However, these were not unchanging characteristics. The most severe problem with which unions had to contend was the influx of 'illegal' (untrained) men into skilled jobs by means other than apprenticeship. Although the problem became most acute towards the end of the nineteenth century it was one of which a union like the Amalgamated Society of Engineers was aware from its foundation in 1851. Its *Rules* had allowed the possibility that if a man had worked for five to seven years at the trade, had shown himself capable of earning the standard rate for the job and could do a proper job, then he would be eligible to join the union and the ranks of the recognised skilled.[14]

The trades which recruited mainly through apprenticeship were, in engineering, the patternmakers, fitters, turners, iron and brass moulders and smiths, while in shipbuilding the central constructive trades of platers, angle-iron smiths, riveters and caulkers did so, as did some others in the yards like the shipwrights. How many apprentices there were cannot be reckoned with any great precision although Charles Moore has estimated that by 1906 they formed 14·6 per cent of the total work-force in engineering, shipbuilding and railway carriage and wagon building.[15] One local example which roughly bears this out is Harland & Wolff's shipyard in Belfast in which they constituted 13 per cent of the labour force in 1892.[16] For the earlier part of the period it is impossible to arrive at a realistic estimate of the numbers, partly because there are no reliable figures for the total numbers working in these industries. However, there is reason to suppose that there was some increase in the number of apprentices from the 1880s but, at the same time, a decline in the quality of what they were learning and were expected to do, as they became increasingly used as cheap labour to be dispensed with once they had served their time.

As to who became apprentices, there is at least one thing which can be said with certainty: all apprentices in these industries and trades were male.[17] But beyond this the issue remains cloudy, although some light has been thrown on the problem, if not on the answer, by recent analyses of inter-marriage patterns within the working class, especially that of Geoffrey Crossick.

In his study of Kentish London Crossick suggested that there was a relatively high degree of inter-marriage among the skilled and to a lesser but significant degree among particular skilled trades, to the extent that over the period 1850–75 something like 42 per cent of men in engineering crafts had fathers in the same trades, while the figures for boilermakers and shipbuilding crafts were 46 per cent and 64 per cent. In other words the contention is that the skilled trades or 'labour aristocracy' were a self-reproducing élite to considerable extent. These findings have been widely quoted but have not gone unchallenged. Thus Roger Penn has argued that in Rochdale at least between 1856 and 1914 there was little particularly significant class endogamy among the skilled. There may, of course, be peculiar reasons why this was so in Rochdale; alternatively there may be peculiar reasons for the pattern in Kentish London. In any event the question cannot be really settled without some large-scale quantitative analysis – although this will not, in itself, indicate the significance one might attach to the findings. But what is also needed is analysis, if at all possible, of not just marriage records – partly because they bear only partially on the problem of apprenticeship recruitment – but also the records of employment and apprenticeship recruitment.[18]

The evidence I have on this question is fragmentary and unsatisfactory; it is the apparently incomplete record of applications to become apprentices at the Armstrong's engineering and armaments company of Elswick, Newcastle between 1856 and 1893.[19] Such evidence as it supplies is insufficient to afford a wholly reliable quantitative assessment; for instance, it gives an incomplete record of the occupations of the parents (usually fathers) or guardians of the applicants, and it similarly gives an incomplete record of the work and educational background of the applicants. But still, it is the kind – if not the quantity – of evidence needed.

What the Armstrong's record suggests is that the chances of skilled

23

workers getting their sons apprenticed into either the same trade or another skilled trade were not much better if at all than those of the unskilled. Thus in the last quarter of 1871, where the father's occupation is known in 45 per cent of 182 applications, a little over 26 per cent of the sons of skilled workers were accepted while 32 per cent were rejected; on the other hand just under 25 per cent of the unskilled were accepted while 16 per cent were rejected. A boy's chances of getting a job at the company were probably best if his father already had a job there, skilled or not. Between 1856 and 1893 some 173 out of 296 boys (or 58 per cent) listed as being taken as apprentices had a father or some other relation working at the company while 51 out of 133 rejected (38 per cent) had kin working there. In other words, what the company probably regarded as an important indicator of the boy's potential reliability and worth was if he had a father (or occasionally a brother or an uncle) with a proven record of reliable work.

What also appears to have mattered was, not surprisingly, evidence that potential apprentices would be trustworthy, respectable and well-disposed to the work which would be required of them. In the marginal notes on the accepted applicants it was often remarked that a boy had had a 'good education' or, simply, 'school'. However, given the limited educational opportunities available, and given that most boys were taken on between the ages of fourteen and sixteen, work experience was also valued. Most of the recruits had previously worked, either in engineering, metal-working and shipbuilding companies or in other trades and occupations, ranging from a grocer's to a joiner's shop. But what was looked for was not so much evidence of specific skills as the requisite social and moral qualities. Thus, for instance, E. Russell and F. Wiggen were rejected in 1871 on the grounds that they did not look 'respectable' while J. H. Innes merely had the terse and imperious comments of Sir William Armstrong registered against his name: 'Doubtful. Rather stupid looking.'

In the case of a company like Armstrong's it was the management, rather than the unions, which controlled entry to the trade: given the generally low levels of unionisation in the company this is not surprising. However, what is uncertain is how general this was. Some unions certainly believed that they had the upper hand in recruitment, at least before the 1890s, and that, in preference, the boys would be taken from the families of the skilled. Thus the Iron Founders said that it was their sons who generally entered the trade; members of the Boilermakers' Society were exerting considerable pressures to get their sons into apprenticeships in the 1880s; and the Shipwrights'

Society in the 1890s was lamenting the apparently recent decline of patrimony and that the members should accept whoever was eligible and disregard the occupation of a boy's father.[20]

What is more certain is that most unions certainly wanted to exercise control over the transmission of skills across the generations. After all, if it has been the formal education system which has been, in the twentieth century and particularly since 1945, a crucial means for working class parents to try to give their children some security and prospects in an unstable and insecure world, in the nineteenth century getting a son, if not a daughter, into a regular trade was thought highly desirable if at all possible. To the trade unions, defending apprenticeship was often seen as one of the means by which a man's 'property in his labour', or 'right to the trade' might be established and sustained. As the ASE declared in its *Rules*, attempting to restrict entry to the trade to those who had served a 'probationary servitude' was a necessary obligation: 'It is our duty . . . to exercise the same care and watchfulness over that in which we have a vested interest as the physician does who holds a diploma, or the author who is protected by a copyright.'[21]

If there was a decline of the specific notion of having 'property in labour' in the latter half of the nineteenth century, what did not decline was the value which skilled men attached to their work. Being skilled was a source of self-identification and pride. It carried with it a sense that their skills were indispensable to production and that it was the properly trained men who were not only the bearers of collective knowledge of the trade but were also the only ones who would execute work competently. The belief that men ought to do the job well was typical among union spokesmen, and was one dimension of the culture of unionism in which it was thought that the market relations between employers and workers should be governed by considerations of rights and obligations, justice and equity.[22] Defending apprenticeship was thought to be central to this. It would be, thought Robert Knight of the Boilermakers' Society, a guarantee against shoddy work and of the pre-eminence of the British economy. Complaining in 1873 of 'speculators' in shipbuilding, who broke the rules of 'fair competition' by taking contracts at less than the 'correct' market rate, Knight accused them of employing 'men, as *mechanics*, who never served any apprenticeship, and who only came to the trade years after they arrived at manhood' because they were cheap. 'These men', he continued, *never* become proficient in their work, because we know for anyone to become a thorough mechanic he *must* be trained to it from his boyhood. We often hear and read about the skill of the English mechanics being on the decline: it is because there are so many pretenders at half-wages. The British artisan of today is equal to any of his predecessors, and if England wants to keep her proud position there must be a wise system of apprenticeship established, which would secure the skill with which our name has been associated all over the world.[23]

When serving their time, or passing through their period of 'probationary servitude', the apprentices learned primarily the techniques of the trade. They would pick up the basics about materials, tools and machines, where relevant learn how to read plans and blueprints, and move progressively from the simplest to the more complex tasks. For instance, railway factory apprentice smiths did the lightest work and 'simple setting and bending, and making of bolts and eyes, rings and links for chains'. Apprentice platers in boiler shops and shipyards generally began as rivet-carriers before moving on to 'marking-off slab and through all the general run of plating'. However, the quality of what was learned and how it was taught was variable. For example, it was observed of engineering apprenticeships in Scotland in the early 1880s that the boys learned in an *ad hoc* sort of way, receiving little help from the foreman or employer; the apprentice 'received no teaching but was allowed to learn by his own observation and practice as best he could'.[24]

Yet what was learned in the workshop was not just technique, but also an identification with the trade and its practices. This meant coming to accept the centrality of the trade as a collectivity, the basic unit of not only trade unionism where it existed but also of many wider social affiliations. As Thomas Wright put it in the 1860s, it was in the workshop that the apprentice was 'taught both by precept and the example of his mates, that he must respect the trade and its written and unwritten laws, and that in any matters affecting the trade generally he must sacrifice personal interest, or private opinion, to what the trade has rightly or wrongly ruled for the general good'.[25] Here too, the codes of sexual identity and behaviour might be reinforced as the boys made the passage to 'manhood'.[26]

While the workshop and the trade were central to skilled labour, the ability of the men to regulate the conditions of their trades were always under pressure, though to a varying extent. Between the 1850s and 1880s there was 'little major change in labour utilization' in engineering. The expansion of the industry was characterised by rising exports, the persistence of relatively specialised product markets, the rapid expansion of the labour force and, in particular, the consolidation of the position of the fitters and turners. In the period 1830–50 the millwrights had generally been forced to accept a five- rather than seven year apprenticeship. And employers dealt a major defeat to the newly formed ASE in the lock-out of 1852 on, among other issues, the use of 'illegal men'. Thereafter the ASE had to abandon a national regulation of apprenticeship, leaving it to the individual branches and districts to determine whether or not working for five years at the trade was the same as a formal apprenticeship.[27]

In these circumstances, the extent to which the union was able to exercise effective control on the issue is uncertain. While 'craft regulation' did not depend entirely upon the establishment of formal trade unionism, it was certainly considerably facilitated by it, and the varying levels of union strength probably did affect the capacity of the engineers to control entry to the labour market. It has been reckoned that the ASE recruited about 58 per cent of eligible workers in Britain in 1861; but densities ranged from 81 per cent in London and the south-east, 70 per cent in Lancashire and Cheshire, down to 31 per cent in Scotland and 28 per cent in the northern counties.[28] Weak unionism enabled – or certainly did not hinder – companies from recruiting unapprenticed men. At Armstrong's in Newcastle, a firm operating in a largely non-union environment before 1871, untrained men were introduced in large numbers in to the ordnance works. It was thought that only about one-third of the workforce were 'mechanics' in 1861, with the other two-thirds being used on repetitive work.[29] On the other hand, given the expansion of the industry as a whole and the reliance of employers on skilled labour, it seems likely that there was a general acceptance by employers of apprenticed men whose initial training would be reinforced by a widening of knowledge and practice in the trade through improvership, migration and following-up.[30]

In shipbuilding the transition to iron and steam and the rise of the boilermakers as the dominant group of trades had entailed the decline of the shipwrights' power and of their ability to maintain the old seven-year apprenticeship. However, it seems likely that the unions, and in particular the Boilermakers' Society, which rapidly established an extremely powerful presence within the yards between 1850 and the 1870s, were able to maintain a fairly strict regulation of a five-year apprenticeship and probably did so to greater extent than the ASE could do in engineering.[31]

What is clearer is that the pressures by employers on apprenticeship regulations began to be much more severe from the onset of economic depression from 1873. In the 'Great Depression' employers were faced with a profits squeeze, rising labour costs, the beginnings of serious international competition from especially the United States and Germany, and a more securely based trade unionism (at least in general). The strategies adopted to deal with these problems in engineering focused on attempts to cheapen and intensify labour rather than to break up the existing divisions of labour and introduce new technologies. One important dimension of this was the heavier use of apprentices. The issue came to a head on Wearside between 1883 and 1885. Whereas the ASE had tried, albeit informally, to maintain a ratio of one apprentice to four journeymen since 1852, it was found that in seven leading shops in Sunderland there were 500 apprentices to 700 journeymen, a ratio of 1 : 1·4, while in some companies the numbers of apprentices actually exceeded the journeymen. The Sunderland men demanded that the ratio be at least restored to 1 : 2 but with the onset of trade depression in 1884 and the determined resistance of the employers, their strike was defeated and with it came, according to Jefferys, 'the abandonment of large-scale attempts to limit apprentices'.[32]

However, the defeat of 1885 did not lead to quite this result. There continued to be battles between employers and the union over the issue. In 1890–91, in response to an ASE ban on overtime, employers on the north-east coast introduced a large number of boys and apprentices into engineering shops and tried to increase their productivity by putting them on to piece rates. Following a strike against these policies, the employers locked the men out and further damaged apprenticeship regulation:

The many disputes which have recently taken place in [the Tyne and Wear district] have left, after settlements, a large residuum of displaced skilled labour. Apprentices have been much utilised during the men's absence, and are so yet – hence the boys' fathers are walking the streets, while the boys themselves are building the engines. This is one method amongst many others, known as cheapening the cost of production and creating surplus labour.[33]

Reinforcing the pressures arising from the economic conjuncture were those of technical change from the 1890s. In engineering this was evident in the central machine and fitting shops and the elaboration of new grades of semi-skilled labour, particularly those working the new kinds of drillers and shapers, and the extension of the number of automatic machine-minders. Although there was no immediate and wholesale introduction of the new machines but rather a 'piecemeal introduction of new equipment', the consequence was, as Zeitlin has put it, 'to call into question the position of skilled craftsmen within the division of labour'. The primary issue of contention became the manning of the machines, an issue fought out in the 1897–8 lock-out by the Engineering Employers Federation. Their success in the dispute, embodied in the Terms of Settlement, dealt the most severe blow to the regulation of apprenticeship yet felt by the ASE, for among those terms was the assertion of the employers' right to employ as many apprentices as they chose.[34]

In shipbuilding the pressures of economic and technical change were similarly there, although the impact of specifically technical changes were less severe than in engineering.[35] Here again, one of the strategies adopted by employers was a cheapening of labour costs by the use of apprentices and boy labour. From the 1880s there were increasing complaints by the Boilermakers about the weakening of the system. In part these focused on the rising ratio of apprentices to journeymen, particularly in years of poor trade like 1894.[36] But they were also about the declining quality of apprenticeships. For instance, it was said in the 1880s that in many yards there was collusion between apprentices themselves and some of the men effectively to limit the training content of apprenticeship. Many of the lads were carrying rivets until they were eighteen or nineteen years old and were encouraged to do so by riveters wanting to retain the services of 'good rivet carriers': 'Our apprentices think (and it is a doctrine that has been taught them by those who ought to know better) that they can carry rivets until [these] ages . . . and then start to learn their trade as an angle-iron smith, plater, riveter, or caulker, and be out of their time at the age of 21.'[37]

However, before 1900 the shipbuilding unions proved more effective than the engineers in regulating apprenticeship. In response to the pressures being felt from the 1880s the Boilermakers' Society attempted to tighten up their control. Between 1891 and 1893 they waged a campaign to insist on a five-year apprenticeship, that it be served in one firm for the whole period, that the ratio of apprentices to journeymen be maintained at 1 : 5, and that no-one be allowed to learn the trade who was not carrying an Apprentice Card. The employers' federation objected strenuously to these limitations but the signing of the National Shipyard Agreement of 1893 was only a partial defeat of the union's aims, at least initially. The five-year term and one-firm rules were adhered to; it was agreed that apprentices should be indentured, but a ratio of 2 : 7 rather than 1 : 5 was agreed to.[38] Yet by the end of the decade the agreement had been effectively defeated.

In 1899–1900, after employers had been violating its terms, the Boiler-makers met the Shipbuilding Employers' Federation and were forced to abandon any restrictions on numbers. The result was an increasing 'swamping' of the trade by apprentices, at least in some areas.[39]

However, the extent of the decline of apprenticeship in engineering and shipbuilding should not be exaggerated, despite the undoubted weakening of its regulation by unions. Sir Benjamin Browne, of Hawthorn Leslie, told the Poor Law Commission in 1910 that 'all our mechanics serve their apprenticeship',[40] and generally More has shown that the ratios of journeymen to apprentices were kept up reasonably well. In 1909 among the shipbuilding and marine engineering trades the average ratio was 3·5 journeymen to each apprentice, while in engineering the average was 2·4. And among the best organised and those who had secured an almost impregnable degree of unionisation – the boilermakers in shipbuilding – the ratio was about 5 : 1.[41]

Why was it that, if there were considerable pressures on apprenticeship, it was not abandoned altogether, or at least diluted much more than it was? Moreover, why did employers not resort to alternative means of obtaining trained labour, notably institutionalised technical education, financed by either themselves or by the state?

There are perhaps three main reasons. First, as I have already indicated, if skills were being diluted, they nonetheless retained very considerable importance. The range of work and reponsibilities of the skilled men were being persistently narrowed but the unevenness and partiality of technical change left them and craft regulation in a moderately strong position in engineering and in a very strong position in shipbuilding. Even in the most technically advanced large firms in engineering, such as in armaments, considerable numbers of craftsmen were required to make and set tools for the semi-skilled and unskilled, to maintain the machinery and do direct production where the new mass production methods were unavailable. Moreover, among the mass of heavy engineering firms the structural organisation of the workshop remained relatively unchanged, not least because in the immediately pre-1914 years they were able to enjoy continuing profitable markets in the empire and elsewhere. And further, where the new machines were introduced the ASE was generally able to capture them for their own members. In shipbuilding, technical changes and shipyard reorganisation did not radically disrupt the exceptionally powerful position of the Boilermakers' society. More-over, and crucially, the industry remained extremely successful and profitable; productivity levels remained higher than in either Germany or the USA and the industry was still producing 60 per cent of the world's new shipping down to 1914.[42]

Secondly, apprenticeship remained a cheap way of training labour and imparting skills. In some cases, the labour of the apprentice could be used by employers to make substantial gains in labour costs. For example, in the early 1900s, savings of 50–60 per cent could be effected by a combination of apprentice labour and new machinery in shipbuilding yards.[43] On the other hand, the value to the employer was complemented by the fact that it was in the interests of the apprentice to work at relatively low wages in order that he might then have access to the ranks of the skilled.[44]

Third, while formal technical education was being made available, its extent and impact were not very significant. The first serious stirrings of interest in state provision of technical education came with the foundation of the Department of Science and Art in 1853.[45] In the 1860s, as some employers and scientists became increasingly aware of the deficiencies of scientific and technical instruction compared with that provided by potential competitors such as France and Germany, there came renewed calls for better state training provision.[46] In 1884 the Royal Commission on Technical Instruction conducted extensive inquiries into the issue, followed by the state subsidy of technical education from 1890. In some ways these initiatives were fairly successful. Thus, by the end of the century, more than 170,000 students were receiving instruction in Department of Science and Art classes.[47] Moreover, they were complemented by the increasing interest of some companies in supporting technical education, at least from the 1880s. However, the impact of these initiatives on the labour force was small. By the 1890s probably fewer than 10 per cent of skilled workers in engineering were affected by formal training, and although the numbers grew thereafter the impact continued to be relatively slight.[48]

The lack of a well developed system of technical education before 1914 may be attributed to a number of factors. As Julia Wrigley has argued, the elaboration of science as a distinctive body of knowledge, with its own institutions and personnel, and the increasing technical division of labour within industry, which includes some degree of separation between 'mental' and 'manual' functions, led to an increasingly narrow definition of the content of technical education. Those attending classes were often subject to a dull, repetitive and abstract imposition of knowledge.[49] Moreover, the relative absence of a

31

strongly directive central state, and what Wrigley has called the 'poor articulation'[50] of the parts of the education system as a whole, certainly hindered the development of systematic technical education. Besides, the central problem – of the absence of a decent basic education system prior to any further technical training – persisted in the years before 1914. The issue was diagnosed by many as being about not only the specific issue of the supply of skilled labour but as a more general social one concerned with, as R. A. Bray put it, 'fit[ting] each youthful citizen, physically, mentally, and morally, to play a useful part in the work of the community'.[51]

Furthermore, if some companies were interested in providing technical education, many remained indifferent. Here the essential problem was the competitive nature of British capitalism. Most firms in engineering and shipbuilding were reluctant to invest in technical education when the benefits might accrue to home or overseas competitors,[52] a reluctance reinforced by the fact that both shipbuilding and engineering remained successful in world markets before 1914.

But above all, what could a formal technical education provide for labour that was not learned on the shop floor? The relative indifference of employers to provision arose partly from the economic and technological rationality of maintaining apprenticeship, partly from the continuing strength of labour organisation, but also from the content of apprenticeship itself. As one shipbuilding employer put it, 'when all is said and done, for the largest proportion of the ordinary apprentices . . . a very high degree of technical education is not an essential in their after life'. And on the side of labour, most unions remained similarly indifferent, although some less than others. The Boilermarkers were 'cool' towards it while the Shipwrights were more favourably disposed to apprentices having a 'theoretical as well as a practical knowledge of their trade, . . . so that they may more thoroughly understand the construction of the vessels they are building',[53] however, the primary interest of the unions was in trying to ensure the continuing training of labour by labour itself rather than by external institutions. And in the end, a shop-floor and 'practical' training in which apprenticeship remained of central importance continued to be the most favoured means of transmitting skills in the engineering and shipbuilding industries. Not least of the reasons for this was because, as the employer B. C. Browne declared in 1915, 'The most important thing for an apprentice to learn is to know *good work from bad*', something the unions had been insisting on for decades, and that to do this, 'he needs to see numerous examples of good workmen all about him whom he can imitate.'[54]

Notes

1 See, for example, E. J. Hobsbawm, 'Artisans and labour aristocrats?' in his *Worlds of Labour*, Weidenfeld and Nicolson, London, 1974, pp. 252–3; C. K. Harley, 'Skilled labour and the choice of technique in Edwardian industry', *Explorations in Economic History*, XI, 1974.

2 Parts of this paper draw on arguments put forward in my 'Time to work, time to live: some aspects of work and the re-formation of class in Britain, 1850–1880' in *The Historical Meanings of Work*, ed. Patrick Joyce, Cambridge University Press, Cambridge, 1987.

3 For discussion about the nature of skill see, among others, Charles More, *Skill and the English Working Class, 1870–1914*, Croom Helm, London, 1980; Anne Philips and Barbara Taylor, 'Sex and skill: notes towards a feminist economics', *Feminist Review*, 6, 1980; Stephen Wood (ed.), *The Degradatin of Work?*, Hutchinson, London, 1982; R. Harrison and J. Zeitlin (eds.), *Divisions of Labour*, Harvester Press, Brighton, 1985; Angela John (ed.), *Unequal Opportunities*, Basil Blackwell, Oxford, 1986, esp. Introduction and essays in Part I; W. Knox, "Apprenticeship and de-skilling in Britain, 1850–1914', *International Review of Social History*, XXXI, 1986.

4 Compare, for example, More, *Skill* with Knox, 'Apprenticeship'.

5 See, among others, J. W. C. Haldane, *Civil and Mechanical Engineering*, London, 1887, pp. 52–3; 80; M. and J. B. Jefferys, 'The wages, hours and trade customs of the skilled engineer in 1861', *Economic History Review* (1st series), XVII, 1947, p. 33.

6 See esp. S. B. Saul, 'The market and the development of the mechanical engineering industries in Britain, 1860–1914', repr. in Saul (ed.), *Technological Change: The United States and Britain in the Nineteenth Century*, Methuen, London, 1970, pp. 146–51.

7 *Newcastle Chronicle*, 24 August 1861.

8 Steel was easier to manipulate than iron: see Keith McClelland and Alastair Reid, 'Wood, iron and steel: technology, labour and trade union organisation in the shipbuilding industry, 1840–1914' in *Divisions of Labour*, ed. Harrison and Zeitlin, p. 170.

9 See More, *Skill*, pp. 124–5.

10 For the Jefferys' estimate see, 'Wages, hours and trade customs', p. 30 n.: this was based on wage figures. I would put the figure for engineering at 40–45 per cent, based on actual numbers employed in three different companies at different times: The Avonside Engine Co. Ltd., Bristol, 1866: see H. H. Creed and W. Williams, *Handicraftsmen and Capitalists*, Birmingham, 1867, Appendix II, pp. 112–17; Palmer's Shipbuilding and Iron Co. Ltd., Engine Works, Jarrow, 1865–82: see P[arliamentary] P[apers] 1886 [C.4797] XXIII, *Royal Commission on the Depression of Trade and Industry*, 3rd Report, Appendix A.IV (i and iv), pp. 298–9; Harland & Wolff, Belfast, 1892; see McClelland and Reid, 'Wood, iron and steel', p. 180. More has estimated the skilled as 53 per cent in 1886 and

49.5 per cent in 1906, although these figures are based on not wholly reliable wage data: see More, *Skill*, p. 186. For shipbuilding, see the figures for Harland & Wolff in McClelland and Reid, 'Wood, iron and steel', p. 180, although S. Pollard and P. Robertson have reckoned 67 per cent for Scotland in 1911, 60 per cent for the North East Coast of England, 1913: *The British Shipbuilding Industry, 1870–1914*, Harvard University Press, Cambridge, Mass., 1979, p. 153.

11 For a general survey of the transformations of engineering see Keith Burgess, *The Origins of British Industrial Relations*, Croom Helm, London, 1976, ch. 1; for shipbuilding, McClelland and Reid, 'Wood, iron and steel'.

12 I am ignoring here the regionally and sectorally uneven developments such as that Tyneside shipbuilding went over more quickly to iron shipbuilding than its close neighbour Sunderland.

13 See More, *Skill*, p. 48. More also notes (p. 77) that in 1909 29 per cent of engineering apprentices and 51 per cent of shipbuilding ones were indentured. Figures for earlier in the period are not available.

14 PP1868–9 [4123–I] XXXI, *Royal Commission on Trades Unions*, 11th Report, vol. II, Appendix H (VI): Rules of the ASE, 1851 revised 1864, 13(3), 13(8) and 14(1).

15 More, *Skill*, p. 101 n. (a).

16 McClelland and Reid, 'Wood, iron and steel,, p. 180.

17 It might be added that the general differentiation of skilled labour had as one of its historical bases the sexual division of labour. For some discussion of this issue see, among many others, Philips and Taylor, 'Sex and skill'. For a brief discussion of the relevance of this to male skilled workers in the period 1850–80, see Keith McClelland, 'Some thoughts on masculinity and the "representative artisan,' in Britain, 1850–1880', *Gender and History*, I (2), 1989.

18 Geoffrey Crossick, *An Artisan Elite in Victorian Society*, Croom Helm, London, 1978, ch. 6; Roger Penn, *Skilled Workers in the Class Structure*, Cambridge University Press, Cambridge, 1984, chs. 10–12; see also John Foster, *Class Struggle in the Industrial Revolution*, Weidenfeld and Nicolson, London, 1974, esp. pp. 125–31 and Appendix 2; Brian Preston, *Occupations of Fathers and Sons in Mid-Victorian England*, University of Reading, Reading Geographical Papers, 56, 1977.

19 In Vickers Collection, Tyne and Wear County Record Office, Newcastle, 1027/4. Apparently, other related records were destroyed by the company in the 1960s.

20 See interview with J. Maddison, General Secretary of the Friendly Society of Iron Founders, Webb Trade Union Collection (LSE Library), A.XIX, pp. 237–8; United Society of Boilermakers and Iron Shipbuilders, *Annual Report*, 1884, p. v; PP1897 [334], X. *Select Committee on Government Contracts*, q. 2,728.

21 Preface to ASE Rules in *Royal Commission on Trades Unions*.

22 For a discussion of this theme, see McClelland, 'Time to work'.

23 Boilermakers' Society, *Annual Report*, 1873, p. v; cf., e.g., PP1886 [C4893] XXIII, *Royal Commission on the Depression*, Final Report, qq. 14,930–31 and PP1893–4 [C6894–VII]; PP 1893–4 [C6894–VII] XXXII, *Royal Commission on*

Labour, 3rd Report, q. 20,683 for similar sentiments from Knight.

24 Alfred Williams, *Life in a Railway Factory* (1915), repr. Alan Sutton, Gloucester, 1984, p. 88; Harry Pollitt, *Serving my Time*, Lawrence & Wishart, London, 1940, p. 31; Pollard and Robertson, *Shipbuilding*, pp. 155–6; for a general discussion of what was learned see More, Skill, pp. 78–87.

25 The Journeyman Engineer [Thomas Wright], *Some Habits and Customs of the Working Classes*, London, 1867, p. 102.

26 See McClelland, 'Time to live', pp. 192–4.

27 See Burgess, *Origins*, esp. pp. 15–16 and 25–40.

28 Jefferys, 'Wages, hours and trade customs', p. 32. The northern counties included Northumberland, Durham, Cumberland and Westmoreland.

29 *Newcastle Chronicle*, 24 August 1861; for repetition work and its effects on apprenticeship at the company see J. F. Clarke, 'Labour relations in engineering and shipbuilding on the north-east coast in the second half of the nineteenth century', unpub. MA, University of Newcastle, 1966, p. 68; *idem*, 'Engineering workers on Tyneside' in *Essays in Tyneside Labour History*, ed. N. McCord, Newcastle Polytechnic, 1977, p. 93; *Royal Commission on Labour*, qq. 25,220; Webb TU Coll., A.XXI, pp. 148–9; Benwell Community Project, Final Report 6, *The Making of a Ruling Class*, Benwell CDP, Newcastle, 1978, pp. 25–6 (citing G. F. Steffen, *Roving in Britain* (1895)); Jonathan Zeitlin, 'Engineers and compositors: a comparison' in Harrison and Zeitlin, *Divisions of Labour*, p. 203.

30 Keith Burgess, 'Authority relations and the division of labour in British industry, with special reference to Clydeside, c. 1860–1930', unpub. paper, pp. 5–6; for discussion of improvers, migration and following-up see More, *Skill*, pp. 71–4 and ch. 6.

31 McClelland and Reid, 'Wood, iron and steel', p. 168.

32 Zeitlin, 'Engineers and compositors', pp. 201–3; J. B. Jefferys, *The Story of the Engineers*, Lawrence & Wishart, London, 1946, pp. 102–3.

33 Evidence of William Glennie, Tyneside district ASE, to *Royal Commission on Labour*, qq. 23,069–70; ASE, *Quarterly Report*, March 1893; Webb TU Coll., A.XVI, p. 171.

34 Zeitlin, 'Engineers and compositors', pp. 222 and 225–8.

32 See McClelland and Reid, 'Wood, iron and steel', pp. 170–6.

36 Pollard and Robertson, *Shipbuilding*, p. 154.

37 Boilermakers, *Monthly Report*, September 1885, p. 10; for complaints about the decline of quality see also, among others, evidence of Alexander Wilkie and Joseph Heslop of the Associated Shipwrights' Society to *Royal Commission on Labour*, qq. 21,462–4, 21,598, and Knox, 'Apprenticeship', pp. 172–3, 177–8.

38 In boilershops the employers were able to insist on no restriction on numbers. For the agreement and its background see D. C. Cummings, *A Historical Survey of the United Society of Boiler Makers and Iron and Steel Ship Builders*, Newcastle, 1905, pp. 127–8; S. and B. Webb, *Industrial Democracy*, London, 1898, pp. 456–7.

39 Knox, 'Apprenticeship', p. 180 for 'swamping' in Middlesborough between 1899 and 1910.

40 Cited in Henry Pelling, *Popular Politics and Society in Late Victorian Britain*, Macmillan, London, 1968, p. 50.

41 More, *Skill*, p. 103.
42 Zeitlin, 'Engineers and compositors', esp, pp. 228–36; McClelland and Reid, 'Wood, iron and steel', esp. pp. 176–8; more, *Skill*, pp. 160–3.
43 Knox, 'Apprenticeship', p. 176.
44 See the discussion in C. More, 'Skill and the survival of apprenticeship' in Wood, *Degradation of Work?*, pp. 114–16.
45 Julia Wrigley, 'Technical education and industry in the nineteenth century' in *The Decline of the British Economy*, ed. B. Elbaum and W. Lazonick, Clarendon Press, Oxford, 1986, p. 167.
46 See, e.g., PP1867 [3898] XXVI, *Schools Inquiry Commission: Report relative to technical education*; PP1867–68 (432) XV, *Select Committee on Scientific Instruction*.
47 G. W. Roderick and W. D. Stephens, *Scientific and Technical Education in Nineteenth-Century England*, David & Charles, Newton Abbot, 1972, p. 14.
48 See the evidence in More, Skill, ch. 10.
49 Wrigley, 'Technical education', pp. 166–9.
50 Wrigley, 'Technical education', p. 182.
51 R. A. Bray, 'The apprenticeship question', *The Economic Journal*, XIX, 1909, pp. 404–5. In the late nineteenth century the issue of the training of 'youth' was increasingly connected with wider fears about the degeneration of the young and the need to instil the virtues of 'citizenship'. For a discussion of these issues in regard to adolescent boys see, among others, John Springhall, *Coming of age: Adolescence in Britain 1860–1960*, Gill & Macmillan, Dublin, 1986.
52 Pollard and Robertson, *Shipbuilding*, p. 149; see also Wrigley, 'Technical education', *passim*.
53 Pollard and Robertson, *Shipbuilding*, pp. 139, 146; evidence of Alexander Wilkie to Royal Commission on *Labour*, q. 21,592.
54 Cited in More, *Skill*, p. 87.

TWO

Technical education and the transformation of Coventry's industrial economy, 1900–1939

David Thoms

Technical education in Coventry received considerable attention and praise from Board of Education officials during the 1930s. In particular, co-operation between employers and the city's technical college was said to have been quite exceptional and responsible for the emergence of what was widely regarded as a highly successful scheme of part-time day classes for engineering students. These had originated at the beginning of the century and in 1914 HM Inspectors commented that: 'From the point of view of numbers and the interest taken in them by employers they are the most important of their kind in the country'.[1] The first day release classes catered for apprentices and were designed to extend over a period of three to four years. In 1929, however, a more ambitious graduated scheme of part-time training was developed which allowed for boys under the age of sixteen to attend college for two-and-a-half days a week with the possibility of progression to an apprenticeship course and preparation for the Ordinary and Higher National Certificates. The Board of Education's annual report for 1930–31 attributed the recent growth in the number of engineering apprenticeship students in Coventry to the success of the first stage probationer scheme, noting that most of the city's large engineering firms released some of their young employees for part-time day classes.[2] The scheme as a whole continued to recruit well during the 1930s and near the end of the decade more than 1,000 students representing some thirty-nine firms attended Coventry Technical College for two half days per week, while similar arrangements had also been introduced elsewhere.[3]

The general expansion of technical education in Coventry coincided with a transformation in the city's industrial base, which moved from the traditional staples of watchmaking and textiles to the new engineering products of cycles, machine tools, motor vehicles and, eventually, electronics and aircraft. The silk ribbon and watchmaking industries suffered intense foreign competition from the mid nineteenth century and in the 1860s there was an outflow of labour from the city as people sought employment in other areas. Cycles provided the initial solution to the employment crisis but also came to serve as the platform for a period of development which elevated Coventry to one of the most dynamic local economies of the twentieth century. Despite periodic setbacks, the story of Coventry's economy from the 1880s was one of relentless growth which lasted for almost a century. During this period the city became associated with firms such as Alfred Herbert, Courtaulds, GEC, Armstrong Whitworth, Standard, Daimler and Rootes, which enjoyed both a national and international reputation. Coventry's engineering industries also played a major part in the rearmament schemes of the 1930s and the war itself. The principal motor car companies, for example, became heavily involved in the production of aero-engines under the shadow factory scheme of 1936, while a wide variety of machine tools and military vehicles and equipment also came to be manufactured in the city. By 1939 Coventry possessed a highly concentrated industrial structure with some 38 per cent of its workers employed in the manufacture of motor vehicles and aircraft.[4]

Coventry's industrial expansion and diversification undoubtedly benefited from local initiatives in the provision of technical education, and it is tempting to argue a dependent relationship, particularly as an exceptionally high proportion of the city's engineering workers were defined locally as skilled. The purpose of this essay is to examine the connections between technical education and industrial change in Coventry from the turn of the century until the outbreak of war in 1939. It is suggested that this relationship was in many respects highly positive. At the very least, co-operation between employers and the education authority demonstrates that there were pockets of local initiative which render the inter-war period less of an anticlimax after the achievements of the nineteenth century than is often supposed. It is also clear, however, that several important qualifications must be introduced before any wider association can be established between technical education and the modernisation of Coventry's industrial economy.

The expansion of the new engineering industries from the late nineteenth century created a growing demand for skilled and semi-skilled labour. As HM Inspectors reported in 1911: 'Coventry is a city in which the advantages of a suitable system of Technical Instruction are almost immediately apparent, as its industries depend to a remarkable extent upon the existence of skilled and intelligent workers.'[5] The pool of labour suitable for transfer from the ribbon and watch trades to engineering was said to have been exhausted by the mid-1890s, thus increasing the potential role of organised technical training.[6] In addition, the likely flow of new recruits from these traditional industries had declined with the fall in the number of young males entering apprenticeships in Coventry. This became noticeable during the last twenty years of the nineteenth century and by 1914 only sixty male apprentices appear in the Coventry Registers compared with 292 in 1880. As Dr Joan Lane has remarked, 'by the outbreak of war, apprenticeship was declining but still effective in Coventry, with technical education playing a significant role especially in the new twentieth century occupations'.[7] The onset of the First World War exacerbated the labour supply problem as a substantial number of young Coventriens volunteered for military service. The recession in the early and late 1920s was a temporary phenomenon. In general, the labour market in Coventry was highly buoyant during the inter-war period with acute shortages developing from the mid-1930s.

Coventry employers adopted a variety of methods to help satisfy their labour requirements. These ranged from the dilution of work from skilled to semi-skilled status to the large-scale recruitment of labour from other parts of the country, including unemployed youths under the government's juvenile transference scheme. Poaching from neighbouring firms was another highly popular strategy and involved design and management staff as well as skilled manual workers. Daimler became well known in the 1920s for the way its bonus rates were manipulated in order to attract employees from other firms, while in 1936 the Rootes Group almost brought another company's jig and tool design department to a standstill by taking on so many of its drawing office staff.[8] A particularly enterprising example of this type of activity involved the works manager of a local engineering firm who, having gained access to the Technical College's academic records, used the information 'to circularise promising students in the employ of other firms, advising them of the advantages of employment at his own particular company'.[9] As rearmament gathered pace from 1936, the labour market in Coventry became a virtual free-for-all with firms outbidding each other in order to attract those individuals with the skills most in demand so that by 1937 the city's engineering workers were said to be the best paid in the country. The Coventry and District Engineering Employers' Association attempted to impose some form of order on the labour market, but with little success, and by the end of the decade the Association admitted that it could no longer keep pace with the rising tide of complaints concerning unfair recruitment practices. It was within this context of a generally competitive labour market from the 1890s that a number of Coventry's leading engineering firms utilised and promoted the development of technical education classes, including those of a part-time day nature.

In common with similar bodies in other towns, the Coventry Mechanics' Institute, which was set up in 1828, was largely middle class and unconcerned with technical training. However, recession in the city's traditional industries eventually promoted the technical education movement locally, and in 1888 a Technical Institute was established in a disused warehouse to provide classes in textiles and horology, though the range of subjects offered was soon expanded. The Institute became rate-aided in 1893 and with more financial support a full-time principal teacher was appointed three years later. The Institute's work increased quickly in the early years of the century with student demand rapidly outstripping the available accommodation. Extensions to the original building in Earl Street were opened in 1926 and in the same year the Institute qualified for technical college status. After deliberating the matter for several years, the local authority opened a new college at the present Butts site in 1935, but a rapid growth in student demand soon put further pressure on teaching space.[10]

The growth of student enrolments in the early years of the twentieth century reflected the changing nature of Coventry's industrial structure, with a marked expansion in demand for classes in mechanical engineering, machine drawing and chemistry. Part-time day classes in engineering began in 1905 and by 1914 were said to be one of the most important and effective parts of the training provided at the Institute, with some 116 students in attendance.[11] Enrolments suffered with the advent of war, but by 1922, 193 Coventry apprentices attended the Institute for one morning and one afternoon per week.[12] To begin with, the part-time day classes received the support of only a small number of firms with the overwhelming majority of students coming from Herberts, Daimler and the Coventry Ordnance Works. Although the number of contributors subsequently increased, the bulk of students appear to have emanated from a limited number of factories and workshops with a particular requirement for highly skilled labour. Thus, when two new science courses for apprentices were introduced in 1929, forty-three of the forty-four students were employed by Daimler, a firm specialising in the manufacture of expensive, high-quality motor cars.[13] Even so, in 1924 it was claimed that 'a larger proportion of employers in Coventry send employees to the Technical School during the day time than probably in any other town in the country'.[14] When the terms of the probationer and apprenticeship schemes were published in 1929, some thirty firms, mostly from the motor vehicle and machine tool industries, were listed as formally supporting the new arrangements and, with the increasingly tight labour market of the 1930s and the active backing of the CDEEA, it seems likely that the general level of support broadened considerably.[15] This appears to be confirmed by the city's apprenticeship registers, particularly with respect to electrical engineering, though it is important to note that Herberts continued to dominate registrations in the 1930s, in some years accounting for around half the total number.[16]

The probationer/apprenticeship scheme was launched in 1929 'in order to provide for selected boys an opportunity to secure the thorough training and education that is necessary to enable them to hold positions of responsibility on the executive and technical staffs'.[17] Boys under sixteen years of age could apply for entry to the probationer scheme through the Juvenile Employment Bureau at the Coventry Education Office or direct to one or more of the participating firms. Entry was competitive and successful applicants were required to take classes in English, mathematics, drawing and science on two half days a week throughout the academic year. Successful students received the Engineering Probationer's Certificate which was endorsed by the CDEEA. Providing that they enjoyed the support of their employers, these probationers had the opportunity to progress to the apprenticeship scheme which involved either a national certificate or trade science course, though the arrangements did allow for transfer in each direction from one programme to the other. All the classes were available in the evening, though selected apprentices were allowed to take the national certificate course on a part-time day basis. The apprenticeship course extended over a period of five years, at the end of which successful examinees received the Coventry Engineering Apprentices Certificate as well as their formal educational qualification. It was the daytime study aspect of the scheme as a whole, together with progression from one level to another, which gave it its uniqueness and stimulated such interest among Board of Education officials and members of the Inspectorate.

The probationer/apprenticeship scheme was a major achievement since it required considerable co-operation between employers and the college authorities, particularly in respect of the day release provision. The rationale behind the scheme was recorded in the minutes of the CDEEA's executive committee when in November 1934 it was noted that 'when the present shortage of skilled workers was visualised some few years ago, the Association, in co-operation with the Local Education Authority, formulated the Coventry Scheme of Engineering Apprenticeship, in the hope that this would assist in remedying the position which otherwise would have been of serious consequence to local industry.'[18] In fact the CDEEA minutes reveal that, by 1920 at least, the Association was being pressed by the local authority to discuss ways of extending apprenticeship training, while in 1926, D. R. Maclachlan, the Technical College principal, made a personal request to meet members of the Association to discuss ways of securing co-operation in the development of a scheme of work which would promote the flow of skilled workers to the local engineering industry. It is clear, however, that the support of the CDEEA was critically important for the successful implementation of the new scheme, and by January 1930 the Association was actively encouraging more firms to participate. Foremost among those CDEEA members who supported the scheme was A. R. Berriman, a Daimler director and a man of high national repute in the engineering industry. According to one Board of Education official, 'it is Mr Berriman who has pushed the whole thing through',[19] while Frank Harrod, Coventry Director of Education, explained that after 'several months of discussion the final scheme was accepted by both bodies largely due to the enthusiasm of Mr. A. E. Berriman, of the Daimler Motor Company, and the keen co-operation of Mr. John Varley, the Secretary of the Coventry and District Engineering Employers' Association'.[20]

The growing popularity of the scheme – by 1934, 527 engineering apprentices and forty probationers were enrolled at the Technical College – enabled it to make a significant contribution to the city's pool of skilled labour.[21] The proportion of skilled manual labour to the work force as a whole was exceptionally high in Coventry, accounting for almost 48 per cent of male employees in 1931 compared with around 31 per cent for England and Wales. The proportion of semi-skilled manual workers in the total labour force actually declined in the 1920s from 45 per cent in 1911 to 24 per cent in 1931.[22] The high earnings achieved by manual workers in the engineering industry appears to provide further evidence of the skilled character of the labour force. Indeed, according to Andrews and Brunner, William

Morris was deterred from expanding his motor vehicle empire in Coventry because of high labour costs, though significantly this did not apply to operations which required a high level of skill, including engine and special project motor body work.[23] Yet these comments on the exceptional nature of Coventry's labour force must be qualified since, as Friedman points out, skilled status in Coventry referred to the payment of a district rate for a particular job, and was increasingly achieved as a result of enhanced bargaining power in a tight labour market, rather than the acquisition of skill *per se*.[24] The apparent high level of skill within the manual labour force in Coventry was thus something of an illusion, since in many cases workers could qualify for the district rate after just a few months' training.

There are other reasons, too, for believing that the significance of the various Coventry schemes for part-time day technical training require some qualification. One of the most important of these concerns the high level of inward migration from the 1890s and the skills which workers brought with them. The cycle boom peaked in 1896, attracting large numbers of young migrants and, as the city's Medical Officer of Health noted, 'houses could not be built fast enough to accommodate the inrush'.[25] Coventry's population totalled almost 70,000 at the turn of the century but by 1911 the figure had risen to 106,349, an exceptionally high decennial increase of around 52 per cent. It was during this period that migration became the dominant element in Coventry's demographic profile, with some 67 per cent of the population growth between 1901 and 1911 representing in-migration from outside Warwickshire. After an initial slump following the end of the First World War, Coventry's population increased rapidly during the inter-war period as a whole, standing at 224,247 in 1939, with in-migration again a major factor, particularly in the 1930s when men were attracted by the growing employment opportunities in the motor vehicle and other light engineering industries. Throughout this period migrants were largely young male adults who came in search of work, thus adding to the city's reservoir of labour. Despite its limitations, certain conclusions may be drawn from the official census data. Up to 1911 most migrants to Coventry came from other urban areas rather than rural or mining districts. Although it is not possible to assess the level of skill which these young workers brought to Coventry, one can at least agree with Lancaster's contention that 'the majority that came were probably familiar with a manufacturing environment which may partly explain the comparative ease of Coventry's industrial transformation from small scale production units to large factories'.[26] Inter-war Coventry became the recipient of migrants from the Celtic fringes and the north of England. One interesting development was a marked influx during the 1930s of Welshmen who left the Cardiff/Newport mining area for employment in Coventry's factories. It was estimated in 1937 that 21·5 per cent of all migrants into Coventry were Welsh. While coal miners probably lacked the engineering expertise of men from specifically manufacturing centres, they were able to find a niche in the semi-skilled jobs which proliferated during the 1930s. Migration was occasionally promoted by employers or by other connections with a particular firm, GEC and Alvis being two examples of this. With relatively easy access from the West Midlands conurbation and other nearby centres of population, Coventry was also a growing centre of commuter traffic. It was claimed in 1929, for example, that some 27,000 workers came in daily, mainly from Birmingham.[27] It seems clear, therefore, that imported labour, much of it skilled or semi-skilled, was a key element in Coventry's industrial growth and diversification from the 1890s, in some instances overshadowing the contribution of the city's Technical Institute and College to the manpower reserve.

Innovations in the management of work were introduced by employers to help alleviate labour supply problems. The extension of working hours through overtime became very popular during the boom of the 1890s, and the pressure upon workers eventually became so intense that in 1910 the five main engineering unions in the city concluded an agreement with the employers which restricted overtime to fifteen hours in any single week. Some employers were forced to regard overtime as compulsory and could find themselves working as many as sixty-nine hours a week over an extended period of time. Overtime remained a popular management strategy at periods of peak production during the inter-war period, sometimes becoming a highly prominent feature of a firm's balance sheet. In 1934, for example, Coventry Motor Panels went into the red because, it was claimed, overtime payments had reached an excessively high level due to the company's inability to recruit additional skilled labour. It is interesting to note that this company, like many others in the city, continued to experience severe labour supply problems during the remainder of the decade, and in 1938 its chairman reported that 'we were compelled to advertise continually through several months and finally had to pay increased rates of wages to induce toolmakers to take up employment with us'.[28]

More important than overtime in promoting the growth of output was the application of machine production which allowed for the substitution of skilled men by semi-skilled workers, including women and juveniles. Dilution was applied before 1914 but acquired new popularity during the First World War as government contracts boosted demand for engineering products and recruitment to the armed forces left many firms with a shortfall of labour. The end of the war brought trade union pressure to restrict de-skilling, but the practice continued and gathered pace in the 1920s as the labour market tightened and economic conditions became generally more competitive. In the motor vehicle industry, for example, female and boy labour was increasingly applied in coachbuilding, particularly in the trim shops, and by the mid-1920s, many firms were recruiting relatively large numbers of married women because the supply of single girls was said to have virtually dried up.

The real solution to the labour supply problem in motor vehicle coachbuilding arrived in the 1930s as mass produced steel bodies made redundant the specialist carpentry skills required by the earlier wooden structures. The 1930s also saw a more general drift towards mass production methods in the Coventry motor industry, particularly with respect to Rootes and Standard, both of which came to concentrate on the volume production of cars. Under the management of John Black, Standard invested heavily in new machinery so that output increased about seven times between 1931 and 1939, while the size of the labour force hardly changed. It was the more specialist luxury and sports car manufacturers, such as Daimler, Jaguar and Alvis, producing a relatively small number of vehicles, which had a proportionately greater reliance upon the traditional engineering skills of the trained and experienced craftsman.

Dilution, in its various forms, was made possible because trade union organisation in key sectors of Coventry's engineering industries remained relatively weak. The assembly side of the motor vehicle industry, for example, was particularly badly unionised and there was very little organised opposition to the introduction of new production methods. Labour disputes did occur in the motor industry and elsewhere, but they were limited in scope and impact. This is partly explained by the awareness among trade union officials of the structural weaknesses and limited membership of their own organisations, but also an appreciation by workers of Coventry's favourable wage rates in an industry plagued by trade fluctuations and seasonal lay-offs.

In addition to daytime engineering provision, the Coventry Institute and College offered a range of classes at different levels and of a technical character, undoubtedly contributing in some measure to the city's industrial transformation. Student demand for technical education seems to have been quite pronounced, reflecting both the city's changing economic base and the apprenticeship traditions of its craft industries. Some indication of the level of student demand is available for the teaching year 1910–11 when just over 50 per cent of Standard V elementary school leavers enrolled at the Institute.[29] Because of the employment opportunities which were available in the city, a substantial number of grammar school boys were also said to enter local industry in preference to university and many of these probably joined the more advanced technical classes. Student demand remained high in the inter-war period, frequently outstripping the available accommodation. Once the new college was opened in 1935 enrolments grew by over 40 per cent in the following four years, rising to a total of 5,910 students, compared with 845 on the eve of the First World War.

The introduction and development of part-time day engineering classes suggests that a number of leading firms adopted a supportive attitude towards technical education and there is evidence to suggest that incentives and pressure were sometimes applied to encourage employees to attend suitable classes. However, HM Inspectors suggested in 1911 that less enthusiasm was demonstrated towards traditional evening classes, and it seems likely that the seasonal nature of employment in the cycle and motor car industries was largely responsible for this reticence.[30] Course attendance was almost certain to be interrupted for workers in these industries by lay-offs during the off-season, while preparation for the period of peak demand meant that overtime working rendered it difficult to secure release in the evenings. HM Inspectors were aware that overtime was a major impediment to the development of technical education in Coventry, but while accepting that seasonal work could not be avoided, they did suggest that some of the tensions could be reconciled by a more flexible attitude among foremen. Seasonality of employment was a factor which continued to be particularly significant for the motor vehicle industry during the inter-war period, though the general increase in the scale of the productive unit probably facilitated a more systematic approach to release for technical training. Even by 1914 Coventry had a number of large employers, including Rudge Whitworth, Courtaulds and Daimler, the latter with a labour force of around 5,000 people, making it one of the largest engineering works in the country. The trend towards large-scale production continued during the inter-war years and was further encouraged by the onset of war in 1939, so that by the end of 1944 almost 80 per cent of the labour force worked in factories of 500 employees or above.[31] Despite this expansion in the scale and complexity of the business unit, the provision for in-house technical training appears to have remained at a very minimal level.

There seems little doubt that the overall growth of student enrolments, both at the Institute and the College, was seriously curtailed by inadequate teaching space. In 1892, only four years after the Institute was opened, a request by local tradesmen for classes in plumbing was rejected because 'class rooms are fully used, and at times inconveniently overcrowded, so that under these circumstances the further development of the Institute is impractical'.[32] During the early part of the twentieth century the Board of Education began to press the Authority on the limited accommodation at the Coventry Institute, and by 1911 this was beginning to feature in HMI reports as a matter of real concern. The situation deteriorated further after the First World War and in 1921 it was pointed out to the LEA that course development was being seriously impeded by lack of space, while in the following year one Board official commented that, 'As to the hopeless inadequacy of the present provision at Coventry for technical education & as to the urgency of increased accommodation & equipment, particularly for Engineering, there can be no question.'[33] In 1925 another internal minute claimed that the Institute 'has been scandalously neglected for the past 20 years by the Authority & it has been a continuous struggle for the past 5 years to bring them up to the present issue'.[34] The students expressed their grievances in a direct manner when in 1933 some 3,000 of them marched to the Town Hall with a petition demanding an immediate improvement in college accommodation. In reporting this demonstration, a correspondent for the *News Chronicle* noted that: 'The college cannot house all the people who seek technical education. Some students are taught in the elementary schools and sitting at ordinary school desks. I heard of a large Coventry policeman who got up at the end of a lesson "waving" the desk at which he sat. It had to be prised off him.'[35] The writer also claimed that although much of the teaching at the college was of good quality, its effectiveness was undermined by the institution's poor physical environment. The building, it was claimed, did not deserve 'to be promoted to the rank of a college'.[36] These were harsh criticisms but, according to one Board of Education official, accurately reflected the seriousness of the situation.[37] The sharp increase in enrolments following the opening of the new college in 1935 appears to support the contention that some potential student demand went unsatisfied because of inadequate accommodation. Yet within a short period the college authorities were again experiencing great difficulty in satisfying student needs and by the end of 1937 over thirty classes were meeting in neighbouring outposts, while enrolments in engineering had been suspended because resources were simply inadequate to cope with the demands placed upon them.[38] After threats by the Board of Education in 1911 to reduce the Authority's grant because virtually nothing had been spent on the Technical Institute, plans for a new building were drawn up and eventually received government approval in 1914. However, these were shelved with the outbreak of war, while progress after the Armistice was retarded when it became known that the proposed Pool Meadow site was not only too small for the new Institute but also did not meet civil engineering requirements. In 1930 the Education Committee approved plans for a new technical college to be constructed on land at the Butts which had been purchased from the Rover Motor Company in 1919. Although the design was regarded by Board officials as rather elaborate, the proposal received formal approval in March 1931, only to be delayed by the national financial crisis of that year. The new Technical College was based on the 1913 plans and was certainly grand in appearance. It is one of the last public buildings in the country to be adorned with Doric columns. More importantly, the college had purpose-built classrooms, workshops and laboratories, a major improvement on the converted cycle sheds which had housed the metallurgy classes in the Earl Street premises.

The long delay in providing the city with a technical college appropriate to its industrial character is perhaps surprising for, as one Board of Education official observed in 1931, 'it is difficult to imagine a stronger case than Coventry for the provision of a suitable facility for Technical education having regard to its great importance industrially'.[39] One possible explanation which circulated within the Board during the mid-1930s was that 'both the Coventry Borough Council and Coventry Education Committee are composed of hard-hearted businessmen who are out to get every penny possible from Exchequer funds'.[40] Yet it should also be noted that during the retrenchment period of the early 1920s little encouragement was given by the Board for the Authority to proceed with its pre-war building plans. The principal explanation for the late appearance of a new technical college was almost certainly the enormous financial and planning problems which the Council experienced from the late nineteenth century as the growing population needed to be provided with schools, houses and other services. Coventry's elementary schools were seriously overcrowded before 1914, and after the war the pressure of excess demand percolated through to the secondary section, so that by 1925 the Authority was said to be about 1,400 secondary places below the Board's target. In housing, land was acquired at Radford in 1923 for the first Corporation housing estate, reflecting the adoption of a more progressive attitude towards the provision of municipal accommodation. Yet the inter-war years remained a period of tension between economic change and social welfare provision for, as the city's Medical Officer of Health commented in 1938, population growth continued to be 'phenomenal'.[41]

Inadequate resourcing is a criticism which could also be applied in some measure to equipment and staffing. Before the Institute became rate-aided it relied heavily upon gifts of machinery and other teaching materials and this tradition continued to influence local authority policy into the twentieth century. With its strong technical bias, the Institute required a substantial input of relatively expensive machinery, preferably of a modern kind. Some firms, such as Herberts and Daimler, appear to have been particularly generous in providing equipment gratis or at greatly reduced prices. However, until the new technical college was opened there appears to have been an ongoing shortage of key materials which retarded course innovation and development. In referring to motor vehicle engineering, HM Inspectors reported in 1914 that 'the equipment for the teaching of this highly technical and somewhat difficult subject is meagre in the extreme'.[42] The introduction of Higher National Certificates in electrical and mechanical engineering was only made possible after the professional institutions took the unusual step in 1924 of circularising local firms in order to encourage additional gifts of machinery and other equipment.

The response of local industry was less than enthusiastic, partly because it was felt that the Authority should contribute its share through the provision of more suitable accommodation. Eventually, some twenty-four firms donated machinery valued at about £4,000 while the local authority invested another £3,000 to bring the Institute's teaching aids up to the required standard. However, as one civil servant pointed out in 1926, it was 'largely as a result of the generosity of local firms' that the Institute was at last equipped for classes at HNC level.[43] A more satisfactory arrangement, at least with regard to machine tools, seems to have been arrived at in the mid-1930s when Herberts provided machinery which was to be replaced by updated models every three years on the basis of an annual rental.[44]

The Institute's first principal teacher, J. H. Belcher, was appointed in 1896. The title was appropriate since he was expected to contribute a full teaching load and, while this was probably acceptable in the early period of Belcher's appointment, it became less so once the Institute's work expanded and the administrative and course development roles became more significant and time-consuming. Belcher exemplified the value of an innovative Principal for he appears to have initiated the original scheme of part-time day classes for engineering students.[45] He also attempted to improve the Institute's work in other ways, but his personal influence must have been limited by a heavy teaching and administrative burden. The situation improved with the appointment in 1908 of a Head of Engineering, though it was not until 1936 that a Registrar was employed to relieve the Principal of responsibility for enrolments, fees and requisitions, allowing him to devote more time to promoting the College's overall academic development.[46]

The recruitment of suitable assistant teachers was another aspect of staffing which occasionally created problems. For example, just before the First World War the Institute found it difficult to retain good staff because, in the buoyant labour market of the West Midlands, salaries were uncompetitive relative to other jobs requiring similar skills. Similarly, a combination of unsatisfactory accommodation and staffing explains why in 1933 the Board of Education refused to approve a proposed Higher National Certificate course in chemistry.[47] Inadequate staffing could also lead to overcrowding and unsound teaching practices. This seems to have occurred in September 1937 when students from different courses were combined for classes in mathematics, creating some excessively large groups.[48]

The general quality of teaching is difficult to assess, though the Board's records suggest that when approval for National Certificate courses was withheld it was normally because of inadequate facilities rather than poor teaching. By the First World War a reasonable proportion of the Institute's students were said to be following a coherent package of classes. Perhaps the most serious criticism levelled at both the Institute and the College was the claim that teaching was too heavily biased towards theory at the expense of practical work. This was a common enough problem in technical education but one which may have been particularly pronounced in Coventry where the persistent shortage of suitable workshop and laboratory space, and the lack of equipment, rendered it difficult to escape from blackboard teaching. Even when the new College was opened, members of the CDEEA continued to complain that the courses were insufficiently practical in character.

The introduction of part-time day engineering classes in 1905 and the appearance of National Certificate courses in the 1920s suggests that in certain respects the Institute maintained a satisfactory pace of course innovation. Moreover, the provision of classes in aeronautical engineering and automatic telephony in 1926 indicates that a genuine attempt was made to adjust to the changing nature of Coventry's industrial economy. Perhaps the most serious criticisms concerning course innovation apply to the first twenty years or so of the Institute's existence when it seems clear that relatively little provision was made for the growth areas of cycles and cars. Thus, although one city Alderman commented in 1893 that 'We do not want to incur the criticism of "too late" of which we heard some whispers a few years ago as applied to our ancient industries in regard to our promising young giant – the cycle manufacture'[49] it was not until 1901, when the cycle boom in Coventry was over, that a class in cycle construction was offered, and then only at the expense of courses in printing technology.

The resource issue was probably the main reason for this delay since the Institute's management committee appears to have appreciated the importance of technical education, noting as early as 1892 that the high proportion of cycle components imported into the city reflected Coventry's lack of a proper training facility in this area of engineering skill. Similarly, it was reported in 1899 that the Institute lacked the resources to introduce a class in motor vehicle carriage building even though the suggestion for this provision had emanated from the City and Guilds of London Institute. A slow pace of development also characterised courses in motor vehicle engineering, and in 1914 HM Inspectors criticised the Institute for not providing suitable instruction in this subject. Motor vehicle technology was taught, but only as part of a general course in mechanical engineering, which was deemed unsatisfactory because it meant that certain important areas of mathematics and mechanics were seriously neglected. This seems a particularly surprising omission since by that time Coventry firms were responsible for an output of around 9,000 vehicles or over 28 per cent of the national total and, with cycles, employed some 12,000 people. In general, course development seems to have become more responsive to Coventry's employment needs during the inter-war period as more resources were placed at the College's disposal, though the failure to introduce industrial management classes of various types is one important deficiency which may have impaired the quality of decision making in the city's numerous business enterprises.

On a related theme, the Authority was also relatively slow to appreciate the potential benefits of the provision of a junior technical school. Although by 1916 one of the city's elementary schools maintained a higher top for boys destined to enter the engineering industry, this was far from adequate for, as one Board of Education official commented, there is 'an excellent opportunity of providing for a large J.T.S. for the Engineering Trades for there is no town in the country more suitable for such a type of school'.[50] When a junior technical school was finally established at the Institute in 1919 it offered two-year courses in engineering and building for boys of 11–13 years of age with the possibility of an optional third year for 13–14-year-olds. By the session 1927–8, 153 boys attended the school and at that time about 90 per cent of leavers joined the engineering industry, some 60 per cent returning to take adult classes at the Institute.[51]

Despite its limitations, technical education in Coventry from 1900–39 made an important and, in some respects, critical contribution to the city's industrial progress, largely because it was in the employers' interests for it to do so. A sluggish local authority was forced to respond to the needs of a dynamic local economy because of the co-operation which developed between the engineering employers' association and the Institute/College management. The pressure which emanated from a number of firms, such Daimler and Alfred Herbert, with a particular requirement for skilled labour, was rendered more powerful because it was channelled through the local employers' association. This was a powerful organisation which represented the interests of a relatively close knit industrial élite.

The probationer scheme and evening trade classes provided a basic level of technical training in a range of subjects relevant to Coventry's new industries. However, this involved skills which were readily imported or acquired on the job. The more advanced form of instruction was the really significant aspect of technical education in Coventry during this period, for it related to a level of expertise which was central to innovation in several branches of engineering and was not easily developed on an in-house basis. Much was achieved, though it remains clear that the local authority failed to provide the level of support for technical education which would have maximised its contribution to Coventry's remarkable industrial transformation before 1939. Although HM Inspectors publicly praised the innovatory nature of the part-time day classes for engineering students which emerged in

Coventry, the Board of Education's records reveal that they were far from satisfied with the local authority's overall provision for technical education. In practice, Coventry, like other authorities, was limited in the level of its expenditure by the parsimony of central government and that of its own councillors. The real problem in Coventry, however, was the city's rate of economic expansion which generated a huge range of competing demands for a limited public budget. The promotion of technical education was simply perceived as a less urgent and politically less sensitive issue than other social needs.

Notes

1 Public Record Office (PRO), Ed. 114/949, *Report of HM Inspectors on the Coventry Municipal Technical Institute*, 1914, p. 2.
2 Board of Education, *Annual Report*, 1931, p. 27.
3 Coventry Technical College, *Report of the Principal for the Year 1938–39*, 1939, p. 11.
4 S. Shenfield and P. S. Florence, 'Labour for the war industries: the experience of Coventry', *Review of Economic Studies*, 1943–5, p. 35.
5 PRO, Ed. 114/953, *General Report of HM Inspectors on the Technical Schools and Evening Schools in the County Borough of Coventry*, 1911, p. 1
6 Medical Officer of Health for Coventry, *Annual Report*, 1896, p. 3.
7 J. Lane, 'Technical training of young persons c. 1850–1914 in Coventry and the Midlands' (Report for the Social Science Research Council, n.d.), p. 14.
8 David Thoms and Tom Donnelly, *The Motor Car Industry in Coventry Since the 1890s*, London, 1985, pp. 107, 108.
9 Coventry and District Engineering Employers' Association (CDEEA), Minutes, 20 July 1936.
10 For a brief history of Coventry Technical College, see H. Temple, *Life Begins at Forty*, Coventry, 1975.
11 PRO, Ed. 114/949, *Report of HM Inspectors*, 1914, p. 1.
12 PRO, Ed. 114/950, *Report of HM Inspectors on the Coventry Municipal Technical Institute*, 1923, p. 6.
13 PRO, Ed. 51/108, E. Jackson to [damaged page], 25 October 1929.
14 PRO, Ed. 90/244, J. Ingles to A. P. Oppe, 3 January 1924.
15 City of Coventry, *Scheme for the Education and Training of Probationers and Apprentices in the Engineering Industry*, 1929, p. 3.
16 These registers have been deposited with the Coventry Record Office.
17 City of Coventry, *Scheme for the Education and Training of Probationers and Apprentices*, p. 1.
18 CDEEA, Minutes, 19 November 1934.
19 PRO, Ed. 51/108, minute signed by W. H. J., 18 October 1929.
20 *Education*, 7 September 1934.
21 *Ibid.*
22 A. Friedman, *Industry and Labour*, London, 1977, p. 204.

23 P. W. S. Andrews and E. Brunner, *The Life of Lord Nuffield*, Oxford, 1959, p. 127.
24 Friedman, *Industry and Labour*, p. 204.
25 Medical Officer of Health for Coventry, *Annual Report*, 1898, p. 7.
26 B. Lancaster, 'Who's a real Coventry kid? Migration into 20th Century Coventry', in B. Lancaster and T. Mason, *Life & Labour in a 20th Century City: The Experience of Coventry*, Coventry, 1986, p. 61.
27 C. Saunders, *Seasonal Variations in Employment*, London, 1936, p. 98 (footnote).
28 Motor Panels Ltd., Chairman's Report, 31 May 1938. I am grateful to the company for granting me access to its records.
29 PRO, Ed. 114/953, *Report of HM Inspectors on the Coventry Municipal Technical Institute*, 1911, p. 2.
20 *Ibid.*, p. 1.
31 University of Warwick, Modern Records Centre, MSS 180/MRB/3/4/28, Midland Region, employment by size of firm, 27 February 1945.
32 Coventry Record Office (CRO), Coventry Technical Institute, Committee Minutes, 13 April 1892.
33 PRO, Ed. 51/108, J. Douglas to W. Gannon, 30 January 1922.
34 PRO, Ed. 90/245, A. S. Barnes to J. Ingles, 27 May 1925.
35 *News Chronicle*, 24 January 1933.
36 *Ibid.*
37 PRO, Ed. 90/245, Eaton to B. Pearson, 27 January 1933.
38 *Birmingham Gazette*, 3 November 1937.
39 PRO, Ed. 90/245, J. W. to Eaton, 23 September 1931.
40 PRO, Ed. 90/245, B. Pearson to Hopkins and Moore, 6 November 1935.
41 D. W. Thoms and T. Donnelly, 'Coventry's industrial economy, 1880–1980', in Lancaster and Mason, *Life and Labour in a 20th Century City,* pp. 24, 25.
42 PRO, Ed. 114/949, *Report of HM Inspectors on the Coventry Municipal Technical Institute*, 1914, p. 6.
43 PRO, Ed. 90/244, W. E. To Gannon, 19 January 1926.
44 PRO, Ed. 90/245, F. Harrod to Secretary, Board of Education, 10 July 1935.
45 *Education*, 20 October 1904. For Belcher's own rationale for the scheme, see *Education*, 24 March 1905.
46 CRO, Coventry Local Education Authority (CLEA), Technical, Art and Evening Schools Sub-Committee, Minutes, 5 May 1936.
47 PRO, Ed. 90/244, J. Walter to Savage, 29 April 1933.
48 CRO, CLEA, Technical, Art and Evening Schools Sub-Committee, 15 September 1937.
49 CRO, Coventry Technical Insitute, Committee Minutes, 4 May 1893.
50 PRO, Ed. 53/337, H. C. B. to Campbell, 16 December 1916.
51 Board of Education, *Education for Industry and Commerce: The West Midlands Metal Working Area*, London, 1929, p. 38.

THREE

The subordination of technical education in secondary schooling, 1870–1914

Meriel Vlaeminke

The last quarter of the nineteenth century was a period of unprecedented activity in British education. At all levels new priorities were being voiced and new demands were emerging, which challenged existing notions of education and created tensions within the administrative structures available to deliver them. The nation's oldest educational resources – the school and university endowments – had been firmly appropriated by the socio-cultural élite which adhered to a model of education which was essentially an intensive process of socialisation for leadership, designed to preserve the perceived liberal–romantic culture and protect civilised values from the evils of industrialism and materialism. Through their ready access to élite occupational status, a small number of successful public schools and Oxford and Cambridge Universities ensured that the education deemed appropriate for the majority of the population was shaped by people who upheld quite different educational priorities for their own social class and who could afford to remain personally aloof from a whole range of pressing educational controversies.

But this privileged corner of the educational world was by the last decade of the nineteenth century facing an increasingly effective challenge from an alternative version of education. Other sections of the population were utilising the haphazard collection of educational resources at their disposal to construct a dynamic and self-contained 'system' of education, which disconcertingly had no apparent desire to emulate the priorities of the élite. By the end of the century this new system was approaching completion and creating a multiplicity of tensions which could no longer be ignored or handled by half-hearted expedients. The majority of endowed schools, despite the reorganisations of the Endowed Schools Commissioners, were in a perilous condition, struggling to find a role and become viable, and urgently seeking a way out of their difficulties. Elementary education under the school boards was breaking its boundaries in all directions, and thereby threatening the existence of the underfunded denominational schools. Attracting older pupils as well as children from a wider range of social classes than had originally been envisaged, board schools offered an increasingly ambitious curriculum supported by more highly trained teachers and more sophisticated buildings and equipment. Carefully nurtured by the self-assured cities of late Victorian England, they formed the foundation on which a framework of further education opportunities – evening schools, teacher training, technical colleges and university colleges – could be constructed. This blossoming of the public education service from below was far removed from the limited intentions of the 1870 Act, and left the central authorities groping for rationalisations and mechanisms to keep pace.

It was against this background that technical education 'made more rapid strides forward than it had done in any period so far'.[1] It had not been a pressing issue while industrialisation was in progress or during the subsequent half-century of world economic dominance. Britain's industrial revolution had succeeded in the absence of any formal encouragement or controls, and it had become a key part of the Victorian gospel not to intervene. Industrialists and entrepreneurs were largely placed outside the mainstream of political and cultural life, a process reinforced by the nonconformist background of many of them, while the intellectual élite had no need to assimilate industry or applied science to its own experience. In England neither the universities nor the schools of the governing class had played any part in the industrial transformation, unlike its continental imitators who had had to learn how to do it and programme their institutions accordingly.[2]

In the latter part of the nineteenth century there were signs that attitudes were changing. A number of more perceptive Victorians, aware that Britain's economic supremacy was coming under challenge, made intelligent guesses at the reasons. Prominent amongst them was the inadequacy of educational provision to respond to the more technically demanding 'second' industrial revolution, in which Britain did not have a fortuitous head start. By the 1890s, they had succeeded in forcing the issues onto the political and cultural agenda. The first input of state money into the endowed schools was to encourage practical science and manual instruction, but it was in the publicly-provided sector that those subjects were positively booming. To the enthusiasts these developments did nothing more than accord science and technical subjects something approaching their rightful place after years of neglect, and there was great delight at what was happening. From the Birmingham witness telling the Cross Commission that 'the little blackguards in the poor districts . . . have an extremely sharp intelligence, and they can be especially awakened by science,[3] to the rejoicing of Samuelson that 'the impetus given to technical education [220 technical schools and colleges started between 1891 and 1893] was beyond the most sanguine expectations of its warmest advocates'[4] real change seemed to be in the air.

Arising as it did from non-élite sources, the technical education movement found its home in a motley collection of institutions – former mechanics' institutes, temperance institutes, town and village halls, libraries, and some endowed schools. The county technical instruction committees of the 1890s played an important part in this movement, notably through their support for new urban technical colleges, but in many respects they were conservative in outlook. Much of their energy and money was devoted to sponsoring scattered evening classes in bee-keeping or wood-carving, and their interpretation of technical education for girls was narrowly orientated towards domestic skills. As far as secondary education was concerned, the committees preferred to make capital grants and finance selective scholarships for the benefit of endowed schools, a relationship which helped to swing the balance in favour of the county councils as the unit of educational administration after 1902. They rarely diverted any money to the publicly-provided sector, where the area of really exciting potential for curricular innovation lay in the school board higher grade departments. From the first such foundation in 1876 (in Bradford), higher grade schooling rapidly developed a clear and widely understood identity, and had by the close of the nineteenth century spread far beyond its origins in the industrial north and midlands. By 1899 some 400 institutions, ranging from large (up to 2,600 pupils of all ages) purpose-built schools to numerous small classes in borrowed premises, can be identified in 237 locations in England.[5] Genuinely local in conception, higher grade schools and classes were supplied in response to a clearly articulated demand – the demand of poorer children for more education than the Education Department provided and than the endowed schools were able or willing to offer. What kind of further education were they looking for and what were the various education authorities in a position to supply?

The old idea that the lower classes were innately hostile towards education has now been largely discredited, but they did have particular requirements, deriving both from cultural norms and from practical necessities. In short, if schooling was perceived as 'a good thing', it must also produce useful results; hence it had to be efficient, cheap and inviting. At a time of expanding employment opportunities – generated by new industrial developments, by the growth of a service sector of employment, and by the emergence of a new crop of sub-professions – the qualifications obtainable through the formal education system became the most important aid to occupational mobility. After something like a generation's worth of school board provision, it seems that much of the early resistance had subsided and a significant adjustment in attitude had occurred. Successful, well-resourced higher grade departments offered unique opportunities to poorer families and yet, organically connected as they were to the public elementary system, posed no formal or financial barriers to entrance. Nor did they demand the kind of long-term commitment to attendance which poorer families were simply not in a position to give. Higher grade school parents were overwhelmingly (80–85 per cent) drawn from the lower middle class and skilled or semi-skilled working class,[6] people whose lifestyles contained a number of inbuilt economic uncertainties, and the headteachers were keenly aware of the financial sacrifices some families were making.

The heads knew too that it was imperative for families' substantial investment in extended schooling to be suitably rewarded, and it was above all in the area of the curriculum, and the manner of its delivery, that the supply had to match the demand. Higher grade education placed a much firmer emphasis on attainment and the formal certification of it than any fee-paying institutions, including the so-called 'academic' grammar schools. All entrants were required to have reached a designated Standard in the Education Department Code (most commonly V or VI, which was generally achieved at the age of eleven or twelve), and each year of every course of study was examinable. This was dictated by the inadequate funding of the schools, which forced a heavy reliance on the grant-earning potential of their pupils, but it does also seem to have accorded successfully with their needs. Compared with their contemporaries in grammar schools, and even more in girls' high schools where only morning sessions were held, higher grade school pupils worked very hard – normally 9.00 a.m. to 5.00 p.m. for forty-four weeks a year – and yet attendance and discipline were exceptionally good. From all sources a consistent picture

58

emerges of an intensive, though not unpleasant, form of schooling which placed a high premium on achievement and measurable results, very different from the liberal–classical tradition which was leisurely both in terms of the aspects of knowledge it favoured and the length of time it took.

Whilst a whole range of examining bodies was utilised in higher grade schools – Nottingham's High Pavement School listed no fewer than twenty – by far the most significant was the Science and Art Department; indeed, without that department the higher grade school movement would not have existed. It was something of a maverick in top educational circles, enjoying a virtually autonomous existence in South Kensington, and with its dedication to science and technical education, its choice of senior personnel and its reliance on examinations, it embodied the antithesis of élite educational priorities. Unexpectedly, it found itself filling a vacuum in the publicly-provided school system, which gave rise to the view that the Science and Art Department was producing a 'lop-sided' or 'warped' curriculum in many secondary schools. This interpretation strongly influenced the restructuring of secondary education after 1902, when there was much talk of a 'balanced curriculum', 'general education' and 'excessive specialisation', terms which are meaningless without knowing the context in which they are expressed. People whose own education would seem to have been conspicuously narrow in curricular terms felt free to indulge in relentless criticism and to issue dire warnings about the future of education, without apparently knowing much about what actually went on in many of the nation's secondary schools.

During the 1890s, the Science and Art Department regulations were progressively liberalised, and although science and technical subjects were still important in higher grade and organised science schools, their head teachers showed a careful regard for constructing as wide an education as teaching resources and examination requirements permitted. Indeed, the striking feature of most schools' prospectuses was the extremely long list of subjects they hoped to fit onto the timetable. At the Leeds Central Higher Grade School, the biggest in the country, all boys and girls studied English, history, geography, Latin, French, mathematics, at least two sciences, drawing, manual instruction and physical education, with religious instruction, German, shorthand, book-keeping, geometry and dressmaking also included at various points during the four-year course. Sciences claimed the largest share of the time – between eleven and fourteen hours (according to age) of a twenty-seven hour week, with two hours for manual instruction – but clearly other subjects were not ignored, and this was before the Science and Art Department's biggest step towards liberalising its curriculum in 1895. The prospectus for High Pavement School summarised its 'Higher Grade Syllabus of Co-education extending over five years' under nine headings – Scripture, Literary, Commercial, Science and Mathematics, Art, Technical Training, Music, Special to Girls and Physical. The school's new premises included large chemistry and physics laboratories 'fitted to meet the latest requirements of an Organised Science School', a science lecture room, laundry, gymnasium, swimming bath and garden, and the facilities of the city's technical centre and cookery school were available for manual instruction and cookery. The stated aim was to provide 'special facilities for learning through "the logic of dirty fingers", as the work of the bench, of the physical and chemical laboratories, and of the laundry and cookery school has aptly been called'. Sir George Kekewich, who visited in 1900, judged High Pavement to be 'a beautiful school . . . this is the kind of school which really needs not inspection but appreciation. I wish all schools were like it.'[7]

What is interesting is that the higher grade school movement increasingly saw itself as pioneering a new style of curriculum, which was useful but not narrowly utilitarian, combining practical, technical, intellectual, cultural, physical and aesthetic pursuits. Its headteachers began to use phrases like 'this renascence of learning' and 'educating the whole powers of man' to validate their work, and stated emphatically that theirs was 'an important type of school' entitled to 'recognition and consideration as national secondary schools'. They were still evolving and experimenting, but certain principles were held dear – that variety was possible without glorifying certain areas of study and demeaning others, that children from humbler backgrounds should not be trained in a particular, limited way, and that the 'dull boys must be as carefully taught as the clever boys'. The heads were of course pleased when a former pupil gained a university degree, but they resisted the idea that universities should dominate secondary education. They saw servicing (with the aid of scholarships) the other variants of higher and continuation education as their special province – the technical colleges, art colleges, pupil teacher centres, evening schools and the like – while also providing sufficient diversity to prepare pupils for the full range of future occupations and training. Civil, mechanical and electrical engineering, surveying, dyeworks, factories, chemical works, architects' offices, art rooms and design studios were specifically mentioned as likely areas of employment. The heads were happy to accept the paramount duty of educating children for 'the practical needs of after life', but passionately argued their right to access to literary culture and to 'knowledge of their own glorious inheritance'.[8] As a definition of the secondary school curriculum – and in particular the place of technical education within it – this approach has, even today, a refreshingly enlightened and thoughtful ring to it.

Is there any evidence that the schools fulfilled these goals, and that their pupils took their more advanced technical and scientific skills with them into the workforce? The allegation that a fairly high proportion became teachers or clerks has sometimes been used to support a view that publicly-provided secondary schooling was a trick – a means by which undeserving children got a form of secondary education 'on the cheap' and then moved into white-collar jobs to which they were not entitled.[9]

There are three responses which show this interpretation to be flawed. Firstly, many school leavers *did* go into occupations where their specialised education was directly applicable. For instance, a group of 145 boys who entered the Bridge Street School in Birmingham produced twenty-seven engineers of various kinds, thirteen chemists, seven laboratory assistants in other schools and colleges, three jewellers, one optician, four architects, four draughtsmen, nine estate agents/auctioneers, two Post Office telegraphists, and ten miscellaneous skilled craftsmen.[10] Secondly, succinct occupational labels are notoriously unreliable, and it seems likely that a leaver who was recorded as an 'architect's clerk' or an 'errand boy in the bicycle works' was hoping to make a career as an architect or a bicycle engineer rather than as a clerk or errand boy. And thirdly, there is of course no reason why a scientific/technical education was a less suitable preparation for teaching, clerical work or the civil service, than a classical/literary one. Indeed, in the case of teaching, the fact that many higher grade school leavers (especially girls) were well qualified in science and mathematics and returned to similar schools to pass on their knowledge, suggests that the late Victorian school boards were closer to a solution to this particular problem than we are today.[11]

The position of girls in this educational environment was also interesting in other ways. The majority of higher grade schools were co-educational, even if some classes within them were segregated, and female pupils and staff were treated as virtual equals. There was never any question of the girls attending less regularly or aiming at less rigorous standards, and attempts to offer them a different, more 'feminine' curriculum were not well received. Middle class visitors to higher grade schools were impressed – and puzzled – by the enthusiasm and competence shown by girls for mathematics and science, including advanced practical work. At Waterloo School in Oldham, for example, twenty girls looked 'uncommonly bright and happy' working alongside forty-eight boys in the chemistry laboratory, while at Manchester Central School the older girls opted in about equal numbers for the advanced science course and for the special commercial course devised to suit them. And Liverpool School Board was astonished to receive a petition from the girls of six board schools 'asking that they might have the same advantages as boys' in attending classes at the new central science school; 120 subsequently enrolled and the headmaster was said to be 'very proud of his girls'.[12] There were some moves to guide girls into biology or hygiene courses, which seems to have been acceptable provided it led to a qualification of equal status, but the real problem area was in technical/practical work. Manual instruction (woodwork and metalwork) was never available to girls; instead it was assumed by the central authorities that they would enjoy – and must learn – needlework and domestic subjects. There are plenty of indications that the pupils, parents, teachers and school boards were less than enthusiastic about this, seeing it as a waste of precious school time. The London School Board's first superintendent of cookery recorded that 'the prejudice against it was almost insuperable, and parents put every possible obstacle in the way of their children attending the classes', and a special report for the Education Department in 1897 complained that 'extraordinary as it may seem in the face of general ignorance on culinary matters, mothers frequently complained that their daughters "wasted their time" in going to cookery lessons'.[13] This apparently insuperable problem of how to provide 'technical education' for girls without condemning them to tedious domestic rituals was to endure for at least three-quarters of a century.

It is evident, then, that by the turn of the century the moribund endowed grammar school was facing a serious challenge from a vibrant, popular and forward-looking alternative model of secondary schooling. Distinguished by their systematic teaching of science and technical subjects within a broad and flexible curriculum, and happily accepting the vocational implications of their work, the higher grade schools were a crucial link in the rapidly developing public education service, in which the technical education movement found its natural home. So how did they fare in the restructuring which comprised Britain's first attempt to organise and define its secondary education system? Was there, as the higher grade school heads anticipated, a fruitful mingling of styles and approaches, drawing on the best experience that was available and producing an integrated but varied network of schools and allied institutions?

Most educational historians have concurred, with a few reservations.[14] They have characterised the educational scene of the 1890s as a chaotic muddle, in which the inept school boards and the unbalanced curriculum were especially in need of reform. They have applauded the early twentieth-century restructuring as a supreme achievement, based on a unique partnership between the central and the new local authorities, who together produced a vast expansion in the secondary field. In this restructuring, the 1904 Regulations were particularly praiseworthy, restoring balance to the secondary school curriculum and embodying the first official conception of secondary education. That conception – the twentieth-century grammar school – went on to accumulate enormous prestige, attracting passionate devotees and often being imbued with almost fabulous virtues. It has been said that English education in the first decade of this century underwent 'a social revolution of the first magnitude'.[15]

This sounds too good to be true and invites further analysis. It is worth recalling who was making the decisions about the future of Britain's secondary education system. At the head of a large Conservative majority, Lord Salisbury, whose 'antiquated notions of what an educational system should be became increasingly irrelevant and increasingly embarrassing',[16] was replaced as Prime Minister by his nephew, Balfour, to whom 'the question of whether the nation's children went to school or not was a matter of deep indifference', and who regarded education as a 'tricky political topic, fraught with pitfalls and full of intricate discussions of detail; not only that but it was boring'.[17] The President of the Board of Education, constituted in 1899, was a low-ranking political appointment and 'the Board' never existed. For its permanent staff, the Board of Education, uniquely among government deparments, retained recruitment by patronage, looking exclusively to the products of the public schools and Oxbridge, and it had been made impossible for a trained elementary teacher to join the inspectorate. One insider concluded that at this time, education was administered by people 'entirely without first-hand acquaintance with the "proletarian" class of education they control. They lack imagination and they lack positive enthusiasm, though many of them burst with brains.'[18]

And yet this inadequate central structure was under increasing pressure to effect major reforms in education; ideas and leadership were going to have to come from somewhere. Into the void moved one of England's most controversial civil servants, Robert Morant. Some have seen him as 'a remarkably able and single-minded administrator', 'one of the greatest of all civil servants', but others have judged him to be 'not quite sane' and 'over-weeningly ambitious, tortuous and indifferent to common standards of honour'.[19] Educated at Winchester and Oxford, Morant had spent most of his working life as the trusted and highly influential adviser to the King of Siam. He thus arrived in the Department of Education (in 1895) with an unusual blend of conventional English upper middle class views about education and a familiarity with unorthodox, autocratic methods of executing policy. He must immediately have seen the opportunities for a conscientious and well-informed policy-maker to cut through the confusion, and his rise in the administration was spectacular and deliberately – as well as unscrupulously – engineered. By 1902, when he outmanoeuvred his senior colleagues to become Permanent Secretary, he was moving in the highest social and political circles and was a close and trusted ally of the new Prime Minister. Politicians certainly held no fears for him. By dint of devoted hard work and single-mindedness of purpose Morant quickly emerged as the experienced expert, appearing to be the ideal man in command of both practical details and visionary plans.

The purpose about which Morant was most single-minded was to generate a clear and lasting definition of secondary education out of the conflicting interests and variants which had developed during the 1880s and 1890s.

Instinctively sympathetic to the survival campaigns mounted by the struggling endowed secondary schools and the voluntary elementary schools, he surrounded himself with a trusted group of hand-picked colleagues, most of them distinguished for their classical scholarship. He consciously closed himself off from counter-opinions of bodies like the National Union of Teachers and the Association of Directors and Secretaries for Education, whom Kekewich had made increasingly welcome at the Education Department. One of Morant's chief victims was the Science and Art Department – and the traditions it embodied – on which the continued growth of the higher grade schools and technical education in general largely depended. 'Technical' and 'secondary' were identified as separate, even antipathetic, forms of education rather than as an integral whole, and under Morant's guidance the former took a poor second place to the latter as specialisation, examinations, and science and technical subjects all fell from favour.

The early recognition of schools as Division A (more scientific, better funded and more popular) or Division B (more literary) was discarded as soon as decently possible; the Science and Art Department's former right to make grants towards the cost of new buildings for technical education was ended, and its examinations were phased out in 1911 and 1918. Theoretically the technical inspectorate and 'T' branch within the central office were equal partners in the new tripartite division of responsibilities, but Morant's profound dislike of technical and vocational education made them very vulnerable. Hostilities culminated in 1908 when the technical Chief Inspector, Buckmaster, suffered the ignominy of demotion and of a blistering and unjustified attack by Morant for his 'evasive statements . . . misleading to the point of being virtually untrue', which Morant chose to publish to the whole technical inspectorate.[20]

The future of British education therefore lay in the hands of a small group of men who themselves shared a common educational and cultural background, and who had limited experience of any possible alternatives. Stemming from a genuine conviction that in the public schools Britain had perfected the training of its leaders, and thereby arrived at the true purpose of education, there was a ready-made blueprint for the extension of state interest into the realm of secondary education. In a number of respects – their selectivity on the basis of social class, their acceptance of the notion of education as a character-forming experience, their aspiration to Oxbridge classical scholarships as the ultimate achievement, their staffing and their independent governors – the endowed schools were the most promising candidates to accommodate that extension. All over the country, schools which in the 1890s had begun to come to terms with science subjects, elementary school pupils and local authority involvement, were encouraged to discard those features and re-emphasise their community of interest with the public schools. Together with schools which had shown something of a collective deathwish by resisting all those advances, they suddenly found that they were the backbone of the new system; status quickly attached to them, and their rescue was complete.

The conditions were not very taxing. Guaranteed a monopolistic position, they entered the state system virtually on their own terms, retaining much of their independence from public control and receiving extraordinarily sympathetic treatment of deficiencies in buildings, facilities, curriculum and teaching skills. At Bristol Grammar School, for example, the Inspectors found a catalogue of imperfections: the curriculum was 'not quite in accordance' with the regulations; the teaching power was 'too exclusively directed' to the classical upper school, to the neglect of boys wanting a 'modern education'; the science syllabus and accommodation were unsatisfactory (the chemistry laboratory recently erected with money from the Technical Instruction Committee had fallen down) and science lessons occupied only two hours per week; there was no art room and no facilities for manual instruction, though the headmaster persuaded the Board that this was acceptable because practical science (of which there can have been very little) 'might be regarded as manual exercise'. And yet recognition as a Division B Secondary School was speedily given in 1903 and was never subsequently in doubt.[21] Examples like this can be found in almost every town and city in England. Few grammar schools were in a healthy state before 1902, and after that date rulings were interpreted in a most generous spirit – including the widely applauded 1904 Regulations on curriculum, the impact of which was far from clear in most endowed secondary schools.

In sharp contrast, all aspiring municipal secondary schools were subjected to minute supervision, backed up by the threat of loss of funding, in the Board's crusade to turn them into pale imitations of the more favoured institutions. The 1904 pronouncement that central grants were primarily designed to 'give impartial encouragement to all well-considered local effort towards developing a general system of Secondary Schools through many channels and in varying directions'[22] was soon proved to have no substance at all as far as curricular choice was concerned. Science and technical subjects were constantly under attack, while the merits of Latin, Greek, modern languages and English were regularly and thoroughly expounded. Excellence in the latter range of subjects was to be a goal for all secondary schools; excellence in the former was commented upon unfavourably, as if a temporary aberration from the past.

It is impossible to find an example of an HMI giving a firm vote of confidence in the science and technical teaching of a school which prided itself on its work in those areas. The good qualifications of the staff and the high standard of the pupils achievement were often commented upon, perhaps because they were such a novelty to the HMIs, but the advice was always to *reduce* the amount of time, the scope of the work, or the level of achievement. Examples are not hard to find. At St George School, Bristol, the work in science was thought to be 'excellent' and 'truly advanced . . . if not somewhat too ambitious', but occupied 'too great a preponderance' in the curriculum. St

George reluctantly decided 'to drop Science Examinations altogether
. . . and adopt an academic Examination', and the time given to
science was 'much diminished'. At Fairfield Road School, also in
Bristol, 'more time than is necessary is allotted to Science, Mathematics and Drawing', though the teaching was of a high standard, with
'ample demonstration and excellent practical development in the
Laboratory'. In Birmingham, George Dixon School was persuaded to
reduce the amount of physics on the timetable, and Waverley Road
was told that its chemistry laboratory was too big, while at Leamington's pupil teacher classes (soon to become the municipal
secondary school), 'too much time is devoted to Science'.[23]

Even more out of favour were commercial subjects and manual
instruction, both of which had a ready appeal for school leavers and
their parents, and which had been positively encouraged by HMIs up
to about 1900. But Morant had a particular loathing for vocational and
technical education, behaving 'almost as if no education at all was
preferable',[24] and after that date there was a steady erosion of the time
and status accorded to those subjects. St George School's manual
instruction was 'of a high order' but should, with drawing, be regarded
as a 'more subsidiary subject', which 'might be dropped or partially
discontinued', and the head of Waverley Road was informed that
machine drawing, book-keeping and shorthand were all unacceptable
items on the timetable.[25] In the new secondary schools, manual
instruction for boys was one of the favoured targets for pruning, to
make room for Latin and more English, though girls were much more
likely to lose science and mathematics time, their cookery and
needlework by contrast being safeguarded. Hence the HMIs visiting St
George School strongly advised that the girls seen doing advanced
electrical measurements in the physics laboratory would be better
employed on domestic science or hygiene, and that in needlework
'mending, patching and darning should be given proper encouragement', in preference to 'fancy, so-called Art work' which 'struck
the Inspector as being of questionable taste'.[26] It should be noted,
incidentally, that what the municipal schools called 'commercial
courses' were not narrowly skills-based or vocational, but were likely
to consist of English language and literature, French, geography,
arithmetic, religious knowledge, art drawing, music, manual instruction, domestic economy, drill, book-keeping and shorthand.[27] But to
Morant, such courses were 'intrinsically bad educationally, and were
provided merely to meet the mistaken view of parents as to what is
good for their boys and girls', while manual work emerged as 'a vexed

question . . . which has given us a lot of trouble', over which reluctant schools should be allowed 'large discretion'.[28]

Instead, the constant drive from the Board of Education and the Inspectorate was to enhance the allotment of time, the qualifications of the staff and the levels of achievement in literary subjects, especially Latin. Each annual report hammered out the message that 'the Board attach so much importance to the inclusion of Latin', and a special pamphlet was produced in 1905 to counteract 'the increasing tendency in Secondary Schools to drop Greek altogether'.[29] It seems to have been taken for granted that a 'real' secondary school could not exist as such unless it taught Latin seriously and continuously, and its progress in municipal schools was always commented upon, usually at length and with forceful exhortations to enhance its place. Not surprisingly their performance was not what the typical HMI was familiar with. Latin at Waverley Road was reported in 1907 to have got off to a good start, but the sixth formers were said to be 'timid', as if they 'feel themselves on perilous ground and . . . hesitate for fear of making a mistake'. And it was urged at Fairfield Road School – where the Bristol Education Committee maintained 'there is no demand for classical education' – that the fourth formers 'ought to be in a position to read Caesar by the Summer Term' of their first year of studying Latin. The 1904 inspection report on George Dixon Girls' School noted with pleasure that Latin was replacing commercial subjects, and the boys' school next door was encouraged to extend Latin throughout the school at the expense of German.[30]

There, as at all similar schools, the biggest criticism was the absence of a specialist classics teacher, which gave rise to the HMIs' recurrent concern that the municipal secondary schools lacked 'a background of scholarship', regardless of their achievements in science or any other subjects. We can now say with confidence that they were wrong, but even in the context of the early twentieth century, England's Board of Education was addicted to the classical/literary style of education in a way which no other country quite shared. Around the same time, Germany was modifying its traditional classical secondary school curriculum to produce one which 'was really rather progressive for its time', and in France a practically-orientated secondary curriculum was flourishing while 'the classical stream entered a period of stagnation and decline'.[31] In the United States, the period between 1890 and 1914 saw dramatic growth in the public education service, including a successful 'blurring of the sharp lines that used to separate academic and vocational education'.[32] And closer to home, the sixteen Welsh education committees responsible for the new intermediate schools launched after 1889 looked 'rather to the continent than to England' and 'were determined that the new schools should not follow the old grammar school tradition'; after 1907 their Chief Inspector fought hard to retain the scientific–vocational character of Welsh secondary schooling in the face of heavy pressure from Morant.[33] Scotland, meanwhile, with its own long-established educational traditions, 'was prepared to deal heavy blows to the classics in order to insist on a proper teaching of science', and with refreshing insight the Scottish teachers argued through their journal that 'any subject could impart "culture" if it was properly taught'.[34] The English Board of Education truly did seem to be out of step with contemporary educational thinking in the modern, industrial, democratic world.

In all these countries there were tensions between alternative styles of secondary education, but England was unique in its exclusive endorsement of the favoured model. It might be thought that if the Board of Education had been genuinely looking to achieve the balance, flexibility and responsiveness to local needs which it said it valued, it would have endorsed the creation of more scientific or technical secondary schools, especially as the classical curriculum was safely ensconced in the prestigious independent schools over which the Board chose to exercise no control.

It might alternatively have reasoned that there was scope for a tier of 'intermediate' schools, lower in status than the secondary school and located within the elementary sector, where science, technical and vocational subjects could predominate. This, it was initially assumed, was to be the role of the higher elementary schools, announced in 1900 and heralded as the eagerly awaited legitimisation of the higher grade schools following the Cockerton Judgment. But it quickly became apparent that they were no such thing. Subjected to minute and confining restrictions, the higher elementary schools were never allowed to acquire an identity or prestige. They found little favour with local authorities, teachers or parents or, indeed, with the Board of Education which had invented them. Only two out of 190 applications were approved in the first year; no more than fifty two of them existed nationwide, and they were abolished in 1918. Even less energy was put into the junior technical schools, which were launched in 1905 and relaunched in 1913 but remained a very shadowy entity, generally consisting of two or three classes of older boys receiving trade instruction. Clearly, in Morant's eyes technical education, in the broad sense that it had been developing in schools of the 1890s, was too popular but delinquent a style of education to be given a home in *any* of the nation's schools, at least while his vision of the secondary school was being 'sufficiently implanted in the public mind'.[35] In the first few years at least, this vision was to be protected from any possible rivals. All other schools were restricted in scope to enhance the status of the grammar school.

Any school with an explicitly technical orientation – or even the word 'technical' in its name –[36] seemed to be an automatic target for the Board's hostility. Many municipal secondary schools were of this type; it was often the natural choice for local authorities seeking to meet the needs of the urban economy and of urban children, and also, in a number of cases, make optimum use of good technical college facilities which were otherwise underused during the day. But whatever the quality of the work and the evident local popularity of such schools, the Board was highly critical of the drawbacks of sharing a building, where 'so many have the right of entry that it is difficult to distinguish between authorised and unauthorised persons' (as at the Birmingham Municipal Technical Day School), or where the school was 'merely an aggregation of scientific and technical classes' with pupils and staff 'constantly meeting and mixing' with others who used the building (as at Bath City Technical School).[37] The Walsall Technical Secondary School in 1905 declared its aim to be 'to develop a boy's whole faculties, by means of a systematic and progressive course of Intellectual Instruction and Manual Training. It is not intended to teach any particular trade, but simply to provide a complete education of both head and hand.' But the HMIs attacked the low fees, the 'ill-suited' building, the shared use of laboratories, the excessive science and mathematics and the head's lack of 'proper' secondary school experience, and forced the school's closure within a year. A senior Board official indulged in some unseemly jubilation: 'I think we may now congratulate ourselves on having extinguished the exceedingly unsatisfactory Walsall Municipal Technical Day School as a Secondary School – let us hope we shall be equally successful with Hanley and West Bromwich.'[38]

In the event, both Hanley and West Bromwich escaped the Board's axe, but only just. Hanley argued strongly that 'in view of the industries of the district it is essential that boys [there were in fact 244 boys and 288 girls at the time] should have every opportunity of receiving a sound scientific education'. Even the visiting HMIs were impressed by the excellent work in science, mathematics, drawing, carpentry and metalwork, and though they wanted more patching and darning and systematic scullery work for the girls and complained that Latin was 'treated somewhat as an intruder on the curriculum', they could not find a sufficiently cogent excuse to drive the Hanley school out of existence. There was a similar story at West Bromwich Municipal Day Technical School, whose determined efforts to remain true to its original aim earned scathing criticism from Morant – 'has shown very considerable adroitness in confusing the issues', and 'would always be well satisfied with anything that was cheap, as they have no objection to shoddy'. Not far away at Handsworth, the endowed grammar school, constrained by its very poor buildings, formed a happy partnership with a new day science school housed in the excellent local technical college, each contributing its specialist teaching and facilities to benefit the pupils of the other. But the Board chose not to make this fruitful arrangement fit its regulations, and within four years the Staffordshire Education Committee was informed that 'the Day Science School of Handsworth has lately been closed, in deference to the expressed wishes of the Board'.[39] The many disputes of this nature between the centre and the provinces reveal much about their deeply conflicting perceptions of the role and purpose of secondary schooling, and – when local authorities showed any resistance – about the autocratic manner in which the new system was delivered to different parts of the country.

Technical institutions supported by endowment received slightly more lenient treatment, at least for a while. For a few years the Merchant Venturers' Technical College School in Bristol earned nothing but praise from the HMIs, but in time its deviance from the grammar school model counted against it and by 1908 the judgement was that 'from every point of view the position of this School as part of the Technical College is regrettable . . . The Merchant Venturers have from time to time threatened to drop the Secondary School and personally I am disposed to think that this might be a good thing.' Ten years later this was accomplished. In Coventry, Bablake School, an old hospital foundation, had carved out for itself a successful role as a specialist science and technical institution with low fees and lots of scholarships, catering for the 'son of artisans, foremen of works (cycle and other) and some sons of farmers' (there were some boarding scholarships). It was reported to be 'highly valued by the people of Coventry' and 'a most valuable feeder for the Coventry Technical Institute and . . . the engineering trades of Coventry'. But the Board decided that 'what is now wanted is to lift the work to a higher plane . . . to enable the scholars to move freely and easily among educated men', by the simple device of raising the fees. There was a massive protest in Coventry, involving public meetings, petitions and letters from individuals, businesses, the Trades Council, nine different trade union branches, the freemen of the city, the Town Clerk's office, and the Guardians of the Poor, but the fees were duly raised and the school's character gradually altered over the years.[40] Coventry was one of a number of cities – Bristol and Nottingham were others – where the Board of Education's policy aroused considerable, though fruitless, opposition from ordinary people, suggesting that they cared very much about the kind of education available to them.

One of the concomitants of defining secondary education as a non-utilitarian, middle class activity was that the educational prospects offered to the majority of the population were dismal. Around 90 per cent of the nation's children in the early twentieth century were destined to spend their entire school career in elementary schools where the curriculum (particularly in science) was deliberately curtailed and where the pupils too old to be drilled for secondary school entrance examinations were something of a nuisance. As one Bristolian said of his last two years of schooling in 1905–7: 'the curriculum was devoid of frills such as Woodwork, Science and French, so it is only to be expected that I have very little to remember. Had we been allowed to continue in "Higher Grade", the last year or two would certainly have given us a wider education. [We] could be said to have been deprived.'[41] It was nevertheless the case that, even where scholarships and maintenance grants were available, thousands of children preferred that dispiriting option to trying for a secondary school place or taking up one they had won – a remarkable comment on what large sections of the population thought of the new 'national' system of education.

The decision to curb all forms of schooling other than the secondary grammar school was an expression of a particular perception of social class, dictated by two strands of traditional thinking. First was the idea that education, especially that provided out of public funds, should be a restricted commodity, available only in such quantities as people 'needed' it, rather than as a liberating, enriching experience from which all might benefit. Such an interpretation of education 'need' requires advance decisions about who should receive what, and the obvious divisions to conservative Victorians were those based upon existing social and occupational groupings. Education as a means of social mobility had a very limited appeal to such people. The capacity to pay fees – on which the Board of Education insisted in every recognised secondary school, whatever the wishes of the local authority – was the most convenient way to select the secondary school population. But the second ingredient ensured that, even for the much larger number whom it was assumed would constitute the labouring classes, any form of technical or vocational training had no place within formal schooling. The profound anti-industrialism of the liberal, gentlemanly, classical tradition in education favoured by England's ruling classes created an ignorance and suspicion of anything which smacked of manual work, applied science or trade instruction. Schooling for all social classes was consequently more to do with producing a certain sort of person than with imparting knowledge or skills (with the exception of domestic skills for girls). Hence elementary education, according to Morant's widely admired 1904 Regulations, was primarily to inculcate habits of industry, self-control, truthfulness and loyalty, and technical education was pushed to the margins of the formal education system, an optional extra which could take place either 'on the job' or as a part-time, largely unrecognised activity. The pioneering work which had been done in developing a broad-based school curriculum which combined general and technical education fitted none of the categories of 'need' as defined by the Board of Education, and so was laid aside in a position from which it has struggled ever since to recover.

This lends weight to a fundamental questioning of the merits of the newly created system of secondary schooling, the success of which was achieved at the cost of so much else in education that overall it represented a diminution rather than an enhancement of opportunities. Undoubtedly technical education was one of the principal losers. No authority on the subject denies that after 1902 technical education at all levels suffered a period of 'comparative neglect', or at best 'only a slow evolution',[42] and at secondary school level the picture was particularly bleak. Even allowing for changes in attitudes over the years, it is hard to accept that the curriculum promoted by the early-century Board of Education was wisely balanced, the essence of a 'general' education. It was, of course, a happy convenience for the Board that the schools which it most wished to get rid of were also those which were identified with the subjects it least valued. Its determination to drive anything too useful or vocational out of the secondary schools reflected a particular approach to learning which was already under threat and which represented a serious mismatch with the needs both of the larger part of the population and, it can be argued, of the nation as an economic and political unit.[43] In the Board of Education as structured and staffed by Morant, there was *nobody* at the higher levels who advanced the claims of science and technical education. At no point in the education system did science and technical subjects even hold their ground under the early twentieth-century Board of Education; far less were they extended or encouraged in the nation's new secondary schools.

Notes

1 M. Argles, *South Kensington to Robbins*, London, 1964, p. 31.
2 As it was neatly put in one case, 'Germany was a land of schools before it was a land of factories'. E. H. Reisner, *Nationalism and Education Since 1789*, New York, 1939, p. 181.
3 Quoted by C. Heward, 'Education, examinations and the artisans' in R. Macleod, *Days of Judgement*, Driffield, 1982, p. 54.
4 Reported in *The Record of Technical and Secondary Education*, III, January 1894, p. 10.
5 See Appendix 1 in M. Vlaeminke, 'The English Higher Grade Schools: a reassessment', unpublished Ph.D. thesis, University of Leicester, 1987.
6 As shown by C. N. J. Scudamore, *The Social Background of Pupils at the Bridge Street Higher Grade School, Birmingham*, unpublished M.Ed. thesis, University of Birmingham, 1976, pp. 118–20; by reference to various schools' admissions registers; and to *Royal Commission on Secondary Education* (Bryce Commission), 1895, VII, p. 273.
7 *Bryce Commission*, IX, pp. 414–5, 422–3; *Prospectus* of High Pavement Higher Grade School, 1895/6/7; *Log Book* of the same school, 23 November 1900; and private letter from Kekewich (Secretary to the Education Department) to the Nottingham School Board Clerk, 4 December 1900. An interesting area which is not explored here is the tensions *within* subjects between the traditional, theoretical approach and more practical, 'modern' interpretations being advanced at the beginning of this century. See M. H. Price (ed.), *The Development of the Secondary Curriculum*, London, 1986.
8 This paragraph is based on speeches made to conferences of the Association of Headmasters of Higher Grade and Organised Science Schools, formed in 1892, as reported in *The Schoolmaster*. It should be noted that heads of co-educational schools sometimes referred only to their 'boys', though in other respects, as will be seen later, girls were treated in an unusually egalitarian manner.
9 A view freely expressed by the endowed school heads through the Incorporated Association of Head Masters, and by various witnesses to the *Bryce Commission*, VIII, e.g.: 'They sometimes go more for the social advantage gained than for a continuance of education' (Mr Douglas Richmond, Endowed Schools Assistant Commissioner, p. 12); 'The impecunious classes cannot expect to get Secondary Education except by means of exhibitions' (Bishop of London, p. 50); and 'Secondary Education is of no value to children of the working classes unless they possess exceptional ability, because it unfits them for manual labour' (Mr P. A. Barnett, HMI, p. 121).

10 *Admission Register* of George Dixon Secondary Boys' (formerly Bridge Street) School. In addition, thirteen went on to further education, thirty-five went into offices, six to the Civil Service, three to banks, six became salesmen/shop assistants, and two joined the Navy.

11 The early-century crisis in teacher recruitment caused by Morant's changes to the pupil-teacher system, coupled with the widespread weakness of science in most grammar schools, especially girls' schools, very quickly produced the alarming dearth of science and technical teachers to which the (Thompson) *Committee to Enquire into the Position of Natural Sciences in the Educational System of Great Britain*, 1918, pp. 5–6, drew attention.

12 *Bryce Commission*, VI, pp. 354, 376, 253, 384.

13 C. Dyhouse, *Girls Growing Up in Late Victorian and Edwardian England*, London, 1981, p. 90; Education Department, *Special Reports on Education Subjects*, London, 1896.

14 Views drawn from J. W. Adamson, *English Education 1789–1902*, Cambridge, 1930; R. L. Archer, *Secondary Education in the Nineteenth Century*, Cambridge, 1921; O. Banks, *Parity and Prestige in English Secondary Education*, London, 1955; H. C. Barnard, *A History of English Education from 1760*, London, 1947; S. J. Curtis, *Education in Britain since 1900*, London, 1952; R. Davis, *The Grammar School*, London, 1967; H. C. Dent, *1870–1970: Century of Growth in English Education*, London, 1970; K. Evans, *The Development and Structure of the English Education System*, London, 1975; J. Graves, *Policy and Progress in Secondary Education 1902–1942*, London, 1942; J. N. Hewitson, *The Grammar School Tradition in a Comprehensive World*, London, 1969; M. Hyndman, *Schools and Schooling in England and Wales*, London, 1978; J. Leese, *Personalities and Power in English Education*, London, 1950.

15 E. Halevy, *Imperialism and the Rise of Labour*, London, 1951 edition, p. 205.

16 T. Taylor, 'Lord Salisbury and the politics of education', *Journal of Educational Administration and History*, XVI, 1984, p. 8.

17 S. H. Zebel, *Balfour: A Political Biography*, Cambridge, 1973, pp. 119–20; and T. Taylor, 'An early arrival of the fascist mentality: Robert Morant's rise to power', *Journal of Educational Administration and History*, XVII, 1985, p. 50. As explained by K. Rose, *The Later Cecils*, London, 1975, and T. Taylor, 'The Cecils and the Cockerton case: higher politics and low intentions', *History of Education Society Bulletin*, 37, 1986, three additional numbers of the Cecil family were actively involved in the shaping of education policy (including directing resistance in the House of Lords after 1906). They shared a devotion to High Church Anglicanism and to anti-democratic Conservatism which was extreme even for the time.

18 F. H. Spencer, *An Inspector's Testament*, London, 1938, p. 313.

19 N. Mackenzie (ed.), *The Letters of Sidney and Beatrice Webb*, II, Cambridge, 1978, p. 138; E. J. R. Eaglesham, *The Foundations of Twentieth-century Education*, London, 1967, p. 39; A. V. Judges, 'The educational influence of the Webbs', *British Journal of Educational Studies*, X, 1961, p. 44; J. Craig, *A History of Red Tape*, London, 1955, p. 155.

20 E. J. R. Eaglesham, 'The centenary of Sir Robert Morant', *British Journal of Education Studies*, XII, 1963, p. 9. The Elementary Chief Inspector resigned

from the service as a result of conflicts with Morant.

21 PRO, Ed. 35/848.
22 Board of Education, *Regulations for Secondary Schools*, London, 1904, p. 10.
23 PRO, Ed. 35/860; St George School, *Log Book*, 29 April 1904; PRO, Ed. 35/846; PRO, Ed. 35/2554; PRO, Ed. 35/2579; Leamington Education Committee, *Minutes*, 14 December 1903.
24 Eaglesham, 'The Centenary', p. 6.
25 PRO, Ed. 35/860; PRO, Ed. 35/2579.
26 PRO, Ed. 35/860.
27 These were the timetabled subjects in the commercial department of the Manchester Central Higher Grade School; schools in Bradford and Birmingham were similar. *Bryce Commission*, VI, p. 265 and VII, pp. 57–8.
28 PRO, Ed. 12/40; PRO, Ed. 12/45; PRO, Ed. 12/50.
29 Board of Education, *Report for the Year 1904–5* and *1906–7*, London, 1905 and 1907, p. 14 and p. 68.
30 PRO, Ed. 35/2579; PRO, Ed. 35/846; PRO, Ed. 35/2554.
31 F. K. Ringer, *Education and Society in Modern Europe*, Indiana, 1979, pp. 74, 139.
32 K. Lindsay, *Social Progress and Educational Waste*, London, 1926, p. 27.
33 L. W. Evans, *Studies in Welsh Education*, Cardiff, 1974, pp. 20–1; and G. E. Jones, *Controls and Conflicts in Welsh Secondary Education 1889–1944*, Cardiff, 1982, pp. 25–9.
34 R. L. Anderson, *Education and Opportunity in Victorian Scotland*, Oxford, 1983, pp. 205, 230; and N. A. Wade, *Post-Primary Education in the Primary Schools of Scotland 1872–1936*, London, 1939, pp. 116–7.
35 Morant's own words in PRO, Ed. 12/40.
36 In the case of one Derbyshire school, an internal Board memo saying. 'I should prefer to get rid of "Technical" out of the name, but I do not like to do so if the Authority have deliberately used it', was met with the ruling that 'we'll call it "Heanor Secondary School" anyway'. PRO, Ed. 35/426.
37 PRO, Ed. 35/2576; PRO, Ed. 35/2158.
38 PRO, Ed. 35/2299.
39 PRO, Ed. 35/2275; PRO, Ed. 35/2300; PRO, Ed. 35/2556. The six schools mentioned in these two paragraphs had all been thriving higher grade schools.
40 PRO, Ed. 35/845; PRO, Ed. 35/2588.
41 A. C. Hone of Merrywood Higher Grade School, quoted in L. H. Clare, *Change and Conflict in Bristol Public Education 1895–1905*, unpublished M.Litt. thesis, University of Bristol, 1975, Appendix I.
42 Argles, *South Kensington to Robbins*, p. 62; S. F. Cotgrove, *Technical Education and Social Change*, London, 1958, p. 68.
43 As it has been by Correlli Barnett, who alleges that Morant 'set out in office not to provide England with education for capability (either general or technical) that could match that of her rivals, but to demolish what little had been gradually built up'. *The Audit of War*, London, 1986, p. 223.

FOUR

Technical and vocational education for girls. A study of the central schools of London, 1918–1939

Sarah King

The English education system of the inter-war years was marked by a 'continuous search' for institutions and courses which responded to national worries about changing economic and social fortunes.[1] Educational policy-makers were preoccupied by the distinction between a liberal, general education on the one hand and technical, vocational instruction on the other. The view most commonly expressed was that vocational training should complement an initial, basic education. However, a powerful current of opinion rejected the notion that technical and vocational education had any place in secondary schools. The widely accepted solution to the problem of defending the academic tradition of secondary schools while simultaneously encouraging technical training for the sake of national rejuvenation was to promote a diversity of institutions ostensibly to meet the diversity of need, talent and aptitude of pupils.

The development of selective central schools during the inter-war years was part of this solution. They were consciously progressive schools to which children gained admittance via an examination, and they sought to provide a balanced combination of a broad general education and a technical, vocational training which would together create adaptable and efficient citizens. They were avowedly to prepare their students, including girls, for immediate employment. But in offering such education under the elementary as opposed to the secondary Code of Regulations, they implicitly and explicitly indicated that technical and vocational education were suitable for a working-class, but not for a middle-class, clientele. Furthermore, the limited understanding of the meaning of technical education for girls embodied in their curricula provides a concrete expression of inter-war

77

gender ideology.

Nevertheless, central schools were acknowledged by contemporaries as the most innovative and successful feature of an education system experiencing few positive developments in an economically stringent era. They were particularly strong in London. Just over 300 central schools eventually operated in England and Wales, but by the mid-1920s the selective central schools of London, on which this paper will focus, were educating almost as many pupils as all the secondary schools of the capital.[2] The selective schools are particularly important for they became in practice secondary schools for the most able working class children, the pupils who were 'most susceptible of cultivation and sensitive of neglect' if not given the correct type of education.[3] Above all, it was generally believed in educational circles that the central schools would lead the way towards future educational progress, as the official pamphlet, 'A New Prospect in Education', stated explicitly in 1928: 'What up to now has been loosely termed the central school is important because along with the general advance we may by its means feel our way to new forms and varieties of post primary education.'[4]

The selective central schools of the inter-war era were modelled upon the Higher Grade Schools which had developed in London during the pre-war period. During the late nineteenth century, the London School Board had set up a number of schools to provide a form of advanced instruction for able elementary sector pupils. As Meriel Vlaeminke has shown in her contribution to this book, these institutions were technically illegal under the 1870 Education Act and a dispute with the Board of Education in 1900–1 resulted in the issue of new regulations imposing strict requirements and limitations on any Higher Elementary Schools. The London County Council (LCC), education authority for the capital from 1904, decided not to seek recognition of its Higher Grade Schools under the new rules but instead to develop the existing schools under the elementary sector code. It thus forfeited a higher rate of grant but retained more freedom to provide in the renamed Central Elementary Schools a 'superior instruction' to give pupils a 'definite bias' towards the labour requirements of the city. By 1918 the fifty-one central schools of London were a proven success and officially acknowledged as such in the 1918 Education Act. The new Act for the first time laid a duty on local education authorities to provide some form of advanced schooling for all able children. The school leaving age was raised to fourteen and children were to be permitted to stay at school until they reached sixteen, thus accommodating a four-year advanced course commencing at eleven or twelve. It was officially accepted and nationally assumed that 'the London Central Schools represent the type of school contemplated under the Act'. The LCC made immediate plans to increase the number of schools to 100, taking 8 per cent of an age group, and the Elementary Sub-Committee congratulated itself upon 'the success which has led to the recognition of the central schools as an essential part of the national system of education'.[5]

It was not long before the ideals behind the 1918 Act began to be tempered by the economic stringency which so constrained inter-war education policy. Although the central schools experienced financial cutbacks, they did develop into a national network. The exact type of institution varied from area to area: for example, Bradford had non-selective 'intermediate schools' and Leicestershire, 'municipal secondary schools' to which all children of a certain age could go. However, in an age of education meritocracy, it was the selective type which were most acclaimed. By the early twenties in many regions a system similar to that of London had developed whereby candidates for both secondary and central schools sat the same Junior Scholarship Examination in either May or November; the best 'A1' candidates were offered places in secondary schools, while those who had slightly lower marks or whose parents could not afford the secondary expenses were allocated to central schools. Each central school had either an industrial or commercial bias to its curriculum, depending on the needs of the labour market in the surrounding area, and therefore there was also often an aptitude test to decide which type of course was most suitable for the pupil.

The development of this type of schooling was in line with the wish of the Conservative Party to maintain a form of élite academic education and to oppose universal secondary education. Major civil servants at the Board of Education also saw true advanced education as being suited only for a minority.[6] In this context the position of the central schools was always ambiguous and uncertain, particularly since it was mainly Conservative politicians who held power at the Board during the inter-war years. The greatest handicap was the constant refusal of the government to include central schools under the secondary code of funding. They suffered disproportionately from inadequate accommodation and equipment, larger classes, lower salaries for staff and shorter holidays than secondary institutions. The central schools also came under increasing attack from the Left as an evasion of the need to provide universal, free secondary education. However, although by the late thirties this type of school was certainly in decline, they could still be described in the influential Spens Report as answering the 'need in a highly industrialised society for post primary schools of a nonacademic type'.[7]

During the inception and early years of the capital's system of central schools, the Municipal Reform Party was in power on the LCC. Like the national Conservative Party, they believed that advanced education was suitable only for a minority and thus demanded that London central schools were highly selective. Only thus could the institutions figure prominently in London's role in the 'moulding of the Empire and in the general advance of humanity'.[8] However, central and local authorities were not always in accord about the role of these schools in the capital. From the start, the Board had insisted that central schools should not be too similar to the secondary system, that they should provide preparation for employment, not for examinations or higher education. There was frequent disagreement with the LCC about whether central school pupils should be allowed to sit external exams or stay at school after the age of sixteen to complete a course. The issue arose particularly over the potential intake of the schools for, by the early twenties, the Board feared that the LCC was increasingly assuming that 'the distinction between the central and secondary schools is a social and not educational one'.[9] It seems to have been widely accepted within the London Education Committee that the vast majority of central pupils would be the children of the 'upper working classes', of 'artisans and clerical workers' and indeed, available written and oral evidence suggests that a large percentage of female pupils did come from such social backgrounds or from lower middle class homes.[10] This group of students, whose parents would be very unlikely to be able to afford secondary school expenses, would previously have been denied any form of advanced schooling. However, as new attitudes about the value of education, about meritocracy and social mobility spread in the post-war era, it was this social group who began to desire and demand an extended schooling for their children. LCC officials seem to have been aware of the strength of feeling, particularly in the relatively prosperous south-eastern suburbs, and saw central schools as a means of satisfying it.[11] The second part of this chapter will suggest that the fact that the London selective central schools developed, in practice, to 'take the place of secondary schools' for male and female pupils of a certain social background means that they provide a significant example of the operation of the interconnected reproduction of class and gender relations in schooling.

It is comparatively recently that historical analyses of education have started to examine gender in all its manifestations and to investigate the impact of schooling in perpetuating the subordinate position of women in society and in the economy. Such an approach is especially important in explorations of vocational and technical training which has traditionally been seen as a way of acquiring the skills which provide access to high-status employment. The exclusion of women from the attainment of marketable 'skills' has reinforced perceptions of females' marginal, low-paid position in the labour market. It may be argued that educational policy and practice can never shape the labour market in a capitalist society and that girls' technical training has simply reflected a realistic appreciation of the limited employment opportunities for women. Mass schooling in a capitalist economy may be vital in reproducing both an adequately skilled work-force and the social relations of production in which females are required as casual labour and domestic workers.[12] However, the sexual division of labour has also benefited and been maintained by men. This complex and subtle interplay between capitalism and patriarchy is particularly significant in the inter-war years, an era marked by the formation of new characteristics of female labour power and by the redefinition of notions of female skill. As new processes in the economy developed, a sexual division of labour emerged in which female workers became associated with new fields of employment, notably with clerical and semi-skilled manufacturing work. Simultaneously the domestic economy underwent change, and new ideals of femininity were 'created' for the post-war consumer society.

It is not the intention of this analysis to suggest a straightforward correspondence between technical education and gendered employment, but the aim is to suggest how forms of technical education can contribute to socialising females into appropriate gender roles and into acceptance of the sexual division of labour. The selective central schools did partially accommodate changing notions about a woman's proper sphere; they did represent an acceptance of the need to prepare girls for economic survival and for some sort of autonomy in an extended range of work. Yet the technical education they provided simultaneously restricted the 'skills' and aspirations their pupils were allowed to develop and imposed an explicit ideology of femininity upon them. The central schools provide an invaluable case study of how, as June Purvis has argued of provision in the 1980s, 'the very words technical and vocational education are gender loaded'.[13]

Although official policy repeatedly stated that 'educational facilities are available alike for boys and girls', the education provided in the LCC central schools was in form and content highly gender-specific. There was an increasing tendency, for economic and educational reasons, for state elementary schools to amalgamate into mixed institutions during the inter-war years, but the strong opinion of both national and local administration was that central schools should remain single-sex. The LCC Inspectorate were 'unanimously of the opinion that mixed central schools should wherever possible be discouraged',[14] The stated justification for this was that: 'Not only is the practical work to which a large proportion of school time is devoted in this type of school entirely different for boys and girls but in such subjects as science, mathematics and drawing the methods of treatment ought to vary considerably with the sex of the pupils.'[15]

Science and mathematics, both of which were supposed to be infused with a technical bias, did indeed receive different treatment in boys' and girls' schools. As early as 1906 the Board had complained that in girls' schools there was 'too much maths, even where only four hours was given to the subject and that they would ask for on the whole a considerable share of time to be devoted to Domestic Economy'.[16] Twenty years later this was still a matter of concern. Inspectorate reports frequently criticised girls' schools which provided 'over-ambitious' syllabi, but conversely praised schools which, like Bloomfield Road, Woolwich, laid emphasis on 'the practical and domestic aspects of the subject'. Similarly, the assumption of girls' innate inability to cope with the theoretical and rational was evident in policy concerning science. Girls' science was always referred to as 'elementary' and tended to be nature study, requiring less expensive resources than the chemistry and physics taught in boys' central schools. The supposed technical bias for girls invariably emerged as a correlation with the domestic aspects of science. In 1925 the inspection of Peckham Girls' Central resulted in a complaint about the lack of emphasis on 'what might be described as science in the home', while Bloomfield Road was praised for providing lessons on science in the home so that the pupils 'in performing operations in cookery and laundry know something of the scientific basis of their work and approach them more intelligently than would otherwise be the case'.[17]

The question of girls' assumed inability to cope with the more complex aspects of science and maths emerged in the debate about the allocation of supplementary junior scholarship to central schools. By 1924 there was concern that girls had won a significantly smaller number of awards than boys[18] and in 1926 the LCC Inspectorate, meeting to consider the problem, were unanimously 'of the opinion that the apparent divergence in standard was no greater than was to be expected from the known inferiority of girls in scoring marks in arithmetic'.[19] A new marking scheme was adopted to adjust girls' marks in the allocation of scholarship in such a way as to 'achieve an approximately equal standard of intellect . . . between the two cases.' This continued to operate through the inter-war period, and available statistics show that the scholarships were indeed given to equal numbers of each sex. Such a scheme is significant. No efforts were made to adjust mathematics teaching in girls' schools or to change the format of an examination which clearly disadvantaged female students. But the decision to allocate scholarships equally does represent a recognition of girls' ability to 'achieve' intellectually and to merit an advanced, vocational education. However gender-specific instruction in schools may have been, the institutions do illustrate some new awareness of what schooling should offer girls.

All the general subjects of the curriculum were to be infused with either a commercial or an industrial bias and thus be 'relevant' to pupils' future vocations. As in the cases of mathematics and science notions of gender differentiation influenced the 'technical' input in each subject. While it was suggested that a suitable geography course for an industrial central school should concentrate on the world distribution of commodities, it seemed that girls would benefit most from lessons about 'the geography of the breakfast table and the Christmas pudding'.[20] It was advised that a good history syllabus could be founded on a study of man's activities and of his overcoming obstacles in the creation of comforts to himself, but the Inspectorate were wary of teaching such achievements to girls and complained that a certain textbook being used in some schools was 'somewhat too difficult and more suited to boys than girls'. English lessons also conveyed appropriate gender characteristics. In 1931, at Peckham Central, the boys excelled in class debate while girls devoted time to performing plays in a 'simple and childlike way'.[21]

It may be argued that the gender-specific curricula of central schools were simply a continuation of the well-documented differentiation in elementary schools and as such are not especially significant. However, in many ways the central schools were a radical educational departure. They were not mere extensions of elementary schools, but represented a deliberate attempt to provide a technically-based education of an advanced nature outside the existing, partially private secondary system. It was repeatedly stated that the ultimate aim of both girls' and boys' central schools was to provide 'vocational training for immediate employment'. It is this aspect of the central schools which is especially significant in any gender-based analysis of technical education, for a girl's vocation in the English education system had traditionally been seen as exclusively domestic. In the immediate post-war period there was an apparent recognition of the need to open up new avenues to women, given the variety of skilled work they had performed in wartime. A 1919 Report stated categorically that: 'Good training is the fact next to good health in increasing the value of women in industry. The removal of all educational disabilities of women and the provision of equal facilities for technical training is urged.'[22] An examination of technical education during the twenty years following this statement suggests that such a positive approach did not materialise in practice. Although new fields of employment became available to some women, the range of work characterised as stereotypically female remained low-status, insecure and poorly paid. While boys were defined in technical education policy according to aptitude and talent, girls were defined as a homogeneous group inherently unsuitable for training in most spheres of work, but innately suited to eventual domesticity.

It was the commercial-bias central schools which were the most numerous and the most popular. By 1925 there were thirty-seven such schools in London along with twenty dual-bias schools. The expansion of women in commercial office work has frequently been cited as evidence that women gained vast new employment opportunities as a result of their wartime experiences. In fact, although it was officially claimed that 'in the case of the commercial, the education given to boys and girls is largely similar',[23] in practice male and female pupils were prepared for very different types of employment. The only guidelines laid down by the LCC for the commercial timetable were that a foreign language should be included and that typing should not be taught during normal school hours since it was not of proper educational value. Instead, 'typewriting' was permitted in the two hours after the end of the school day. In practice this regulation seems to have been relaxed; the Hadow Report stated that in the third year of a commercial course shorthand and book-keeping were taught, while in the fourth and fifth year typing and office-work lessons were added. However, the stipulation that pupils must attend after school hours for typing was particularly significant for girls since it is clear that the main aim of their commercial education was to teach the monotonous, low-status elements of office work.

Clerking had traditionally been a male sphere of employment and the lower grades of office work were recognised as being a valuable training for boys who could later win promotion and rise up an employment hierarchy. However, for the large number of women who went into office work during the inter-war years, this idea of an avenue of promotion did not seem to apply. In 1931 a Board of Education pamphlet, 'Education for Salesmanship', lamented that the employment of office girls rather than boy clerks meant that there were no longer candidates for advancement within firms. Formerly there had been a group of boys who had 'constituted a pool from which potential salesmen, managers and other responsible officers of the firm were fairly certain to emerge', but girls did not fulfil this need.[24] It seems apparent that commercial central schools were to produce a generation of office girls to answer the growing need for low-grade workers and a group of adaptable, commercially-trained boys who could fulfil a variety of roles in the economy. This distinction was seen to affect explicitly the curricula of central schools: 'It is doubtful whether boys and girls ought to do exactly the same kind of work seeing that the proportion of pupils who will become shorthand typists is much larger in the case of girls.'[25] The girls should thus be given a large dose of subjects which were not deemed truly educational: 'The acquisition of mere speed in shorthand is perhaps hardly the province of the central school though it may be justifiable to devote more attention to speed in the case of girls for whom it has more definite and immediate value.'[26]

Such notions materialised in the actual timetables which commercial central schools for girls provided. It was reported in 1924 that at Greenwich Park Central pupils were sacrificing all other subjects for speed in shorthand and that the fifth year were having seven hours of shorthand lessons a week. In 1937 Peckham Central was criticised for its ambitious syllabus which allowed girls to move beyond basic office skills to commerce for forty minutes a week. The Inspectorate felt that such education was not suitable for girls and that 'the sections on the stock exchange and insurance might be deleted and the English banking systems should be treated in the simplest possible terms'.[27]

It was certainly widely accepted that girls, on leaving commercial central schools, would have little choice but to enter mundane, low-status work. The Central Schools Employment Committee in its Annual Report of 1933 stated that the demand for girls to perform 'office work of a routine nature' was considerable although the prospects in such employment could only at best be regarded as fair. The LCC 'Guide to Employment for Boys and Girls' wrote of the great opportunities and promotion prospects in commercial employment for males, but went on to state that 'the prospects of girls in clerical and commercial life are far more restricted', although 'typists, including shorthand typists, are all women'. The Guide even implied that it was the fault of the office girls themselves that there were so few opportunities for them. Girls were 'often conscientious routine workers but, perhaps through want of opportunity or ambition are inclined to be too easily satisfied in holding positions where there is little or no responsibility'.[28]

The tendency to see divisions in the labour market as 'natural' and 'inevitable' extended to the belief that girls were innately suited to use the new office equipment being developed during these years and to tolerate monotonous, low-skilled work. 'Education for Salesmanship' commented of typewriters that it had been found that 'the use of these aids . . . is a task peculiarly suitable for girls'.[29] Employers apparently recognised such qualities and preferred female typists 'because of the special aptitude for certain types of office work'. Noting this the Central Schools Employment Committee undertook to circulate information about new machinery to schools as quickly as possible because 'although routine and mechnical in character, good progress can usually be made by the girl who has the opportunity of mastering an installation comprising several machines'.[30] There seems to have been little dissent about this attitude from teachers and at their second national conference in 1936 commercial teachers accepted 'the sharp differentiation between the position of men and women in the field of commerce . . . women in business are expected to be Peter Pans, that is to do routine work and not aim at promotion . . . it follows that the question of training girls for commerce chiefly turns upon the question of office arts.'[31]

Yet commercial education remained immensely popular with the clientele of the central schools. It was the technical training which parents desired and demanded for their daughters. Ballard, an acknowledged expert on central schools, declared that 'if parents were allowed to choose the bias for their children they would almost to a man (and to a woman) choose the commercial bias'.[32] During the late 1920s concern mounted at the LCC that the popularity of commercial central schools was so great that they were providing 'serious competition' for girls' secondary schools. In 1929 an exchange took place concerning evidence from headmistresses that parents of secondary girls were seeking the addition of commercial subjects to the time-table, a demand to which the LCC resolutely refused to agree. The problem was deemed to be so serious that a special report to the Higher Education Sub-Committee in December 1929 suggested it was important to accentuate the differences between the two types of school for girls rather than to 'assimilate the curriculum of the secondary to the central schools'.[33] London headteachers repeatedly reported that parents were always willing to pay for commercial examinations, and oral evidence confirms the concern and interest of parents about their daughters' vocational education and the economic rewards which it might bring. It is quite clear that many of these parents had to make considerable sacrifices to keep their daughters in central schools, particularly in the final two years when their offspring could have been earning. This represents a significant new outlook on the appropriate schooling for girls.

Thus the commercial-bias courses in London's central schools for girls demonstrate both the limitations and the potential of this educational experiment. They did offer to a certain group of girls training in a new field of employment which would provide some benefits absent in traditional women's work. The girls were permitted to enter a former male sphere and to use modern equipment not previously associated with femininity. Office work did offer social status; better wages than the girls might otherwise have earned, even if they were lower than those of male colleagues; the freedom to wear their own clothes and to work set hours, and possibly the chance to have their 'own space' at a desk in the office. All these things had frequently been denied to women in employment. The great popularity of the commercial courses demonstrates the contemporary perception that this was desirable employment. Yet the schools were reinforcing the still rigid sexual division of labour in which females were confined to low-status work and denied the advancement which the acquisition of commercial 'skills' gave to boys. The central schools prepared girls only for a specific sphere, thus relieving males of 'inappropriate' mundane work, while providing a steady supply of workers required in the administrative and commercial enterprises of the capital.

Overwhelming popularity was not the problem of the industrial-bias central schools, although places were still sought after as a form of advanced education. Indeed, the LCC became so concerned that the attractions of commercial courses could engender a shortage of workers for other areas of the labour market that a special investigation was set up in 1927. It was resolved that the name 'industrial bias' should be changed to the more appealing 'technical bias', and that a non-commercial side should be introduced into *all* central schools – scientific and industrial for boys, domestic for girls.[34] The aim of the industrial or technical institutions was supposedly to produce workers to fill the particular labour needs of an area – for example, the engineering works of south-east London. Women in industry in England during the eighteenth and nineteenth centuries had worked overwhelmingly in the needle trades, laundry and millinery. Any industrial 'skill' required had been learnt once in employment as an apprentice, not in school. The First World War had demonstrated the ability of women to undertake a variety of skilled work in industry, but in the aftermath of the conflict women were soon once again defined in official reports and policy as a homogeneous group engaged only in unskilled labour or 'semi-skilled work such as box-making in which the skilled work is assigned to men and only the less skilled is done by women'.[35] Although in reality women were to provide a large proportion of the labour force in the new inter-war industries, the need to train them was largely dismissed since it was assumed that as craftsmanship was eliminated and manufacturing processes simplified, the new work of a routine character could be performed by any woman. Lord Eustace Percy, President of the Board of Education, expressed a widely-held sentiment in the pamphlet, 'Education and Industry': 'Let us ask ourselves what opportunities for education we are offering to the boy. It is of boys and men that industry is mainly thinking and it will save some complications if I confine myself to them.'[36]

Nevertheless the technical selective central schools were theoretically to provide girls with training for skilled employment, although it was admitted from the start that the relationship to provision made for boys would have to be 'distant'. In practice, the training girls received in these schools emphasised the domestic subjects considered appropriate feminine preserves and taught 'skills' which might be transferred to the home. Assumptions were thus made about the limited span of women's working lives which were simply not based on fact. In spite of all the hurdles placed before them, the percentage of women in paid employment increased during the inter-war years and females continued to constitute at least 30 per cent of the labour force. Throughout the period, as many girls as boys left elementary sector schools to enter employment. Moreover, the notion of female dependence was contradictory, for almost a fifth of all adult women did not marry between 1921 and 1939, largely because of the demographic imbalance between the sexes inherited from the nineteenth century and augmented by war casualties. It seems probable, given the attitudes expressed by women towards employment during the war, that many more would have chosen to remain in paid work if they had been given the training, opportunity and freedom to take skilled, well-paid employment.[37]

The LCC placed few restrictions on the curricula of technical-bias central schools other than that domestic subjects and handwork should be included. From the inception of the system there had been uncertainty as to how the vocational bias could actually materialise in the curriculum. The London Inspectorate commented in 1912 that:

In the Girls' Schools the industrial bias is more negative than positive in character. The bias shows itself more in the exclusion of certain subjects such as French and shorthand than in definite training of an industrial type. This is almost inevitable. The majority of the girls will either stay at home or enter the higher ranks of domestic service.[38]

Little had changed by 1926 when the Hadow Report summed up the technical courses as 'more time' spent on needlework, art and domestic subjects.

A great deal of time was indeed devoted to sewing. However, the opportunities for employment for central school pupils in the needle trades were limited for it was still usual for a girl to enter a workshop at fourteen and acquire skills as an apprentice. The central school girl was not put at an advantage in the labour market by staying on at school until the age of sixteen. A 1936 report acknowledged that 'technical bias for girls often resolves itself into the preparation of girls for entry into the needle trades at the age of sixteen at a wage appropriate to the age of fourteen'.[39] Employers on the Needletrades Consultative Committee made clear to central and local authorities that they required fourteen-year-olds with good eyesight. The central schools were not providing satisfactory employees, particularly since the sewing lessons which girls were 'compelled to undergo' were causing a loss of 'visual activity'.[40]

Nor was this type of schooling a route towards further training for girls. In spite of the insistence of the Board that pupils be prepared for immediate employment, it became increasingly accepted that central school education could lead onto either full- or part-time further education. The influential President of the Board, Eustace Percy, became a champion of this idea and in 1925 discussions took place about the possibility of instituting school-learning scholarships for central school fifth-year pupils of whom there were approximately two thousand in London at that time. From the start it was recognised that awards for girls would be a problem for 'there do not seem to be the same openings for girls as there are for boys in the higher walks of industry'.[41] Brereton, a former LCC Inspector and champion of central schools, suggested that the solution was a list of approved courses in such subjects as photography, hairdressing, dressmaking, tailoring and domestic subjects to which girls could win scholarships *if* it was shown that such courses 'can be justified in the ultimate economic interests of girls entering upon them at 15½–16 years of age. Indeed it may prove that a shortened course of six months to a year in these special women's trades is all that is to be justified on the technical side for girls.'[42] The question of girls' scholarships was then postponed for future consideration but the matter does not seem to have arisen again.

Although LCC policy-makers clearly recognised the problems of providing technical education for girls which would serve as 'definite and immediate remunerative preparation for skilled employment', throughout the inter-war years the courses remained unchanged. There was no solution to the problem of what occupational bias to offer apart from an extension of the home-based crafts which girls had always been taught. It is apparent that there was a strong link between the extended vocational training of this type in central schools and the inter-war ideology of domesticity. This is, of course, a continuity with the pre-war era, but a dominant element in the twenties and thirties was the emphasis placed on domestic skills as preparation for paid employment.[43] The well-trained woman would enter the labour market for a limited period and then return to the home, a well-prepared housewife ready to buy the new labour-saving devices of a consumer society.

The emphasis on domestic skills was not, of course, new or confined to central schools. What was new was the context of inter-war Britain in which there was a great deal of uncertainty and confusion about gender roles. Although this chapter has urged that war did not open up vast new employment opportunities for females, there was a contemporary belief that women *had* achieved a major breakthrough and that, having experienced social and economic independence, they would seek a permanent escape from the home. This belief excited alarm in certain quarters. The roots of such fear were both economic and emotional and help explain both the great opposition of the male trade unions to women doing a variety of skilled jobs and the pervasive propaganda stressing the joys of domesticity. There was also national concern about the 'servant problem', i.e. the great unpopularity of service among young women. An enquiry into the supply of servants in 1923 saw a clear connection between the solution to the problem and training, for 'although theoretically many people consider that all women are potential domestic workers, in practice there is such a strong resistance to employing untrained women or girls'.[44]

It was explicitly accepted that the advantage of the selective technical central school was that an extended domestic training could be provided for intelligent girls who would become skilled domestic workers and later exactly the sort of wives and mothers which the nation needed. The 1923 report on domestic service noted approvingly that in practically every central school 'provision is made for a more or less continuous course of domestic training'. The LCC Inspectorate and officials constantly stressed that these schools provided more advanced domestic training than other educational institutions, while in 1926 Hadow commended the sheer amount of lesson time spent on domestic life. Oral evidence confirms that the timetable was dominated by cooking, laundry, cleaning and sewing.[45]

The connection of such domestic lessons to females' paid employment was explicit, although both Central and local authorities frequently claimed that it was 'contrary to fact' that these courses trained girls for service. A 1929 Board report on technical training for girls stressed that the aim of this schooling was certainly not to train servants, but paradoxically continued 'the most encouraging feature of all is that once a girl is trained she appears to rise above the distaste for domestic employment'.[46] The Central Schools Employment Committee was certainly keen on this type of vocation for female pupils and felt that 'every encouragement should be given to girls to take up such work and steps are accordingly being instituted to obtain attractive posts'.[47] The London 'Guide to Employment' told its readers that although domestic work was commonly considered work for which women were 'naturally fitted', the fact that a large part of the work was skilled must not be overlooked. The Guide stressed the joys of interesting and intellectually demanding household gadgets and pointed out that job prospects were good since 'a working housekeeper is frequently employed by an unmarried man'.[48]

The central schools also had a role to play in producing a new generation of modern housewives. Inspector Brereton felt that domestic instruction should be extended even further since 'so much unhappiness existed today from girls not knowing how to run their home properly'; his sentiment was widely supported. The idea of the working class housewife changed during the inter-war years to include notions of 'enlightenment' and 'self-fulfilment'. The enlightened housewife would buy new mass-produced goods and gadgets while demonstrating how happiness could be achieved through the efficient performance of her daily tasks. This message was to be conveyed to central school pupils: 'As the enlightened housewife organises her work to minimise drudgery and avoid waste of time, the domestic subjects class should set a high standard in this direction. The cultivation of a happy and intelligent attitude in home affairs should be impressed upon girls.'[49] It was in the national interest, moreover, that the girl learned that the home was the centre of family life and that, in her role as mother, her prime task was to ensure the well-being of her family. The headmistress of Peckham Girls' Central received great praise in 1934 when she set up a 'technical' course in childcare involving the study of feeding, toys, infants' clothes and home nursing. The Inspectors claimed approvingly that students went on to train as nurses after such schooling, but statistics show that most in fact went into private homes, usually as children's maids. Nevertheless, this was seen as exactly the type of instruction which a technical institution should provide and the Education Committee was certain that every girls' central should develop 'a course of this kind'.[50]

A recurring problem in any analysis of formal schooling and its effects on pupils is the difficulty of establishing exactly what occurred within the classroom walls, exactly how policy was put into practice by individual staff. This is particularly so in the case of the London central schools, as a great deal of freedom was given to teachers to organise timetables, curricula and experimental teaching. Great emphasis was always laid on the need for a certain type of teacher for the central school, teachers who would have knowledge of the world of employment into which children would enter. In practice it seems that many who did work in these establishments had similar backgrounds to those who taught in grant-aided secondary schools. By 1934, 45 per cent of selective central school teachers were graduates.[51] The limited sources available for the inter-war years suggests that female teachers generally came from a slightly higher social class than their male counterparts. It thus seems likely that many women teachers in central schools would have been of middle-class origin. The effect of these women on the girls they taught is significant. The National Association of Teachers in Selective Central Schools tended to stress that they provided 'in the full sense of the word a liberal education' and criticised the 'materialistic' aim of preparing pupils for work.[52] In 1934 the Association made a strong attack on the pressure put on girls by constant domestic lessons. In the book, *The Selective Central School*, they pointed out that many girls were already under strain from tending younger siblings at home, and stated that 'the policy that ought to be pursued in an age of sex equality is a matter demanding serious and unbiased thought'.[53]

However, other sources imply that the comparative freedom of the staff sometimes resulted in more emphasis being laid on traditional female virtues. Their journal, *The Central School Teacher*, emphasised 'the general uplift aesthetically and economically which the next generation must receive if the girls have thorough domestic training'.[54] In 1931 an article stressed that the teacher should aim to show 'that the welfare of the country depends upon the good housewife'.[55] To this domestic ideal were added other appropriate elements of inter-war femininity – the central schools were to teach 'good manners', 'culture' and 'ladylike bearing'.[56]

Yet in spite of the stress on domestic lessons for girls, the subject remained educationally of low status. The London girls' buildings often offered inadequate facilities and equipment while boys' schools were provided with laboratories, woodwork rooms and sometimes power-driven machinery. The inspection of Charlton Central in 1936 pointed out that 'the boys have good handicraft rooms in a separate building but the girls have no domestic subjects room'.[57] At Bloomfield Road, Woolwich, domestic lessons were practically impossible because of the noise from the metalwork room. Thus, female students received the message that the domestic training on which they spent so much time was of low status within the hierarchy of subjects on the curriculum.

In conclusion, the selective central schools of London did offer new opportunities to some girls, and did represent a new outlook on appropriate vocational schooling for women. The forms of technical education offered girls in the central schools marked a new acceptance of the need to train females for limited economic independence, and there is evidence that some of the girls who went to central schools were able to enter new spheres of employment. However, the technical training provided in central schools simultaneously reflected and contributed to a strengthening and remoulding of the sexual division of labour both in paid work and in the home. Even the new areas of paid employment for which the central schools prepared women were characterised by relatively low status, low pay and insecurity. Domesticity was still perceived as a girl's ultimate destiny. Educational policy-makers were endeavouring to accommodate objectives which were not altogether compatible. In response to the social and economic pressures of the inter-war years they wanted to make working-class girls more employable. But they were committed to doing so without either challenging the gender stereotyping embedded in the labour market, or altering women's conventional role within the domestic economy. In short, technical and vocational education for girls in the central schools gave expression to tensions within the ideology of femininity which developed during the inter-war years, deepened during the Second World War, and have not been resolved today.

Notes

1 H. Silver, 'The liberal and the vocational', *Education as History*, Methuen, London, 1983, p. 158.

2 For example, in 1924 the total population of London central schools was 27,179, that of secondary schools (both aided and maintained) 31,282. London County Council (LCC), *London Statistics, 1929–30*, LCC, 1931.

3 Board of Education Consultative Committee, *The Education of the Adolescent* (Hadow), HMSO, London, 1926, p. 44.

4 Board of Education, *The New Prospect in Education*, HMSO, London, 1928, p. 3.

5 Greater London Record Office (GLRO), EO/PS/1/10, *Development of education in public elementary schools*, 17 December 1919.

6 For a full discussion of this see D. W. Dean, 'Conservatism and the national education system', *Journal of Contemporary History*, VI, 1971; and G. L. Savage, 'The civil service and secondary education in England during the interwar period', *Journal of Contemporary History*, 18, 2, 1983.

7 Board of Education Consultative Committee, *Secondary Education*, (Spens) HMSO, London, 1938, p. 73.

8 LCC, Report of the Elementary Education Sub-Committee, 16 March 1927.

9 PRO, Ed. 97/208. Note written by Pelham, 11 October 1923.

10 There are notorious difficulties in categorising women according to social class. In this paper the class terms used by contemporaries have been used.

11 Although including some declining and economically depressed areas such as Deptford, in general the south-east was prospering with the expansion of new industries.

12 For an analysis see A. Wolpe and A. Kuhn, *Feminism and Materialism*, Routledge, London, 1987.

13 Letter from June Purvis, *Times Educational Supplement*, 17 October 1986, p. 17.

14 PRO, Ed. 97/207, *Notes on the Inspection of Ten Elementary Schools*.

15 PRO, Ed. 97/207, *Report on the London Central Schools*, 1914, paragraph 11.

16 GLRO, Ed. PS/1/2, *Education Officer's Report*, 19 July 1906.
17 LCC, Inspectors' Report on Bloomfield Road Central, Woolwich, 1918.
18 This discrepancy was the result of the ending of the probationer bursaries which had previously been awarded mainly to girls. These were a particular type of supplementary scholarship given only to those undertaking to enter teaching. The supplementary scholarships were available for pupils of thirteen to fourteen years of age.
19 GLRO, EO/PS/1/3, Memorandum, Chief Inspector Spencer, 8 February 1926.
20 GLRO, EO/PS/1/15, *Report by the Chief Inspector*, unsigned notes on bottom of the report.
21 LCC Inspectors' Report, Greenwich Park Central, 1918; Peckham Central, 1931.
22 Parliamentary Papers, *Report of the Women's Advisory Committee on the Domestic Service Problem*, 1919, Cmd. 67, p. 170.
23 GLRO, EO/PS/3/19, *Proposed London Survey*, 1925.
24 Board of Education, *Education for Salesmanship*, HMSO, London, 1931, p. 68.
25 PRO, Ed. 97/207, *Report on London Central Schools*, paragraph 11.
26 *Ibid.*
27 LCC Inspectors' Report, Peckham Girls Central, 25 July 1937.
28 London Advisory Council for Juvenile Employment, *A Guide to Employment for London Boys and Girls*, HMSO, London, 1928, p. 43.
29 *Education for Salesmanship*, p. 68.
30 Central Schools Employment Committee, *Eighth Annual Report*, 1933.
31 *The Central School Teacher*, November 1936, p. 10.
32 GLRO, EO/PS/31/19, *Proposed London Survey*, 1925.
33 GLRO, EO/PS/2/4, *Report to the Higher Education Sub-Committee*, 12 December 1929.
34 By 1935 there were seven schools providing an industrial bias and forty-nine with a commercial bias. The remaining schools in London were dual bias.
35 Board of Education, *Trade and Domestic Schools for Girls*, HMSO, London, 1929, p. 15.
36 Board of Education, *Education and Industry*, HMSO, London, 1928, foreword.
37 J. Lewis, *Women in England*, Wheatsheaf, London, 1984 provides more details about women in the inter-war period. The marriage bar was in operation in many areas of employment during these years.
38 PRO, Ed. 97/207, *Notes on the inspection of public elementary schools*, 1912.
39 GLRO, EO/PS/1/12, *Survey of central school accommodation*, 1936.
40 GLRO, EO/PS/2/12, undated note.
41 GLRO, EO/PS/3/19, memorandum on proposed leaving scholarships, 1925.
42 *Ibid.*
43 For a discussion of the pre-war period see C. Dyhouse, 'Good wives and little mothers: social anxieties and the schoolgirls' curriculum 1890–1920', *Oxford Review of Education*, III, 1, 1977.
44 *Report to the Ministry of Labour into the present conditions as to the supply of female domestic servants*, 1923, paragraph 14.
45 Eight women who attended central schools in London during the inter-war period were interviewed by the author in 1988.

46 Board of Education, *Trade and Domestic Schools for Girls*, HMSO, London, 1929, p. 13.
47 Central Schools' Employment Committee, *Report*, 1933.
48 London Advisory Council for Juvenile Employment, *Guide*, Domestic Service Section.
49 GLRO, EO/PS/2/12, memorandum on handicraft in senior girls' schools, undated, p. 3.
50 LCC Inspectors' Report, Peckham Girls' Central School, 1937.
51 National Association of Teachers in Selective Central Schools (NATSCS), *The Selective Central School*, University of London Press, 1934, p. 74.
52 PRO, Ed. 97/208, memorandum on the position of central schools in the elementary system of London, undated.
53 NATSCS, *The Selective Central School*, pp. 29–30.
54 *The Central School Teacher*, December 1929, p. 13.
55 *The Central School Teacher*, November 1929.
56 Women who attended central schools recall the constant emphasis on 'ladylike behaviour'.
57 LCC Inspectors' Report, Charlton Central School, 1936. Inspectors' reports frequently mention the inadequacies of equipment for practical subjects in girls' schools. In December 1929 *The Central School Teacher* commented that while equipment in boys' schools was 'uniform with laboratories and woodwork rooms . . . the old elementary notion prevails that the attendance of a few of the girls at a cookery centre is sufficient'. Similar differences appear to have applied to scientific subjects. The Greater London Record Office holds photographs of well-equipped, modern laboratories for boys but girls were denied any such provision.

FIVE

Technical education and secondary schooling, 1905–1945

Bill Bailey

Following the 1944 Education Act local authorities were advised by the Ministry of Education to provide three types of secondary school – grammar, modern and technical – in order to fulfil their responsibilities to provide education according to the age, ability and aptitude of pupils in their areas, up to the age of fifteen. But in 1958 only 3·7 per cent of secondary pupils were enrolled in Secondary Technical Schools in England and Wales, this figure representing 279 schools and 95,194 pupils,[1] and numbers of schools and pupils were in decline. H. J. Reese Edwards' definitive study showed that from a high point of 319 Secondary Technical Schools in existence in 1948 there were just 268 in January 1960.[2] The reality was that the technical schools never became an effective third force in the system of secondary education for all. National secondary provision was bipartite rather than tripartite.

Explanations for this lack of commitment to technical education can be found in the post-war circumstances of local authorities. In particular they were haunted by considerations of cost and by doubts about selection. The Spens Committee had anticipated the technical schools remaining in their parent institutions, the technical colleges, but this was seen as a handicap after 1945 both because it prevented them developing their own ethos and corporate life, and because it encouraged perceptions of them as 'vocational'.[3] However, to build and bear the costs of the schools as separate institutions would involve the LEAs in heavy expenditure on specialist teachers, buildings and equipment. There was also considerable uncertainty about determining a rational and reliable means of selecting pupils for the technical schools. While the Norwood Committee claimed to have identified three types of child, albeit as 'rough groupings',[4] there was apparently no fair way of actually identifying those who should be allocated to technical schools, and opinion was divided on the optimum age of admission. In April 1946 a senior Ministry official, A. A. Part wrote: 'The psychological experts, with few exceptions, seem to think that it is not practicable to select children adequately for Secondary Technical Schools at an age earlier than thirteen.[5] Practice varied. Of the 268 schools in existence in 1960, 145 admitted at eleven, fourteen at twelve and 101 at the age of thirteen.[6] Many felt that eleven was too early an age at which a decision about children's occupational futures – and its corollary, the beginning of a technical bias to their education – could be made.

These doubts and uncertainties are redolent of unresolved issues concerning the place of technical and vocational education in school provision, inherited from the pre-war years. The larger explanation for the weak position of secondary technical education after 1944 must therefore be found in its earlier history. The important themes are the relationship of the Junior Technical Schools, whose origins lie in the years before the First World War, to the development of academic Secondary Schools; the view of the Board of Education that technical education was an essentially local concern; and the preoccupation of the technical associations, which were campaigning for expansion, with more advanced forms of technical education.

The early development of full-time junior technical courses took place in conditions unfavourable to their development. After the Cockerton Judgment (1900) and the 1902 Education Act the main thrust of the Board of Education's efforts was to consolidate the academic curriculum of the schools run under the new Regulations for Secondary Schools. In the first place this required the destruction of the Higher Grade Schools, and thus the setting aside of the alternative curriculum for older elementary pupils pioneered in these schools. In the words of the Historical Chapter of the Spens Report: 'The most salient defect in the new Regulations for Secondary Schools issued in 1904 is that they failed to take note of the comparatively rich experience of secondary curricula of a practical and quasi-vocational type which had been evolved in the Higher Grade Schools, the Organised Science Schools and the Technical Day Schools.'[7] The official policy of restriction was maintained after 1904 by the prevention of the emergence of any alternative to the academic course of secondary education, through for example the Board's Minute for Higher Elementary Schools. This formed a procrustean bed for local authorities wishing to develop provision for older elementary pupils.[8] However, under Article 42 of the Board's Technical Regulations in force from 1905 onwards it was possible for grant aid to be paid in support of Day Technical Classes for young people who had completed their elementary education, and it was under this Section that a number of full-time trade schools were established in the London area. The first was opened for the furniture and woodworking trades, at Shoreditch Technical Institute. It was for boys aged thirteen to sixteen and provided a pre-apprenticeship course, broadly half of the curriculum general, the other half technical.[9] The aim was to send the boys out to trade workshops as apprentices or as improvers. This was followed by schools preparing for skilled posts in engineering trades established in the Poplar, Hackney and Paddington Technical Institutes. Similar schools – full-time with a technical bias – had been started in the London Polytechnics when they opened in the 1890s; by the 1900s these had been changed into secondary schools of the conventional kind – and had moved out of the Polytechnics' premises into their own buildings.

By 1907, fifteen day technical schools of this type had been founded in LEAs in the north of England,[10] but it was in London that these full-time technical classes were mainly concentrated. The particular conditions in the capital helped to explain this: the decline of apprenticeship in some of the dominant trades; the concentration of employment opportunities in a wide range of skilled occupations, and the easy availability (especially to boys) of 'blind-alley' jobs at comparatively high rates of pay. In 1912 the London County Council was maintaining sixteen trade schools (ten for boys and six for girls) and by this time two types of school were evident: (i) the 'trade school', which prepared for specific occupations such as cabinet-making, the needle trades (assumed to be female) and the meat trade, and (ii) the pre-apprenticeship school preparing boys for particular industries (mainly engineering and building) without specialisation in particular trades within these industries. These two variants were to typify junior technical courses until the end of the Second World War.

Tables 5.1 and 5.2 show the increase in junior technical schools up to 1939. Under the revised Regulations for Further Education issued in 1926 Junior Commercial Schools were recognised. These prepared their pupils for entry into work as shorthand typists and clerks. There were also ten Junior Housewifery Schools preparing girls for 'home management'. The relative opportunities for boys and girls in the junior schools as a whole are not easily established from the Board's statistical reports. However, as part of an HMI Review in 1937 a snapshot picture of the schools and their pupils for 1935–6 was given

Technical education and the state

Table 5.1: Secondary Schools and Junior Technical Schools 1913–38 (England and . Wales)

Year	Secondary Schools		Junior Technical Schools	
	Schools	Pupils	Schools	Pupils
1913/14	1,027	187,647	37	—
1918/19	1,081	269,887	69	—
1919/20	1,141	307,862	78	9,811
1920/1	1,205	336,836	84	11,235
1921/2	1,249	354,956	89	12,256
1922/3	1,264	354,165	89	12,206
1923/4	1,270	349,141	87	11,988
1924/5	1,284	352,605	89	11,954
1925/6	1,301	360,503	92	12,704
1926/7	1,319	371,493	104	19,333
1927/8	1,329	377,540	107	20,200
1928/9	1,341	386,993	112	18,877
1929/30	1,354	394,105	120	20,217
1930/1	1,367	411,309	189	21,998
1931/2	1,379	432,061	194	21,945
1932/3	1,378	441,883	203	22,470
1933/4	1,381	448,421	213	24,130
1934/5	1,380	456,783	223	25,609
1935/6	1,389	463,906	232	27,354
1936/7	1,393	466,245	243	28,747
1937/8	1,398	470,003	248	30,457

Source: To 1925/6, Board of Education, *Statistics of Public Education, England and Wales* (annually); from 1925/6, Board of Education, *Annual Report.*

and this is reproduced in Table 5.3. This shows that rather more than two-thirds of the places in the schools were taken by boys, with girls forming the majority of pupils in the Trade and Junior Commercial Schools. The courses took place in Technical Colleges and Institutes in which the *senior* technical courses were housed. A pragmatic justification for the provision of junior technical schools – all full-time day schools – was the use they made of facilities (specialist accommodation and teachers) which otherwise would be used only for evening class students.[11]

The Association of Teachers in Technical Institutions (ATTI) supported their growth, a prominent theme in discussions leading to the formation of the Association in 1905, there having been an absence of policy for technical education in the early years of the Board of Education. At annual meetings speakers regretted the official emphasis on secondary and university institutions which assumed the

Table 5.2: Junior Technical Schools

Year	England		Wales	
	Schools	*Pupils*	*Schools*	*Pupils*
1926/7	101	18,704	3	629
1927/8	104	19,541	3	659
1928/9	108	18,243	4	634
1929/30	115	19,537	5	680
1930/1[a]	177	21,066	12	932
1931/2	182	21,003	12	942
1932/3	191	21,445	12	1,025
1933/4	200	23,090	13	1,040
1934/5[b]	208	24,532	15	1,077
1935/6	216	26,071	16	1,283
1936/7	226	27,395	17	1,352
1937/8	230	29,036	18	1,421

Source: Board of Education, *Annual Reports.*
Notes
a From this year onwards a school is taken to be a group of pupils under a separate headteacher: previously a school had been counted as an institution in which a junior technical school (or more than one) was run.
b From this year the Schools of Nautical Training were included as they were administered under the Regulations for Further Education from 1 April 1934.

Table 5.3: Junior Technical Schools and pupils 1935/6 (England)

	No. of schools	Boys	Girls	Total
Junior Technical Schools	97	13,972	—	13,972
Junior Technical (Trade) Schools	37	859	2,419	3,278
Junior Housewifery Schools	10	—	495	495
Junior Commercial Schools	50	2,184	3,915	6,099
Total	194	17,015	6,829	23,844

Source: Board of Education, Educational Pamphlet No. 111, *A Review of Junior Technical Schools in England*, 1937.

superiority of literary forms of education which were 'a preserve of the elect'. In order to create a more modern system of education the Association was discussing, in 1909, a policy paper which proposed four types of school 'beyond the primary stage': Technical Secondary and Commercial Secondary (13–17) Schools, Day Trade Schools, and Secondary Schools 'of the present type'.[12] The Board's Consultative Committee were seen as the upholders of the traditional view and the ATTI resolved to urge upon the Board that technical education be represented on the Committee.[13]

At its Annual Meeting in 1910, ATTI members were discussing the imminent publication by the Board of new Regulations for the full range of work covered by the Board's Technical Branch. Papers relating to these have not been generally known to historians of education.[14] A total of 131 memoranda, prepared by Technical Branch Officers and Inspectors, formed the basis of a review and projected rationalisation of full- and part-time, vocational and non-vocational courses and classes in technical institutions. They reveal a determination on the part of Morant and the principal officers and HMI of the Technical Branch to follow through their policies for elementary and secondary education with similar regulations for further and technical education. They show, firstly, a wish to substitute a simpler means of determining central government grant for the complex system inherited from the separate codes operated by the Department of Science and Art and the Education Department up to 1900. The review involved also the creation of a framework of provision via the Board's Regulations into which the local authorities could build their local systems of classes and institutions. The proposed Regulations covered the wide-ranging area of work falling outside the secondary schools and universities, forming what the Board was beginning to refer to by the term 'Further Education'. This work was categorised under seven main headings: (i) evening schools; (ii) full-time courses in Technical Institutions, (iii) Day Technical Classes (full- or part-time); (iv) Schools of Art (mainly evening work); (v) Art Classes; (vi) Junior Technical Schools; and (vii) University Tutorial Classes.

The Board's proposals were for a comprehensive plan for further education, related to elementary and secondary schools and to universities, to be prepared by each LEA. This 'Scheme for Further Education' would have at its centre the local authority undertaking its duties to provide vocational and non-vocational courses ('technical instruction' and 'disinterested studies making for wise living and good citizenship'). The position and status of larger institutions doing advanced work would be recognised with a new title – the Local College. To these a single inclusive block grant would be paid; other work, mainly evening classes located in other premises like elementary and secondary schocls, would be aided by an inclusive grant paid to the LEA. Thus a great deal of laborious and detailed administration would be eliminated – in particular, by making the number of teacher hours the unit of audit instead of the number of hours of students' attendance. The Local College would become 'the centre and crowning point' of the local system of further education.

Although these proposals were generally welcomed by representatives of local authorities and the technical associations (who strongly supported the idea of Local Colleges),[15] they were never formally adopted or fully implemented. Board of Education papers at the Public Record Office do not clearly explain the non-implementation, though it can be surmised that post-war reaction and economies affected the seeing-through of this ambitious and expensive scheme. There was also resistance to certain principles inherent in the plans from bodies associated with the world of adult (non-vocational) education; the Ministry of Reconstruction Adult Education Report (1918) significantly opposed the handing of responsibility for such classes to local authorities where, it was assumed, narrow, utilitarian values would dominate.[16] For whatever reason, the draft plans for the comprehensive development of post-compulsory education were dropped. The central authority for education in the Morant era had worked on a large scheme of review and development, but, not for the last time, plans for the development of further education were not put into effect. There was, however, a need to review the unplanned growth of the junior technical schools.

The development of full-time junior technical courses after 1905 had been accompanied in some localities by their consolidation as a permanent feature of provision. Although Article 42 relating to full-time day technical classes had provided the basis for their development, the need for clearer definition and consolidation of these schools had been a strand in the officials' thinking on the new draft Regulations. As mentioned above, fuller Regulations for Junior Technical Schools had been discussed with LEAs and in 1913 the Board issued a separate set of Regulations to take effect from 1 August 1913. These Regulations, in contrast with the positive and, in many ways, constructive framework outlined above, were restrictive in their spirit and purpose. The 'new' junior technical schools were to prepare ex-elementary pupils for specific occupations or trades through courses of no more than two or three years' duration. They were to develop in ways which would distinguish them clearly from secondary schools and from central schools with an industrial bias. Initiative for their establishment would lie with the LEAs and their size was to be limited according to the ability of local industrial firms to absorb their pupils in appropriate positions. Parents were to be required to sign their agreement that their children were destined for artisan employment in the occupations for which the schools prepared. The teaching of foreign languages was excluded, hence pupils could not proceed to matriculation. The schools were not to prepare pupils for advanced technical courses, the professions or the universities, for 'no pupil may be allowed without the express consent of the Board, in advance, to enter for any examination in any secular subjects other than one confined to pupils of the school'.[17]

With some small amendments these Regulations remained operative for junior technical schools until they were superseded by the Secondary School Regulations of 1945. The schools were administered by the Board's Technical Branch and inspected by HMIs attached to that Branch. Thus three branches of the Board had responsibility for post-elementary courses: the Secondary Branch, the Elementary Branch (Higher Elementary and Central Schools) and now the Technical Branch. Just as after 1904 a separation had been introduced between elementary and secondary education, there was now a division of responsibility between these two and the newly recognised technical schools. That this was intentional is shown in the summary above of the principal conditions placed on the schools. These were intended to keep them 'true to type' and so prevent any tendency for them to develop as rivals, through imitation, of secondary schools 'proper'. In contrast with similar institutions in some European countries (Fachschulen in Germany, Écoles d'Apprentissage in France), the junior technical schools were clearly a part of the educational system, though indirectly linked to industry by the parental certificate as to the pupil's future artisan employment and the ability of local employers to absorb the schools' pupils. These factors and conditions were to limit the development of these schools in later decades.

Furthermore, a policy objective of separation and differentiation in post-compulsory institutions was clearly evident. The distinctive purposes of the Secondary, Higher Elementary and Central Schools, and of the Junior Technical Schools, were expressed in terms of their different curricula, related to the social class origins of their pupils, and to their occupational destinations.

During the 1914–18 war, deficiencies in the British use of scientific research compared with Germany's had been exposed; not only the wartime emergency, but future economic survival, required better use of existing facilities and their expansion. Wartime reports contained explicit criticisms of failings in the developing system of national education under the direction of the Board of Education. At the outbreak of the war the Board's Consultative Committee had been considering a brief on the provision of scholarships for higher education, essentially from secondary schools to universities. After a suspension of sittings in 1914, the Committee resumed its deliberations with a significantly broadened agenda. The war had made apparent the need for scientific and technological instruction and for research. The importance of extended education in post-war national reconstruction was amplified with recommendations for increasing the number of scholarships. Although the Report dealt mainly with scholarships from secondary schools to universities, the Committee did take evidence on the preparation of lower grades of worker. The role of secondary schools in producing clerks was underlined. 'To this extent it is true, as is often said, that we train our young men to become clerks and not for any other useful employment.'[18] This led the Committee to the view that it was necessary to expand post-elementary courses related to other occupations like those in the junior technical schools, but the Committee noted that, in evidence they had been told that 'the Board of Education was opposed to the treatment of Junior Technical Schools as an alternative to Secondary Schools'.[19]

In their report published in 1918, the Prime Minister's Committee on Natural Science chaired by J. J. Thomson expressed similar views to those of the Consultative Committee. One of their conclusions was a call for a reconsideration of the position of the junior technical schools, but in the main Report they took their analysis further. They referred to the extent of overlap between branches of the Board in the administration of post-elementary institutions: 'In fact, into the secondary pie three fingers are put.'[20] The official separation prevented 'a fruitful differentiation of Secondary Schools', the Committee argued; there was room and a need in the system for schools for 12–16 year olds in which no foreign language would be compulsory, and which would have 'a definite bias' towards practical education.[21] The junior technical schools should be developed, concluded the Committee, into such a form of secondary school. In seeing the junior technical school as an alternative in an expanded system of secondary education, the Thomson Committee was putting forward a view which was to become widely accepted in the inter-war period, although in practice the structure of the system remained the same despite some developments within it.

The recommendations of the Reports referred to above, along with those of other proposals for 'reconstruction', were largely not acted upon in the waves of post-war reaction and 'economy'. Many of the terms of the 1918 Education Act were also not enacted, so that, although most LEAs prepared their 'schemes' of educational development in line with the Board's Circular 1096,[22] the Board of Education never gave the statutory approval which would have placed upon the LEAs the duty to implement them. But the suspension of the Act and the setting aside of proposals for reconstruction did not mean that local systems came to a complete standstill. On the one hand, the pressure of unsatisfied demand for places in secondary schools led LEAs to add to the number of schools and places. On the other, the raising of the school-leaving age had the effect of changing the system and, with raised public educational expectations, of changing the perspectives of some progressive thinkers. In particular, the consolidation of up to three years of full-time education for all eleven-year-old children presented the local authorities with the task of providing appropriate places for these new pupils. The Act had provided for advanced instruction for the new age groups and this encouraged some authorities to follow the lead of others like Surrey and Leicester to establish non-selective central schools to which pupils not attending secondary schools at eleven were transferred for the remaining years of their full-time education. In areas where junior technical schools existed, there was a second, small selection at thirteen plus.

The changing outlook is shown in an article, in the *Manchester Guardian*, in October 1925 by R. H. Tawney.[23] At the recently-held North of England Education Conference, the question of adolescent education had been widely discussed. There was unanimity as to the gravity of the situation in which 80 per cent of fourteen-year-olds were allowed to take up full-time employment (it was disastrous to 'the physique, the intelligence and the character of these young people') and agreement that the remedy lay in extending education into the 'critical years' from fourteen to eighteen. But there were at the conference two 'schools of thought' with regard to the form of provision to be made. H. A. L. Fisher and Robert Blair had favoured part-time continuative education from fourteen to sixteen, while Aldermen

Jackson and Conway had argued for full-time 'post-primary' education from eleven to fifteen and eventually to sixteen. Tawney's perception was that this divergence of view could be explained historically. The old school followed the thinking of Michael Sadler (1907), the Poor Law Commission (1909), the Consultative Committee (1909) and the Lewis Committee (1917).[24] All these emphasised the consequences of the neglect of adolescent workers and proposed continuative education as what the Consultative Committee had called a 'protective sheath' against social evils. The framers of the 1918 Education Act had reflected this thinking in the Day Continuation School clauses.

Tawney's perceptive point in his 1925 article was that these Reports ignored recent developments in post-primary education, which was understandable given that the main focus in each case was the injury to their health and character of workers aged fourteen to sixteen. The figures for school attendance given in the Lewis Report were for the school year 1911–12 and Tawney pointed out that developments since that time had given a turn to the discussion which could not have been foreseen. Between 1911 and 1920 the number of pupils in secondary schools had doubled. In 1917 it was perhaps difficult to anticipate the effects of raising the school-leaving age or the increased numbers staying on at school until fifteen and later. In their 'schemes' the LEAs had planned for an increase in post-primary (i.e. post-eleven) provision and, in some cases, in order to meet legal obligations, had begun to reorganise the elementary school course with a break at eleven for those who did not transfer to secondary schools. The new circumstances had altered the terms of the debate away from continuing day-release from work for the majority of young people, to a better educational and economic solution in which extended full-time education had become the obvious and preferred alternative. After all, the Day Continuation School had failed, in Tawney's words, 'to strike the imagination of parents and educationalists'. It was, he concluded, better to have a system which would be 'a reality as far as it goes, and which can later be extended, than to erect a pretentious structure which has no strong hold on those who pass through it'.

In an age of persistent juvenile unemployment the economic and educational case for extended full-time as opposed to continued part-time education came to be accepted more widely, and for the remainder of the inter-war period the principal focus of concern and debate continued to be the education and training of the adolescent. For some groups the day continuation school remained the preferred objective but even among these there was wide agreement as to the raising of the school-leaving age to fifteen. Discussion therefore came to deal increasingly with the provision and organisation of secondary education for all children. The policy of elementary school 'reorganisation' was seen as a small but significant change in the direction of providing secondary education for all. The significance lay in the break at eleven plus – an acceptance of a difference between primary and post-primary education – even if in many places it meant little more for children than transferring to the senior department across the school yard. Logic, if not fairness, required one set of regulations for all post-eleven (*i.e.* secondary) schools.

The junior technical school did not fit easily into the emerging system, particular issues being the age of entry and its curriculum focus. Justification for the school so far had been largely based in its vocational strengths, leading to specialist slants to the courses and a determination to recruit pupils no earlier than thirteen. Any incorporation of the schools into a post-primary system would require change in these two respects. The reduction of the entry age to eleven would increase the school's size and would require the schools to provide general courses from eleven with specialisation in the later years – unless, as was most unlikely, opinion changed to accept vocational preparation from eleven onwards. A change of entry age would also demand scrutiny of the allocation of responsibility for the junior technical schools in the Board and the wisdom of the 'three fingers in the pie'. The Hadow Report 1926, despite submissions from the technical associations that the entry age be reduced to eleven, recommended that the schools continue to recruit at thirteen and that they should be developed 'in accordance with the needs and requirements of certain local industries'.[25]

During the 1920s the policy of the Board with regard to the junior technical schools was unchanged. In 1926, as part of the large revision of the Board's Regulations, those for junior technical schools were incorporated into the new Regulations for Further Education.[26] In draft form these proposed a change of name – to Junior Vocational School – a move which was successfully opposed by the technical associations. A writer from the ATTI pointed out that the use of the word 'vocational' would be deeply resented because it suggested 'bare trade introduction . . . and nothing else'.[27] More importantly, the new Regulations allowed the teaching of a foreign language if a case could be made that it was vocationally necessary, and the requirement on the parent to sign the certificate as to occupational intentions was dropped. However, these small steps in the direction of liberalising the junior technical schools did not initial a period of major expansion (see Table 5.2). The increase in the number of schools after 1930 is largely explained by the decision to count each school separately; previously a college which housed more than one school had counted as one.

As might be expected, the technical college associations continued to advertise the strengths of the junior technical schools and press for their expansion and development. Most annual conferences featured debates and resolutions calling for the recognition and growth of these schools as alternative (i.e. parallel) secondary schools, with an entry age of eleven.[28] Offended by the Board's wish to lower the status of junior technical schools by changing their name and by the 'dismissive' references to the junior technical school in the Hadow Report, the ATTI organised their own survey of these schools.[29] This was completed by early 1929, chiefly by means of a questionnaire completed by members in regions. In general the data collected were what would be expected. Courses were mainly two years in duration with thirteen as the age of entry. The schools were held mainly in the local Technical College and examples of pupils transferring to and from secondary to junior technical school were very few. A modern language was being taught in only a few places – as in junior commercial schools; in some places French classes were organised outside school hours. Gateway School at Leicester, with an entry age of eleven and a language offering of French, German and Latin, was highly exceptional.

The ATTI Council decided to make policy on junior technical schools a main item of the 1929 Annual Conference. Resolutions were passed calling on LEAs to develop their provision of such technical schools spanning the eleven to sixteen age range (with free interchange of pupils between schools at thirteen) and with a modern language included in the curriculum.[30]

At about this time the Board began its own review of junior technical schools which it published as an educational pamphlet in 1930.[31] The Board's intention in publishing this pamphlet was to answer calls, such as those from the ATTI above, for a modification of the aims and curriculum of junior technical schools in the light of changes in state education especially since 1918. In this the pamphlet drew on the recommendations of the Hadow Report (1926) and on its own view as to the distinctive characteristics of the schools as they had been consolidated since 1913. The Consultative Committee had confirmed the views of witnesses that any very large development of junior technical schools was impossible given their fundamentally local characteristics, that is, the close connection between the school and the pupils' future employment, based on an assessment of local labour needs. It was impossible for a large proportion of children to know their future occupation with any certainty. Considerations of cost also prevented any great expansion. As far as the lowering of the entry age was concerned, the authors pointed out that this would involve either a radical change in the curriculum and organisation of the schools or a grave injustice to the pupils. The injustice would result from an occupational decision taken too early, while it would be found 'exceedingly difficult' to give a general education from eleven to thirteen with progressive specialisation thereafter. The latter task, it was stated, required specialist staffing and equipment to be found in a senior technical institution rather than in the same school in which younger pupils were receiving a general education. The conclusion was, therefore, that the status quo should be maintained. The junior technical school should not be absorbed into 'the new system of post-primary schools' with a lower age of entry. Only in so far as it remained 'true to type' would it retain its popularity.[32]

If the Board expected this view of the place of the junior technical school in schemes of 'reorganisation' to dampen arguments for change they were to be disappointed. Even as the Pamphlet was being prepared, the Board were approving the Workington LEA's proposed junior technical school with eleven as the age of entry.[33] However, a proposal from Smethwick LEA for a school admitting at the same age was turned down early in 1931. This led the Director of Education for the Smethwick LEA, S. Childs, to take to the annual conference (1931) of the Association of Education Committees (AEC) a motion that LEAs be allowed to experiment with aspects of the organisation of junior technical schools including the entry age.[34] The Board replied to the AEC in February 1933, saying that 'the problem of pre-employment training for industry and commerce' had been continuously engaging the Board's attention and that they had found no reason to think that a school of the kind contemplated by Smethwick would be 'a useful contribution to a solution of this problem'.[35]

If the Board was unwilling to go along with suggestions for development from some progressive educationalists and LEAs, it responded more positively to ideas put forward by its Chief Technical Inspector, Arthur Abbot. The claim that pre-employment education had been 'continuously engaging' the attention of the Board was a reference to the preparation of another pamphlet, 'Trade Schools on the Continent' published in October 1932.[36] This was the report of a visit by two Technical Inspectors – Abbot and J. E. Dalton – to France,

Belgium, Czechoslovakia and Holland in order to investigate full-time pre-employment schools.

In May 1931 Abbot passed a paper on 'The Future Development of Technical Education' to the head of the Technical Branch, Charles Eaton. This paper contained some thoughts on the implications for technical education of recent changes in the educational system. In particular Abbot emphasised 'the development in duration and character of full-time education' over the previous twenty-five years which was already affecting technical education. Like Tawney a few years before, he identified the extension of the school-leaving age to fourteen, the 'large number of Central Schools', the increase in junior technical schools and the four-fold increase in secondary schools. These developments, in his view, constituted 'not merely an educational achievement but a social and economic change of first-rate significance'.[37] The effects on recruitment to industry and commerce were considerable. The increase in secondary school places (and of the number of children staying on) reflected parental aspirations for better, 'black-coated' jobs for their children. This was reinforced by industry's regulations about the age of commencing apprenticeships and, as long as these were unchanged, the number of secondary school boys entering skilled trades would be small. This change was already affecting technical colleges which were now teaching (in their day and evening classes) 'a larger proportion of ex-secondary or ex-central pupils than they were ten years ago'. Data were not easily obtained on this, but he had found on a recent inquiry at two large technical colleges (Derby and Halifax) that the proportion of students with a prolonged full-time education was half the total number of students.

If this information was at all typical then major changes were taking place in the colleges and in industry. In the past, industry had recruited mainly from the elementary school, and the technical colleges had assisted many youngsters of ability and determination to get into higher and better-paid jobs. The new situation, if consolidated, would mean that higher posts would increasingly go to ex-secondary pupils, either at the time of entry to work, or in the later competition for promotion. The inevitable consequence, in Abbot's view, would be a 'check to the vertical mobility' of labour; if correct, this would be a new phenomenon in England. As well as having social consequences, this would affect attendance at evening technical classes, since the traditional students' main motive of ambition would be displaced. If this expectation was fulfilled the question of the vocational training of the artisan and the foreman would have to be faced. The easy way, based on the view that the British workman was, of course, the best in the world, would be to let workers pick up their training in 'the ordinary rough and tumble of the works', but Abbot's view was that only 'the unimaginative or insularly complacent' could feel confident that this was an alternative to the systematic training provided in many European countries in écoles d'apprentissage, Fachschulen, and Écoles Professionelles – the equivalents of Trade Schools in England and Wales.

Eaton accepted the importance of the trends identified by Abbot and agreed that the key problem was the ex senior elementary fourteen-year-olds destined for skilled positions 'who must be provided with some alternative incentive and interest in their work'.[38] With Permanent Secretary Pelham it was agreed that more information about Continental schools of the trade school type was desirable and that the two inspectors should visit France, Czechoslovakia, Belgium, Holland and Germany from 4 October to 8 November 1931. The visit was delayed by the political crisis of the autumn and eventually took place between 14 January and 17 February 1932. A draft of their report was ready in May 1932 and it was published in October of that year.[39]

As well as containing much detail of the organisation, finance and curriculum of trade schools in the four countries the report stressed a number of general points. The interest and investment in technical education in relation to national development was the basis, in these countries, of the fuller development of full-time technical schools. In England and Wales the relatively late development of state education had resulted in many part-time (evening) schools for those in employment. On the Continent these schools taught the practice of trades, while here the emphasis was on the principles underlying workshop practice. This was partly the result of the trade schools being a part of the industrial system, rather than being a part of the educational system as was the case in the United Kingdom. Interesting though these contrasts were, the pamphlet concluded that what was necessary was not an 'abrupt departure from our tradition', but the development of the provision of technical education which had hitherto failed to keep pace with changing conditions in industry. The 'preliminary training of the rank and file' should continue to take place within the education system, with a recommendation that more young employees should be released during the day for attendance at technical classes since evening classes were not a satisfactory means of instruction in 'a modern industrial state'. Most importantly, the report recommended more of the two types of junior technical school, and in particular it stated that there was no justification for the restriction of the trade school to the area of the London County Council. On the question of the age of entry, the report confirmed Board policy by reference to the success of the schools (here and abroad), which was stated to be the result of selection at about the age of thirteen.

Of course, the recommendations in the pamphlet were not intended to be taken as a statement of the Board's policy with regard to technical education. The introduction clearly stated that the pamphlet contained information to which the attention of the local authorities should be directed. The prefatory comments did, however, include the observation that changes in industry and the 'reorganisation' of education required a reconsideration of the 'system of technical education',[40] the first public recognition by the Board of the need for policy review and change. This can be seen as a shift in the Board's position with respect to post-primary education and the officials' expectations of the Consultative Committee chaired by Sir Will Spens as it began its work on its new brief in late 1933. The terms of reference presented to the Committee in November 1933 were: 'To consider and report upon the organisation and interrelation of schools, other than those administered under the Elementary Code, which provide education for pupils beyond the age of 11 +; regard being had in particular to the framework and content of the education of pupils who do not remain at school beyond the age of about 16.'[41] This wording indicated the kind of recommendation expected of the Committee; importantly their attention was directed to schools other than elementary. They were, therefore, to consider the secondary and junior technical schools and, presumably, to ignore the elementary system which accommodated the majority of children in the central schools and senior classes.[42] Clearly some kind of change in the status of junior technical schools was anticipated, an impression strengthened by the addition of two principals of technical colleges to the Committee's membership. This can be seen as a decision to broaden the representative base of the Committee and to include people 'competent' in the area of technical education. For nearly thirty years the technical associations had pointed out the inadequate representation of technical education which in 1933, before the new additions, stood at one representative from a London college.[43] Also significant was the reaction of Charles Eaton, head of T Branch, when the terms of reference were under discussion. He informed the Permanent Secretary that he and E. G. Savage (Chief Inspector and Senior Technical

Inspector) were 'perturbed' at the proposed terms on the grounds that it was too early to attempt an examination of the place of the junior technical schools in 'the general educational framework'.[44] Clearly they had an understanding of the lines along which the Committee's deliberations would run; they preferred to wait a few years and first see the results of a series of full inspections of junior technical schools which Savage had initiated.[45]

In its Report, after five years' research and deliberation, the Spens Committee's recommendations followed the Board's expectations in calling for a number of the existing boys' junior technical schools orientated towards the engineering and building industries to be raised to secondary status. These schools – to be named Technical High Schools – were to recruit at eleven plus through the competitive examination used in selection for the Secondary Grammar Schools. The basic course was to be a five-year one, from eleven to sixteen, with the curriculum of the first two years 'broadly of the same character'[46] as in other secondary schools so that transfer of pupils could take place at thirteen; a modern language would be included, preferably German. A new leaving certificate which was to have parity with the School Certificate was to be introduced for Technical High School pupils.[47] The Committee had no doubt that the Technical High Schools should be housed in Technical Colleges; where possible the buidings of the College and of the Technical High School should be physically connected to facilitate use of equipment and teachers. The number of schools to be granted the new status was not mentioned and the other types of junior technical schools were not to change.[48]

If this recommendation was foreseeable and welcome to the Board, the Committee's firm call for a single Code of Regulations to cover all schools for children over eleven was not. On this point the Committee had received and endorsed the views put forward in evidence to them by teachers and administrators via their associations: that the logic of educational development required the establishment of a system of secondary education for all children.[49] That the principal officers of the Board did not share this view was shown in their discussions of the Report and briefing of their political masters on the government's response to it. The Permanent Secretary drew up a memorandum justifying rejection of the proposals for free universal secondary education the grounds of cost.[50] This was the approach adopted by the Parliamentary Secretary, Kenneth Lindsay, in the Commons in February 1939; the Board of Education could not adopt the wide-ranging recommendations on secondary education as these would

114

involve the central government and local authorities in greatly increased expenditure. In the meantime the Board would act on the Committee's other 'important and constructive' proposals, including Technical High Schools.[51]

Even as the Board was working on its public response to the Spens Committee's Report its Technical Branch was attempting to give momentum to a policy of improving the accommodation of Technical Colleges. In 1936 a 'Drive' to increase and improve facilities for technical education had been launched as part of the National Government's election commitment in 1935 to encourage educational development across 'a broad educational front'.[52] Given competing demands on national and local resources, this had resulted in mixed success and by late 1938 the President decided to submit a Memorandum to Cabinet which, if its proposals were agreed, would provide additional finance for LEAs' projects. As part of the general case made for the expansion of technical education this memorandum made particular reference to the evidence that the engineering and construction industries needed more sixteen-year-old boys from technical schools. There is evidence that up to the summer of 1939 the Board approved eleven new junior technical schools,[53] but with the declaration of war in September, the Board's officers' attention turned to immediate concerns and the drive for technical education was shelved, as were the recommendations of the Spens Committee's 1938 report.

When in 1940, in their evacuated quarters in Bournemouth, the officers turned their attention once more to planning educational development, they used as their starting point the agreed policies of the 1930s. The Spens recommendation for a single code for the universal system of secondary education for all – with grammar, technical and modern schools – was the basis of the Green Book's proposals for discussion. Although the tripartite structure was not mentioned in the White Paper of 1943, nor in the 1944 Education Act, it was the selective and divided system, supported by the Norwood Report's theory of 'rough groupings' of children, which the new Ministry promoted in its post-war pamphlets for the guidance of LEAs.[54]

The limited progress made after 1945 in establishing the technical schools – what the Crowther Report in 1959 called 'the alternative road' – has been outlined at the beginning of this chapter. Despite some (temporary) increase in the numbers of technical schools, it could at no stage be claimed that they formed a third element in the secondary system. While cost was certainly a factor in this 'failure', it is clear that the broad issue of their relationship to other types of secondary education which had divided planners during the inter-war period had not been resolved in a way which made their expansion either practicable or desirable. The Ministry's priorities lay in the provision of secondary modern places alongside the grammar schools, and the local authorities which had to implement 'secondary education for all' on the ground followed this cue.

Responsibility for the technical schools was transferred in 1945 to the Secondary Branch which stressed the case for general education up to fifteen rather than vocational preparation. Through this administrative change the technical schools lost the support of the Technical Branch, which in any case had not pressed for the inclusion of the technical school in the secondary system. Simultaneously the technical associations led by ATTI withdrew their interest in the technical schools and focused increasingly on institutions providing post-school education and training. Thus they pressed the cause of senior courses with the Ministry's new Further Education Branch. There were structural reasons for their doing so. Junior technical schools represented the lowest category of work in the Burnham classification, whereas concentration on higher courses could earn for an institution designation as a Local College, or in the terminology of the Percy Report (1945), a College of Advanced Technology.

The technical schools thus lost their potential supporters inside and outside the Ministry. An Association of Heads of Secondary Technical Schools was rapidly formed in 1947 to defend the schools and attempt to elaborate for them a *raison d'être*. Not surprisingly the Association inherited a sense of grievance similar to that experienced by earlier enthusiasts in the ATTI.[55]

To conclude, the marginal position of technical schools after 1944 was rooted in inter-war uncertainties about just what form the technical education of adolescents should take. Should specific trades or general principles be taught, and from what age? Was the trade school, the Technical High School or the post-school technical college the model to follow? These issues were much debated between the wars, as we have shown, but responsibility for the failure to resolve them ultimately rests with the central educational authority and can be explained in terms of its commitment to a hierarchical secondary system geared to selection for 'liberal' education and ill-equipped to discriminate between its rejects or to provide them with forms of secondary education defined in positive terms, rather than as the negation of grammar school provision. The junior technical school of the years before 1914 could be said to have had a clear rationale as a pre-apprenticeship school end-on to elementary education ending at fourteen. But once eleven had been established as the entry point for secondary education, dominated by a 'non-vocational' philosophy, the logic of the preference of the Technical Branch of the Board of Education and the technical associations for entry at thirteen plus and for advanced work geared to skilled apprenticeships was to take technical education out of the school system. It was unlikely in this context that many LEAs would follow the Ministry's somewhat hypocritical advice and throw themselves behind the creation of Technical High Schools alongside Secondary Grammar and Modern Schools. When, in the 1960s, LEAs embarked on another phase of 'reorganisation' – establishing secondary comprehensive schools – the few remaining junior technical schools were absorbed without significant resistance.

Notes

1 From Ministry of Education, *15–18, A Report of the Central Advisory Council for Education (England)*, London, 1959, Table 5, pp. 16–17.

2 Reese Edwards, *The Secondary Technical School*, London, 1960, Appendix 2

3 PRO, Ed. 136/789, *The Secondary Technical School*, Minute, A. A. Part to Permanent Secretary, 2 April 1946

4 Board of Education, *Curriculum and Examinations in Secondary Schools*, Report of the Committee of the Secondary Schools Examinations Council (Norwood), London, 1943, p. 2.

5 PRO, Ed. 136/789, Minute to Permanent Secretary, 2 April 1946.

6 Edwards, *Secondary Technical School*, Appendix 2, pp. 194–8.

7 Board of Education Consultative Committee, *Secondary Education, with special reference to Grammar Schools and Technical High Schools* (Spens) HMSO, London, 1938, p. 66.

8 Board of Education Consultative Committee, The Education of the Adolescent (Hadow), London, 1926, pp. 26–31. There were only thirty Higher Elementary Schools in England and fourteen in Wales, in 1919.

9 The information about London schools in this paragraph is from London County Council (LCC), *Eight Years of Technical Education and Continuation Schools (mostly evening work)*, Report by the Education Officer, London, 1912.

10 Board of Education, *Memorandum on the place of the Junior Technical School in the educational system*, Pamphlet No. 83, London, 1930, p. 11.

11 Cf. P. F. R. Venables, *Technical Education, Its Aims, Organisation and Future Development*, London, 1955, p. 98 '. . . the junior technical school was a 'godsend to fill up the place in the daytime'.'

12 ATTI Papers, MSS 176 T 1/1/4, Council Minutes, April 1909. These are held at the Modern Records Centre, University of Warwick.

13 *Technical Journal* (journal of ATTI), No. 5, April 1909 and No. 10, July 1910.

14 The T[echnical] Revision Memoranda are held in the Library of the Department of Education and Science. Geoffrey Sherington, *English Education, Social Change and the War, 1911–20*, Manchester, 1981, pp. 13–14, refers. The Board had formally announced its intention to issue new Regulations in the Prefatory Memorandum to the Technical Regulations for 1909–10.

15 That is the Association of Technical Institutions (ATI) representing the governors, the Association of Principals of Technical Institutions (APTI) and the ATTI. These three groups were to agree and publish a 'Policy for Technical Education' in 1932 (reissued in 1937 and 1945). The 1937 issue contained twenty-two recommendations including: the organisation of technical education on a regional basis; the increase of junior technical schools as a form of secondary education; the increase in senior full-time courses; improvements in accommodation especially libraries, etc.

16 Ministry of Reconstruction, Adult Education Committee, *Final Report*, London, 1919, Cmd. 321, see especially paragraphs 306–9.

17 Board of Education, *Regulations for Technical Schools in England and Wales in force from 1 August 1913* (Cd. 6919), paragraph 6 (g).

18 Interim Report of the Consultative Committee on Scholarships for Higher Education, 1916, Cd. 8291, p. 12.

19 *Ibid.*

20 Report of the Committee appointed to enquire into the position of National Science in the Educational System of Great Britain, 1918, Cd. 9011, p. 43.

21 *Ibid.*

22 Board of Education, Circular 1096, Draft Suggestions for the arrangement of schemes under the Education Act, 1918.

23 The article appeared on 16 October 1925.

24 Michael Sadler, *Continuation Schools in England and Elsewhere*, Manchester, 1907; *Report of the Royal Commission on Poor Laws and the Relief of Distress*, 1909, Cd. 6004; Report of the Consultative Committee on Attendance, compulsory or otherwise, at Continuation Schools, 1909, Cd. 4757; Final Report of the Departmental Committee on Juvenile Education in Relation to Employment after the War, 1917–18, Cd. 8512.

25 Board of Education, *The Education of the Adolescent*, p. 66.

26 Board of Education, *Statutory Rules and Orders, Regulations for Further Education*, 1926.

27 *Times Educational Supplement* (Technical School Notes), 3 July 1926.

28 The *Technical Journal* for these years reports ATTI Conference debates and resolutions.

29 ATTI Papers, MSS 176 T 1/1/9, 19 January 1929.

30 *Ibid*, 16 March 1929.

31 Board of Education, *Memorandum on the place of the Junior Technical School* (see note 10).

32 *Ibid.*, p. 30.

33 ATTI Papers, MSS 176 T 1/1/9, 25 May 1931.

34 *Education*, 16 June 1931.

35 *Education*, 27 November 1936.

36 Board of Education, *Trade Schools on the Continent*, Educational Pamphlet No.

91, London, 1932.
37 PRO, Ed. 121/247, 1931 Inquiry: JTS Abroad, Minute A. Abbott to C. Eaton, Principal Assistant Secretary, 9 May 1931.
38 *Ibid.*, Minute, C. Eaton to H. Pelham, Permanent Secretary, 28 May 1931.
39 *Education*, 28 October 1932, carried a leading article on the 'Abbot Report'. The pamphlet did not report on Trade Schools in Germany.
40 Board of Education, *Trade Schools on the Continent*, Prefatory Note.
41 Board of Education, *Secondary Education*, p. iv.
42 This point, along with many other insights, is made by Joan Simon in her two-part article, 'The shaping of the Spens Report 1933–38: an inside view', *British Journal of Educational Studies*, XXV, 1977.
43 The serving member was R. L. Roberts, Chair of Governors, Northern Polytechnic. The newly appointed members were H. Schofield, Principal of Loughborough Technical College, and J. Paley-Yorke, Principal of Poplar School of Marine Engineering.
44 PRO, Ed. 24/1226, Consultative Committee Memoranda 1913–34, Minute C. Eaton to E. H. Pelham, 15 July 1933.
45 These inspections provided the data for the Board of Education's Educational Pamphlet No. 111, *A Review of Junior Technical Schools in England*, published in 1937 while the Consultative Committee's report was awaited. It provided a descriptive account of the schools and significantly was critical of the premises in which many of them were housed, finding them 'quite unsuitable for full-time schools of [sic] boys and girls between the ages of 13 and 16 years' (p. 28).
46 Board of Education, *Secondary Education* (Spens), p. 275.
47 *Ibid.*, p. 279.
48 *Ibid.*, p. 374.
49 B. Simon, *The Politics of Educational Reform 1920–1940*, London, 1974, pp. 257–8.
50 PRO, Ed. 136/131, The Spens Report, Board's Examination of Recommendations etc., Memorandum prepared January 1939.
51 B. Simon, *Politics of Educational Reform*, p. 268.
52 For a full account of this initiative see Bill Bailey, 'The development of technical education 1934–1939', *History of Education*, 16, 1987, pp. 49–65.
53 PRO, Ed. 138/4, *Draft History of Education during the War, vol. II*, D. S. Weitzman.
54 Ministry of Education, *The Nation's Schools, Their Plan and Purpose*, Pamphlet No. 1, London, 1945.
55 Gary McCulloch, Edgar Jenkins and David Layton, *Technological Revolution?*, London, 1985, p. 48.

SIX

Technology, institutions and status: technological education, debate and policy, 1944–1956

Martin Davis

The contribution of technology to British economic performance in the nineteenth and twentieth centuries has been widely debated. Whilst acknowledging the importance of economic factors in the development of the British economy, this chapter concentrates particularly upon policy towards technical and technological education in the immediate post-war years. Three factors are explored in depth: the debate about the aims and purposes of this education; the problems of status, and the minefield of institutional pressure groups through which policy innovation had to tread. It argues that the interaction of these elements seriously frustrated the development of technological education and that a more *dirigiste* approach by government was needed, which implied strengthening the powers of the Ministry of Education to include responsibility for the universities. Nor were either industry or the professional institutions clear about the kind of education they required. Their uncertainties linked directly to the debate between advocates of a broadly based expansion of technological education and those who sought to raise standards by creating the small number of peak institutions. Government decisions in the mid-1950s implied the pursuit of both aims simultaneously.

Although the Ministry of Education's Technical Branch was aware in the 1930s of skill shortages, it was the Second World War which heightened awareness of deficiencies.[1] Dependence upon American expertise and emergency schemes to train workers in new skills reinforced concern about British backwardness. War underlined the need to improve the quantity and quality of technical training and to raise the calibre of industrial management. Yet improvement faced formidable obstacles – the uncertain status of technology, university and the professional institutions' attitudes, and the limited powers of the Ministry of Education. Was the need for more technologists, more technicians or for both? What was the distinction between technical and technological education and what were the implications for training? And yet it was religious issues and the nature of secondary education which dominated the background to the 1944 Education Act. Correlli Barnett rightly comments that the 'crucial question of providing the nation with an education for capability from primary school to technical university equal to that of her competitors was squeezed away to the sidelines'.[2]

The debate about technical and technological education will be traced from the Percy Committee, which reported in 1945, to the White Paper *Technical Education* of February 1956. Particular emphasis will be laid upon the activities of the National Council for Education in Industry and Commerce (NACEIC) established in 1947–8 and its efforts to create a new national award in technology to assist expansion. However, it is important to stress that, despite the widespread contemporary belief that there was a shortage of technologists in Britain, this assumption was not rigorously tested at the time. There is independent evidence, for example Charlotte Erickson's study of the steel industry, that the leaders of British industry were less qualified technologically than their American and European counterparts; whether this was the outcome of the failure of technological education and the source of its continued weakness, or was rooted in wider economic and social trends in British society, is perhaps an unanswerable question.[3]

The Percy Committee

The Percy Committee, which reported in 1945, received evidence suggesting that the output of technologists needed to be increased well beyond 1939 levels. As the Hankey Committee noted: 'We are entering an age in which organising and scientific capacity may well make the difference between victory or defeat in war, between prosperity and decline in peace.'[4] The Ministry's own estimates for 1939 were 9,100 students in technical education over the age of seventeen and 1,600 (25 per cent) over twenty-one. Most students were part-time and wastage rates were about 50 per cent. University output in 1943 had been 1,051 first degrees and sixty-five higher degrees in applied science and its maximum was reckoned to be 1,600 per annum (1,354 excluding polytechnic and external degrees), whereas about 3,000 per annum were needed.[5] But though the figures on supply were reasonably accurate (allowing for some double counting), those on anticipated demand were rough estimates partly derived from comparisons with American and German wartime achievements. Other evidence stressed the need for new forms of training for management which would include practical experience. Sir Charles Darwin, a member of the Committee, argued that university engineering students had no systematic training in advanced technology.

Status issues also emerged. Attention was drawn to public-school bias against technical and factory employment, 'partly due to the past recruitment of industrial executives from non technicians and the bias of secondary schools generally towards nonfactory employment'. The City and Guilds noted that in the German steel industry most directors and works managers had university or *Hochschule* education.[6] Ironically, the Federation of British Industries (FBI) stressed the value of the communal life of the universities and made no reference at all to the significance of technological education.[7] The Committee suggested that the status of technical and technological education outside universities would be raised by a new and prestigious award, but could not agree upon its title. Advocates of degrees in technical colleges pointed to justice, parity of esteem and national and international recognition, but were opposed by upholders of the university degree monopoly and those who saw a diploma as more appropriate to industrially-orientated higher education. The Committee of Vice-Chancellors and Principals (CVCP) proposed a 'high technological diploma – not a degree nor with the letters of a degree – but with letters of its own'.[8] The Percy Committee also considered a B. Tech. proposal but this was abandoned under university pressure. The final report included both viewpoints but the balance was undermined by the Chairman, Lord Eustace Percy,[9] who asserted that 'the reputation of a university degree would be undermined if there was a dual standard, one for universities and another for "municipal colleges of technology" which do not claim maturity and do not even aspire to independence'.[10] This is perhaps not surprising coming from a man who, though a former President of the Board of Education, had preached the superior values of a pre-industrial world and called for a return to 'the standards which have always governed societies before they acquired great wealth through trade – societies, for instance, like seventeenth century England before the emergence of the Indian "nabob" '.[11]

The Percy Committee was a disappointment to the Ministry of

Education. It did identify many of the problems – the need for new forms of training, the high failure rates in technical colleges, above all the lack of focus and direction in technical education, but was less fruitful of solutions. The damaging consequences of the inferior status of technical education, the need for a national award and for a new sandwich course was accepted. The principle of parity of esteem was acknowledged but then not granted. The Committee recommended upgrading some technical colleges but set out no clear criteria by which they should be chosen. Its inability to agree on the awards issue meant that it never examined technologies beyond traditional engineering, though it was just these areas, not linked to the professional engineering institutions, which most needed support and educational development. Unable to interest the universities very much in technological education outside their ambit, the Committee fell back upon the expansion of regional advisory councils for further education with academic boards, consisting of LEA, university, industrial and technical college representatives. Policy advice at the national level was to be left to a new National Advisory Council. Not only did Percy fail to solve the problem about expanding technology, it even left a future institutional focus vague. Above all, its debates underscored the powerful influence of the universities, the weak and underpowered position of the Ministry, and industrial uncertainty about the future labour force required. Percy thus left an unfinished agenda, not a programme for action.

Similar issues were explored by the Barlow Committee (1946), which recommended doubling the output of university science graduates but also discussed technical education. Sir Walter Moberley, Chairman of the UGC, expressed doubts to Barlow about the university sector's ability to expand, suggesting that the state 'would have largely to rely on technical colleges and similar institutions'. The Committee noted that 'in liberated Europe, where university education had stopped entirely during the German occupation, the universities were already handling two or three times the number of students which they had before the war', and added drily that 'the university authorities had been concerned more with the size they would like to achieve than with the real requirements of the nation'. Despite this, Barlow wished technical colleges to concentrate on providing more technicians, a view which ignored the reality of the mixed provision of a very wide range of courses from craft to university degrees which characterised the technical college system.[12]

The National Advisory Council

The National Advisory Council had to tackle the issues of the award and expanded provision, of specialisation versus increased provision, against a background in which technologists and technicians were taught in a wide array of institutions. Resolution of these issues was needed to meet the challenge thrown out by its chairman, Sir Ronald Weeks,[13] who claimed that the battle for peace would be lost ' . . . if we cannot in the time mobilise and increase all our available resources of manpower and skill to solve the problems of production which at this present moment are on our doorstep'.[14] But policies for technological education, particularly the creation of a new national award, required negotiation with powerful pressure and interest groups. The Ministry, acutely aware of university attitudes, sought to avoid the degree controversy whilst seeking to create a prestigious award for technical colleges viewed as essential to raise recruitment. Both the National Council and the regional advisory councils were dominated by educational interests, whilst industrial representatives did not exceed 20 per cent.[15] This composition was not well attuned to winning the vital support of industry and the engineering institutions.

Like Percy, NACEIC debated demand. Anxiety about shortages was reinforced by the perceived need for a different kind of engineering education, aimed at creating a more professional manager. Quantitative issues were treated very generally – with few statistics and less analysis – but some broad assertions were made. The output of chemical engineers was 'wholly inadequate' and a four-year chemical engineering degree was needed. The annual output of electrical engineers was believed adequate, but apprenticeships in smaller firms needed improvement. Physics required an 'engineering physicist' combining theoretical and practical training, whilst the rubber industries anticipated a doubling of demand for highly trained personnel with growing awareness of the need for scientific training. NACEIC considered closely the views of the Tizard Committee (1948) which suggested industry would benefit from the introduction of those '. . . who had specialist training in some branch of engineering or other applied science, following upon a sound education in the fundamental sciences'.[16] Tizard believed that this could be achieved by the expansion and concentration of technological education in universities or new colleges, perhaps analogous to MIT or Imperial College. The National Council took expansion for granted as a desirable good but its nature remained vague in the extreme. By and large it was the educationalists in the Ministry and in the colleges who were concerned to expand provision, both in their own interests and because of awareness of greater and, they believed, better provision abroad.

Improved and expanded provision was handicapped by a failure to define differences between technicians and technologists and to establish an appropriate ratio between them. Only the Institute of Electrical Engineers offered a definition in which the *technologist* was described as undertaking work in industry which required a high degree of personal responsibility, whilst a *technician* carried out responsible work in accordance with the established practice whilst under the general direction of a technologist. However, even the IEE had only reached these definitions after much debate and they pointed towards the separate education of technician and technologist, although in the British system differing courses, from craft to technology, were commonly taught in the same institution. Nor did they ask if the employment of engineers in industry reflected these distinctions.

The Treasury highlighted the need for more three-year apprenticeships at eighteen plus. Graduate apprenticeships were sharply criticised. 'There is seldom time on the shop floor to teach the graduate apprentice the skillful [*sic*] manipulation of hand and machine tools, consequently he can only be usefully employed on the less skilled work.' Graduate apprentice schemes were devised 'more for the purpose of selecting future executives for the firm from a field of promising graduates than of providing all-round fundamental practical training'. And the Treasury perceptively observed that: 'It is possible that much of the technical alertness of American production is due to the fluidity of staff there and the resultant high degree of cross fertilisation of ideas.'[17]

If demand was uncertain what was the supply? The broad trends in university and technical college output can be seen from Tables 6.1, 6.2 and 6.4, while Table 6.3 gives an analysis of the distribution of different qualifications awarded in technical colleges in 1949.

Wartime and immediate post-war growth had been in *part time* certificates and much provision was outside the universities. In 1948, 38 per cent of all London University degree students in science and 58·1 per cent in engineering were in the London polytechnics, with one technical college having *more* engineering students than any constituent college of the university.[18] A similar development was noted by Gerstl and Hutton. Amongst IME members in the younger

Table 6.1: Ordinary and Higher National Certificates and Diplomas awarded in science and engineering, 1945–55

	ONC	OND	HNC	HND
1945	5,135	116	1,844	60
1946	5,544	130	2,069	82
1947	5,805	110	2,479	61
1948	7,997	N/A	4,509	N/A
1949	9,483	348	4,147	287
1950	10,581	337	4,961	293
1951	10,617	299	5,564	351
1952	11,302	253	6,226	250
1953	10,898	214	6,452	312
1954	11,957	361	6,827	248
1955	13,458	412	7,371	229

Sources: Derived from Ed/46/700, 17 March 1949, Ministry of Education, *Annual Surveys and Technical Education*, Cmnd. 9703, 1956.

Table 6.2: University degrees awarded in science and technology

	Pure Science	Medicine	Dentistry	Technology
1938	7,661	11,883	1,488	5,288
1947	12,516	12,496	1,584	8,767
1948	14,544	13,414	2,144	10,146
1949	16,099	14,094	2,547	10,884
1950	16,917	14,147	2,724	10,993
1951	17,168	14,201	2,885	10,591
1952	17,053	13,910	2,889	10,215
1953	17,001	13,511	2,715	9,993
1954	16,971	13,239	2,564	10,036
1955	17,327	13,088	2,583	10,586
1956	18,133	13,341	2,651	11,379

Sources: Derived from Annual Abstract of Statistics.

age groups in 1962 a substantially higher proportion of HNC holders, as opposed to graduates, was identified:

7 per cent of nongraduates: Age 55+
20 per cent of nongraduates: Age 35–44
32 per cent of nongraduates: Age under 34[19]

Certainly the technical colleges were responsible for a significant proportion of the output of highly qualified personnel in science and,

Table 6.3: Degrees, Higher National Certificates and Higher
National Diplomas awarded in technical colleges, 1949

	Science	Engineering	Other technologies
Degrees			
Internal	296	413	—
External	155	308	—
Total	451	721	—
HNC	203	3,851	525
HND	—	144	143
Total	203	3,995	668
Grand total	654	4,716	668

Source: Adapted from PRO/Ed 46/753, Draft Cabinet Paper, 'The
Establishment of a Royal College of Technologists', 23 November
1950.

Table 6.4: Technical college students as percentage of university students in 1949

	Pure science	Engineering
Degrees	2·9	7·1
Degrees, HNC & HND	4·7	34·6

Source: Calculated from Tables 6.2 & 6.3.

particularly, technology. Therefore their future was not marginal but
central to British provision and distinctions which allocated technology to universities and technician education to technical colleges
were not sustainable in practice.

The degree and university attitudes

The second central issue was the nature of the award. The National
Council's Steering Committee commented that '. . . the overwhelming prestige attached to a university degree offered little hope
that what would be in effect a rival qualification could establish
itself . . .' and asked 'whether any member felt that anything less than
a degree would provide a desirable solution to the problem of an
award'.[20] The weight of evidence submitted pointed in the same
direction. The Association of Education Committees wrote that 'there
is pressing need for a qualification having the prestige of a degree'.[21]
Yet how could this be reconciled with university preservation of

degree monopoly? A possible compromise was affiliation or sponsorship between universities and technical colleges, but difficulties soon emerged. A draft minute of the joint UGC/NACEIC Committee which recommended integration of technical colleges and local universities by mixing of staff and students was described by the UGC Secretary as 'extremely controversial'.[22] Ministry scepticism was aroused since it was felt that many technical college students taking London external degrees would have benefited from a course of 'moderate honours degree standard' which 'universities either don't or don't want to provide'. Many university courses were alleged to be made up of snippets of fundamental science together with a hotchpotch of engineering technology.[23]

University attitudes varied from the wholly unyielding CVCP to the slightly more flexible UGC, whose Chairman wrote in September 1949 of the issue of technical college qualifications: 'In the first place we are certain to be assured that anything less than a degree will not satisfy the technical colleges. [Sir Charles] Darwin has expressed this view on numerous occasions and I wonder whether we shall eventually get by with anything less than a B.Tech.' If established it was essential to make it clear that university technology 'stood for something different in character'. He suggested the UGC should prepare a note, 'if only as an answer to those who think that all technology should be handed over to the technical colleges'.[24] A CVCP meeting in March 1949 regarded proposals to link universities and technical colleges as 'only too likely to put a veneer of quality on top of an unsound structure'. The Vice Chancellors underlined their opposition to degrees in technical colleges. 'Any scheme which bestows labels that do not mean what the public is led to expect them to mean will soon be exposed to disrespect; the immediate sufferer from these will be the bearers of those labels, the next will be the begetters of the scheme, and the eventual victim will be the nation.'[25]

This rigidity did raise unease. Sir Edward Appleton, Secretary of the DSIR, wrote, 'I felt that the VCs Committee were becoming inclined to adopt too much of [an] . . . Ivory Tower . . . attitude about the B.Tech.' Universities should regard this problem as 'a great opportunity rather than an irksome task, and that if they were interested in Applied Science at all, they should not shirk the responsibility it involves'.[26] This appeal must have struck home for in discussion between the UGC and the CVCP it was agreed 'informally and confidentially that, if pressed the universities would not oppose the establishment of a B. Tech. – for which they do not hold the responsibility'.[27] However the offer remained in a sealed envelope, until opened by the author of this chapter, so the issue was never pressed. Whilst it is easy to exaggerate individual proposals it seems possible that the debate over titles which haunted technical education until the Robbins Committee reported in 1961 might have evolved along different lines had the award of B. Tech. been established in technical colleges in the early 1950s. As Antony Part was to say in the Ministry's oral evidence to Robbins: 'We found that degree is a magic word.' If status is important in the self-esteem of institutions and student course and career choices, then the determination of universities to safeguard the degree monopoly was damaging.

The engineering institutions

The National Council now sought alternatives which, to quote Sir Ronald Weeks in December 1949, would enable technological studies to achieve 'in the eyes of the nation as a whole, the position of prestige and importance which it should enjoy'. A Royal Institute of Technology, with categories of membership and sharing some of the functions of a learned society, as well as validating a new award, was proposed. It would act 'as a national forum, comparable in some respects to the Royal Society in the fields of pure science, for the discussion of many common problems in technology which are daily arising from invention and research'.[28] Crucial to success were the attitudes of the three engineering institutions, the Institute of Mechanical Engineers (IME), the Institute of Civil Engineers (ICE) and the Institute of Electrical Engineers (IEE). Relations between them, the Ministry and the National Council soon became deeply embittered and the centre of powerful lobbying on all sides. In keeping with their traditional practice, the three Institutions acted jointly, though the IEE appears to have taken the lead on this issue.

The institutions believed that the proposed Royal Institute of Technology threatened their standing and suspected that Ministry officers had left consultation with the Institutions to last in order to neutralise their opposition. A letter from the President of the IEE to Guy of the ICE on 24 November 1949, stated:

As I understand it Bray's [a Ministry official] policy is to tackle every possible opponent separately and to come to the Professional Institutions last . . . knowing his single-minded purpose, I felt he must have realised that Associate Membership of the RIT would be disliked by us just as much as the idea of another kind of degree has been disliked by the universities.[29]

The ICE also believed that the Ministry had missed the point: it was not status that mattered, but improved buildings and equipment; status came from recognition of courses by the professional institutions. The Institutions also distrusted the development of technology in technical colleges as threatening technological studies in the universities with their broader culture, seen as vital to the status and influence of the engineer. The National Council proposals raised unease and the Secretary of the IEE drew attention to pressures seeking to exclude the education of engineers from universities. On the one hand, certain physicists and scientists believed that universities should be restricted to research and teaching in pure science, on the other pressure was for larger technical colleges to be allowed to award degrees in technology.[30] Nor could the Institutions have been reassured by a *Times* editorial in December opposing university expansion in technology: 'The right way forward was slowly to raise the status of technical colleges to good technological institutes.'[31] The IEE believed that the situation needed 'careful watching . . . not only as a matter affecting their own interests but also as one affecting the national interest', particularly since the aim of the Royal Institute was to give national recognition to colleges which had not won this on 'their own merits'.[32]

The Institutions' distrust owed something to their origins. As Buchanan notes, in sharp contrast with the Continental tradition, they did not rest upon graduate entry. Examinations for membership were only slowly introduced around 1900. 'The way was gradually opened to entry for people with college and university qualifications, though to an extent very limited in comparison with other parts of Europe.' And Buchanan goes on to argue that the development of so many separate engineering institutions weakened the capacity of professional engineers to advance their own broader interests and suggests that they suffered from a 'professional inferiority complex'.[33] In a *draft* letter to IEE members of the Regional Advisory Council about the NAC proposals, Professor Pippard commented: 'The continental system by which qualifications to practice [*sic*] is conferred by State Diploma does not appeal to professional engineers in this country . . .'.[34] And the complex negotiations which had to take place between the three Engineering Institutions – and a lesser level of contact with some other professional associations – do underline the real handicaps of institutional proliferation.

This insecurity is highlighted by the IME response to the NAC Report. 'For many years the chartered professional bodies of this

country holding a unique position and being democratically constituted, have successfully looked ahead and assented to requirements in
the education of the new entry into the professions which they represent.' And, in a remarkable rewriting of the IME's own history, argued
that 'the Engineering institutions have forged an uphill battle to secure
recognition of the fact that an engineer is not made by his academic and
theoretical education only, and there are still those who would dispute
the necessity for practical training and practical knowledge'.[35] Similar
concerns were voiced by the ICE which feared that the establishment
of the Royal Institute of Technology might reduce entry to the professional bodies by 30 per cent and that an 'un-British process of superim-
position of a direct competitor would be established to carry on the
principal activity and purpose of existing autonomous learned
Societies and Institutions'.[36]

The validity of these fears for which there is no explicit evidence in
NAC papers is difficult to judge. The Institutions' perceptions about
tactics may have been well based, since the Ministry was painfully
aware of the minefield through which any new proposals would have to
pass, but the central strategy was to strengthen technology in the
technical colleges. Indeed, the IEE's memorandum upon the NAC
proposals sums up Ministry motivation well when they argued that the
colleges 'will not be able to recruit the most suitable material for entry
to the courses, nor collect staffs and teachers of appropriate standing',
without a suitable award. It is important to note also the paradox in the
stance taken by the engineering institutions for their concern ought to
have led them to welcome the proposed Royal Institute of Technology. Their anxiety about a threat to the role of technology in the
universities is not proven. Anxiety that the enhanced powers of
government would begin to erode the engineering institutions' powers
to control the recognition of qualified engineers arose from a misunderstanding of the National Advisory Council's proposals.

Although the Minister, George Tomlinson, received a joint deputation of the Engineering Institutions in December 1949, they came
away with the belief that the Ministry would press ahead with the RIT
proposal. Overall the IEE was 'alarmed at the dangers inherent in the
establishment of the Royal Institute of Technology which, they feared,
would take over the functions of the major engineering institutions'.[37]
The Ministry had not anticipated this response and there appears to
have been a breakdown in communication since members of the
professional institutions served on the NACEIC and on the regional
advisory councils which considered the National Council's Report.

Although the Institutions felt they were being ignored, the NACEIC itself said: 'It has never been our intention that the vitally important work of the major professional institutions should be ignored. Indeed we cannot imagine the possibility of a new body being established without considerable help and cooperation from existing institutions.'[38] Negotiations continued, and in July 1950 the IME welcomed a statement that the proposed Royal Institute would not function as a professional institution. Despite unease, the Institutions did concede that some account had been taken of their views when the National Council's proposals were published.[39]

Other reactions to the NACEIC report

Other reactions to the NACEIC report varied. Educational interests were broadly sympathetic. Supporters emphasised the urgency of the achievement of parity of esteem. The National Association of Labour Teachers argued that it was a denial of equality of opportunity that students on similar courses to universities should obtain an inferior award.[40] Supporters were outweighed by opposition from the professional institutions, the City and Guilds and the FBI. Three broad strands can be identified: those who denied the need for an award; those who favoured an award but not the Royal College (as the Institute was now called), and advocates of upgrading a few colleges. As the Institution of Production Engineers put it, 'financial aid . . . should be concentrated at first in a comparatively small number of establishments, with potentialities for fairly rapid development into centres of higher technological education'.[41] The FBI favoured a Technological Grants Committee, as did the Royal Institute of Chemistry. The Federation argued broadly along the lines of its 1949 report, *The Education and Training of Technologists*, in which, in contrast with its views in 1945, it did stress the need for integral industrial training and the development of a small number of technical colleges along lines analogous to Imperial College, but rejected a national award. The AUT offered support for the selection and removal of a few technical colleges from LEA control, but otherwise technological education should be restricted to the universities. Technical colleges 'were overloaded with low grade courses and poor material, are lacking in general amenities and have no real atmosphere of science and culture'.[42] There was no doubt much truth in this view but it did not address the issue of how the general standard of technical education might be raised.

Sir Frederick Handley Page, speaking on behalf of the City and Guilds, was concerned that: 'In this country we have at present a widespread and fairly high level plateau of technical education, but we have no peak institutions. We therefore lack a certain drive, intensity of purpose and inspiration which would come from peak institutions of Technology.[43] The Ministry claimed that this view was 'based on sheer ignorance of what is being done in technical colleges or on the assumption that the admitted defects of these colleges cannot be overcome'. This proposal took no account of the 'desirability of living local association with industry such as can be developed in technical colleges as they exist today and assume the only local contact with industry worth talking about is that which can be established on a national scale'.[44]

Despite these representations, the Ministry pushed ahead, rejected the idea of technological universities and accepted the NACEIC Report. The White Paper, *Higher Technological Education*, of September 1951 proposed a chartered College of Technologists without the use of the title 'Royal' and restricted to the approval of courses and awards.[45] Thus, by the October 1951 General Election, agreement had been reached on the establishment of the College of Technologists, and after six years of debate a grudging basis for a new policy had been won. But the defeat of the Labour government threw policy into flux.

Conservative policy

Government policy between 1951 and 1956 first abandoned the proposal to establish a College of Technologists, but then reversed policy and returned to the essence of the 1951 plan. The new Minister, Florence Horsburgh, soon came under renewed pressure from the engineering institutions and received a deputation in December 1951.[46] Lord Cherwell, the Postmaster General and Churchill's pre-war and wartime scientific adviser, attacked the College of Technology proposal in a letter to the Minister in November 1951. 'So far as I know the most important institutions consulted about this proposal have been strongly opposed to it. What is needed is better teaching for technologists rather than a body which tells them how good they are! In any case there seems no urgency in going ahead with the formation of this proposed college.'[47] And in advocating the case for technological universities to the Chancellor of the Exchequer he argued: 'The Technical Colleges are in quite a different category – they train the

NCOs of industry, not officers.'[48] Within a few months a Ministry official wrote: 'It is now clear that there is to be a sharp and proper distinction between developments in universities and in technical colleges respectively.'[49] Whilst the Minister announced in the House of Commons on 11 June 1952 that the Royal College of Technology would not be established it also agreed that central government grant support for technical college courses in technology should be raised from 60 to 75 per cent.[50] As a Ministry officer wrote in January 1952: 'After all that has happened we concluded that it would be best to get on first with the proposal for better grants for selected colleges and courses.'[51]

The National Council was deeply disappointed and in January 1953 wrote to the Minister to express the 'grave concern of a *substantial majority* of members of the Council that the government had not seen its way to accepting the Council's . . . recommendation that a College of Technologists should be established'. The Council stated 'emphatically' that the College was essential to the future development of higher technological education.[52] When the delegation was received on 18 February 1953, it was informed that the Ministry believed that a national award was urgently needed and 'even the professional institutions were beginning to realise this', but there was still too much opposition to the Royal College of Technologists. Would the National Council reconsider titles, constitutions and functions? NACEIC members argued that frustration was building up, but above all the student was the key factor because unless he was offered 'an award which would be widely accepted as evidence of his qualifications he had no incentive to take the course'.[53]

Some evidence that professional institutions were becoming more flexible does emerge despite the refusal of the Minister to meet them in November 1952, because government policy towards the universities had not yet been settled. In a joint memorandum, the three engineering institutions stressed their commitment to the principle of an independent national body.[54] However, they remained, 'wholly opposed to the setting up of the Royal College of Technologists'. They now pressed for the development of a few selected colleges – Royal Colleges of Technology financed through a Technological Grants Committee, but this was rejected by the Minister who stressed the urgent immediate need for better technological education. 'It would be most unwise to forefeit the contribution which . . . some technical colleges can make just because it is not *immediately* practicable to adopt the plan of establishing colleges wholly devoted to technological as distinct from technical work.'[55] The Minister asked the Institutions to accept the government policy.

NACEIC now proposed 'A National Council for Awards in Technology at Technical Colleges' awarding a Diploma in Technology. The Institutions were reported as 'ready to help in clothing the skeleton' and admitted 'they had been dubious of the NAC's intentions as regards standards but had been reassured'.[56] It was agreed that the engineering institutions should be represented in a personal not an institutional capacity. Yet difficulties still persisted and the institutions approached the Ministry again, pressing the need for the selection of colleges rather than courses. Colleges should have greater independence and staff need to be refreshed 'by exchanges in a Common Room fully representative of all the sciences in which the technological applications are based'. They proposed independent bodies to select the colleges, co-ordinate the examinations and control the awards.[57]

Upgrading was also debated at the Joint Council of Professional Scientists on the Future of Higher Technological Education in September 1954, but Ministry officials argued that this would lead to colleges losing touch with industry's needs. When it was suggested that six colleges should be upgraded, the Ministry pointed out that there were twelve major polytechnics in London *alone* and no major college had more than 50 per cent of advanced work. The revised NACEIC proposal was acceptable since it concentrated on the award and sidestepped the issue of upgrading. The establishment of the National Council for Technological Awards (NCTA) was announced on 14 July 1955. The struggle to establish a national award in technology for technical colleges was at last won.

The White Paper *Technical Education*

The government was not unsympathetic to the development of a small number of advanced colleges of technology and this concern to strengthen technological education, reinforced by a belief in the danger of British backwardness, led to the White Paper *Technical Education* in February 1956. An important driving force in the new policy was the Minister, Sir David Eccles and Antony Part, who was transferred to the Ministry. In an interesting background paper written at the end of 1955, Antony Part showed awareness of the speed of technological change; 'success not stability is the goal of our century', he wrote, and 'the technician of 1975 may need to know nearly as much as the technologist of today'.[58] To this broad vision was added concern at the poor quality of much technical college accommodation and the slow pace of improvement: 'Many of our technical colleges have old and inadequate buildings, and others are housed in a number of separate and often scattered premises', and 'more and better facilities are needed for approved courses in advanced technology'. Education for economic growth was strongly emphasized: 'Unless we can get every intelligent youngster on to the further education ladder our hopes of meeting industrial needs will not be fulfilled.' The case for increased expenditure on technical education was put forward: 'The universities are the first barrel in our gun. The technical colleges are the second . . . the technical colleges have rendered great service to education, industry and commerce. Their potentials are wide but their present scope is limited.'[59] It is also fair to say that an element in the new thinking was a refutation of Lord Cherwell's renewed advocacy of a technological university, which the Ministry saw as too narrow and too much influenced by Continental precedents. Of his view that universities were not alive to the need for more scientists and technologists, the Ministry said 'nothing could be further from the truth', and noted that the technological university controversy had been 'highly prejudicial' to action.[60]

The White Paper draft stuck an upbeat note: 'The prize will not go to sheer numbers but to the best system of education'; but whilst acknowledging the need for more technologists and technicians, it warned against the more extravagant comparisons with other countries which should be viewed with as much suspicion as official wartime statistics of aircraft losses. The economic implications of investment in technological education were spelled out: 'If we consider the problem of our balance of payments, it is clear that the supply of trained personnel is the key to the expansion of exports of high quality goods and to the winning of contracts for capital goods on which our ability to pay for a growing volume of imports must depend.'[61] Implicit also was a more *dirigiste* approach whose problems are revealed in the Minister's own comment: 'We need more central direction but . . . if we do not butter up the local authorities we are in for trouble.' And echoes of earlier controversies are revealed in a letter from a UGC official to Part commenting on unease at describing the output of the technical colleges as technologists 'as the expression "technologist" in many people's minds means a man who has had a university training'.[62] He suggested that technologist should be used in the White Paper to describe someone who had studied engineering or applied science to the standard of a university pass degree, whereas the Ministry preferred the definition to encompass membership of a professional institution. The Ministry stressed that the White Paper set out a policy of concentrating advanced work in a limited number of technical colleges and Eccles argued to the Prime Minister that the 'emergency is bringing to light new methods of training, such as sandwich courses, which are the equal of traditional methods'.[63] The White Paper provided for a new tier of Colleges of Advanced Technology (the CATs) above a hierarchy of local, area and regional colleges established by Circular 305. Advocates of specialisation had made some impact upon government policy but Ministry officials could also point to the establishment of the Diploma of Technology and the 75 per cent grant for advanced courses, not restricted to the CATs, which took account of the reality of the dispersed provision of courses in technology. The Ministry advocated a broad brush approach, expanding the education of technicians as well as technologists.

Three major strands ran through this debate. The first was the problem of distinguishing technical from technological education. Professional institutions believed in this distinction and that it necessitated education in separate institutions. The Ministry doubted whether this was desirable and knew that it was not immediately practicable. The 1956 White paper did, however, mark the beginning of a policy of separation which was to be pursued for the next three decades. The second was the aim and purpose of technical and technological education: to raise status, to raise standards, or to expand numbers to assist in industrial development and contribute to national economic growth? Here there was much confusion and the central issues were often obscured by institutional lobbying.

The third area was that of status, and provides some evidence for the assertions of Wiener and Barnett. Wiener has advanced the hypothesis that British élites were unsympathetic to manufacturing capitalism and this in turn hindered the progress of technological education, contributed to the low prestige of the engineer in comparison with continental Europe, and played a part in 'Britain's psychological and intellectual deindustrialisation'.[64] More powerfully, Correlli Barnett in *The Audit of War* has made a strong prosecution case for technological backwardness and the poor technological training of industrial leaders. He asserts that these deficiencies have been responsible for Britain's failure since 1945 to learn from the lessons of the Second World War, and, indeed, for a propensity to learn the wrong lessons. Both Ahlstrom and Gerstl and Hutton have suggested that the limited prestige and status of engineering in British society has been linked to the *ad hoc* way in which the British engineering institutions emerged and, in particular to the lack of prestigious higher education institutions of engineering – apart from Imperial College – to compare with Zurich, Berlin, Gothenburg, MIT and the Polytechnique. It is often overlooked that these institutions were often originally inferior in status to universities and only gradually won equality, in the German case by about 1900, in the Swedish by the 1920s. Moreover, there was a significant increase in the social class background of students entering these institutions during the nineteenth century.[65] Ahlstrom suggests that 'in Germany and France scientific and technical education was approved for the élite', whereas 'in Britain it was approved by the élite'.[66] The British tradition was not only to produce far fewer advanced students in engineering and technology, but their education took place both in universities and in technical colleges. Thus I would agree with Ahlstrom's view that Britain was very unfortunate that separate institutions of technology did not generally develop. It can be argued that British policies in this field after 1945 partly echoed continental experience half a century earlier.

In broadly similar vein, Gerstl and Hutton argue that, 'because engineering departments were part of universities, for social and political reasons they did not grow as rapidly as they should have done'.[67] Moreover, in examining the membership of the IME in the early 1960s, they comment that the number of university graduates amongst IME members was 'remarkably low' and, equally significant, 20 per cent of the members of the graduate members of IME had taken the London External degree, available in some technical colleges.[68] Respondents to their survey argued that 'courses at universities were too academic and those at technical colleges too vocational' – much the kind of criticism made by the Ministry between 1944 and 1956. Less than one third of the IME members surveyed claimed satisfaction with their status: '. . . regardless of the degree of personal achievement . . . the majority of engineers are disatisfied with the status of their profession.'[69] In a ranking of professionals the general public's view placed the engineer eighth out of ten, and a survey of sixth-form boys by Oxford University's Department of Education in 1961 indicated a very similar ranking. Those boys achieving the highest grades at Advanced Level predominantly entered science degrees rather than engineering; comparative studies with Holland and France showed much higher ranking for engineering, and also indicated that it attracted a greater share of high examination grades. Lawrence and Bayer's comparisons of A level and Arbitur grades in the 1970s yielded similar results. The attitude surveys in the Finniston Report indicate that the term engineering was markedly less prestigious in British than continental societies.[70]

Whilst scepticism has been expressed about the status hypothesis, it is striking that many of these issues do appear in the debate about technological education. There was anxiety about the low status of technology within and outside universities and its implications for management. The belief was held by many in industry and the engineering institutions that university social and cultural attributes were as important as technological qualifications. Thus the future status of technological education required that it should *not* be developed in technical colleges, with their associations with the grimy world of industry. The first draft of the Percy Committee had noted: 'It is generally recognised that in many leading countries of the world technological qualifications stand higher in public esteem than they do here, and industrial progress and development are proportionately more rapid and more widespread.'[71] Yet in their response to Percy, the engineering institutions stressed the need for personal qualities and for social and athletic facilities corresponding to those of the 'older' universities.[72] The FBI, in its evidence to Percy, echoed similar concerns and in discussion with the Committee noted '. . . the especial nature of university life was thought to be its residential character . . .'.[73] Similar issues emerge in the NACEIC debate. In a draft report NACEIC claimed that development would be frustrated unless 'technology is accorded in the minds of industry and the public generally a status as high in relation to industrial development as pure science enjoys in relation to fundamental discovery'.[74] And in its final report the National Council stressed that a key reason for the establishment of the Royal College was 'to assist in securing for technology generally the high status which its economic importance justifies in the industrial field'.[75] The institutions saw the Royal College proposals as a threat to their autonomy, and the university world stood full square for the degree monopoly but was unable to choose between expansion of technology in the universities and encouraging the development of selected technical colleges. The arguments for selective development were probably more status-induced than resting in a belief in the specific need to increase the output of technologists. And when the CATS and the Dip. Tech. were established they were so concerned to achieve comparability with universities that their output grew very slowly. Those in the technical college world and the Ministry who wished to create a prestigious award argued their corner so strongly because they believed the enhanced status of colleges would increase the quantity and quality of students applying and bring in train more resources and a further access of prestige and power. But even the Ministry, with its broader concerns for public policy, did not really explore in depth what might be the appropriate balance between technicians and technologists, and it accepted as a perceived rather than established truth the need for expansion.

Industrialists did not clearly assert evidence of increased demand for technologists. This does not mean that no such demand existed. Possibly the relatively low proportion of technologically trained members of British boards of directors reinforced an élite industrial culture less perceptive about future needs for technologists than that of competitors. Some in the industrial world were also sceptical of the attitude of civil servants. As one principal of a civil engineering firm wrote to the Secretary of the ICE in 1949: 'They often gave me the impression that they are not quite sure whether the general run of professional engineers is a man who goes around tightening up a few nuts and bolts, or occasionally does a little wiring.'[76] Even so it was the largely classically trained members of the Technical Branch of the Ministry who sought to expand provision. Their problem was that they were of low status even in the hierarchy of the Ministry.

It may well be true that shortages of technologists and technicians were important in the 1940s, fifties and sixties, resulting in failures in design, the increase of import penetration and the loss of export markets, as some of the deindustrialisation debate suggests. Though there were many other reasons for the relative economic success of leading industrial competitors, they certainly had a history of technological education, larger in volume and superior in prestige to that available in Britain. In particular the tendency in Britain of highly motivated and qualified school leavers to prefer pure science to applied science and technology probably did have significant consequences. The 1956 White Paper comparisons with other industrial countries may have been fanciful and overheated, but the sense of urgency which Sir David Eccles brought to policy was not.

If status concerns were one debate, the limited powers of the Ministry were also significant. The *ad hoc* development of the Ministry's powers gave it less capacity to shape policy than in other industrial countries. No doubt this experience, followed by that of the establishment of the NCTA and the Dip. Tech. in the later 1950s, contributed to the Ministry belief that the UGC should be brought under their wing. Certainly the difficulties in technical and technological education policy in this period make a powerful case for greater *dirigisme*. The increase of the Ministry's powers in all areas of education has been a consistent theme since the 1950s.

The crucial issue between 1944 and 1956 was an inability to pursue the central economic aims and purposes of technical and technological education – the expansion of a highly qualified labour force to meet the challenge of industrial competitors. This issue was asserted in the Percy debates and again in the White Paper of 1956. But between these debates there lies a wasteland when this issue was obscured by the manoeuvring of vested interests, concerned with status and institutional autonomy. Key pressure groups such as the CBI and the engineering institutions seem themselves to have lost sight of economic issues. And whilst the educational world did see expansion and the provision of a prestigious award as in their own interests, equally it could be argued that these were desirable in national terms. The broad versus national front strategy was important but it is not clear whether the advocates of selection were genuinely anxious to increase the output of technologists or to safeguard the status and influence of technology by restricting it to universities or exclusively technological institutions. The years between 1944 and 1956 saw progress on the central issue of expansion delayed and distorted by institutional lobbying and confusion between the need for technological expertise necessary for a period of rapid industrial change and the acquisition of enhanced status for technological education in British society. And government lacked the power to resolve the impasse until the re-emergence of belief in the contribution technical education could make to economic progress in the mid-1950s.

Notes

1 K. McCormick, 'The search for corporatist structures in British Higher Technological education: the creation of the National Advisory Council in Education and Commerce (NACEIC) in 1948', *British Journal of the Sociology of Education*, 7, 1986, p. 297.
2 Correlli Barnett, *The Audit of War*, London, 1986, p. 282.
3 Charlotte Erickson, *British Industrialists Steel and Hosiery 1850–1950*, London, 1959, ch. 2.
4 PRO, Ed. 46/296, Higher Technological Education (HTE) 7, Interdepartmental Committee on Further Education and Training (Hankey Committee).
5 PRO, Ed. 46/295, Percy Committee 17, 14–15 June 1945, *The Present Position of Technological Education* (undated).
6 PRO, Ed. 46/295, Percy Committee 4, 27–8 July 1944.
7 PRO, Ed. 46/295, Percy Committee 14, 27 April 1945.

8 PRO, Ed. 46/295, Percy Committee 9, HTE 38, *CVCP, Note on Relations between Universities and Technical Colleges*, (submitted with oral evidence, 26 October 1944).

9 Lord Eustace Percy. Born 21 March 1887, MP 1921–37. Parliamentary Secretary, Board of Education 1923, Minister of Health 1923–4, President of the Board of Education 1924–9, Rector of the Newcastle Division of the University of Durham 1937–52.

10 Ministry of Education, *Higher Technological Education: Report of a Special Committee Appointed in April 1944*, 1945 (Percy Committee), p. 25, item 4.

11 M. Wiener, *English Culture and the Decline of the Industrial Spirit*, Cambridge, 1981, pp. 104–6.

12 PRO, CAB 124/533, Barlow Committee Meeting, 8 January 1946.

13 Sir Ronald Weeks. Born 13 November 1890, Pilkington Brothers 1912–14 and 1919–45. Army 1914–18 and 1939–45 (general), Chairman Vickers 1948–56 and Chairman NACEIC 1948–56.

14 PRO, Ed. 46/699, National Advisory Council (NAC) 1, 1 June 1948.

15 P. F. R. Venables, *Technical Education*, London 1956, pp. 137–8, 141 and K. McCormick, 'The search . . .', p. 309.

16 *Higher Technological Education*, Report by the Advisory Committee on Scientific Education, 25 June 1948.

17 PRO, Ed. 46/700, NACEIC Standing Committee 2, 15 November 1948.

18 PRO, Ed. 46/700, NACEIC Standing Committee 6, 28 November 1949.

19 J. Gerstl and S. P. Hutton, *Engineers, the Anatomy of a Profession*, London, 1966, p. 42.

20 PRO, Ed. 46/700, NACEIC Steering Committee 3, 14 January 1949.

21 *Ibid.*, Steering Committee 4, 17 March 1949, *Preliminary Report on Higher Technological Education*.

22 PRO, Ed. 46/737, Draft Minute First Meeting, 3 September 1949, Ross (UGC) to Mcluckie (NACEIC), 21 September 1948.

23 *Ibid.*, Mcluckie to Gibson and Bray, 21 September 1948.

24 PRO, UGC 7/864, CVCP, *Qualifications for Students of Colleges of Technology*, May 1949.

25 PRO, UGC 7/864, Meeting with Vice Chancellors and Principals, 25 March 1949.

26 *Ibid.*, Sir Edward Appleton to Trueman, 14 July 1949, Appleton to Manson, 13 July 1949.

27 *Ibid.*, Note of a Discussion Between Deputy Chairman and Sir Hector Hetherington on 19 July 1949.

28 PRO, Ed. 46/742, NACEI Council, 16 December 1949.

29 ICE 3030/7, Vol. 2, *IEE, Memorandum for a National Association of Higher Studies in Technical Colleges, 3 December 1949*. (Note that whilst I have used archives from all three engineering institutions, the ICE has the most extensive, including substantial correspondence.)

30 PRO, Ed. 46/700, Standing Committee 6, 11 November 1949.

31 *The Times*, 26 November 1949.

32 IEE, Education Committee, 24 February and 23 March 1949.

33 R. A. Buchanan, 'Institutional proliferation and the British engineering

profession, 1847–1914', *Economic History Review*, 2nd Series XXXVIII, 1, February 1985, p. 57.
34 ICE 3030/7, Vol. 2, Professor Pickard (IEE), 30 December 1949.
35 *Ibid.*, IME Report to NAC, 2 December 1950.
36 *Ibid.*, IEE Memorandum for a National Association for Higher Studies in Technical Colleges, 3 December 1949.
37 *Ibid.*, 14 December 1949.
38 PRO, Ed. 46/700, Steering Committee, 11 November 1949.
39 IEE, Education Committee, 11 June 1950, Minute 53.
40 PRO, Ed. 46/752, National Association of Labour Teachers to Minister, 16 January 1951.
41 *Ibid.*, Institute of Production Engineers to Tomlinson (Minister of Education), 1 January 1951.
42 *Ibid.*, Ed. 46/752, AUT to Mcluckie, 7 July 1951.
43 IEE Education Committee, 16 April 1951.
44 PRO, Ed. 46/752, Flemming to Maud, 23 April 1951.
45 *Higher Technological Education*, Cmnd. 8357.
46 PRO, Ed. 46/752, Internal Ministry Memorandum on Deputation, 17 December 1951.
47 PRO, Ed. 46/755, Cherwell to Florence Horsburgh (undated by hand early November 1951).
48 PRO, Ed. 46/754, Cherwell to R. A. Butler, April 1952.
49 PRO, Ed. 46/752, signed Flemming, 4 June 1952 (on back of AUT Memorandum to Florence Horsburgh, 15 January 1952).
50 *Hansard* Fifth Series, Vol. 502, H. C. Debates 5.s., Written Answers p. 34, 11 June 1952.
51 PRO, Ed. 46/754, *Higher Technological Education*, 2 January 1952.
52 PRO, Ed. 46/750, I. O. Mcluckie to E. L. Russell and others, 12 January 1953.
53 *Ibid.*, extract from Standing Committee minutes, 18 March 1953 and Council Meeting, 30 March 1953.
54 *Ibid.*, Florence Horsburgh to the Presidents of the Engineering Institutions, 27 June 1953.
55 *Ibid.*, Ministry of Education Internal Memorandum, 18 February 1953.
56 *Ibid.*, Note of a Meeting at Vickers House, 1 December 1953.
57 *Ibid.*, Institutions to Minister of Education, 6 May 1954 and attached Memorandum JACE/59.
58 Ed. 46/1001, AAP (Antony Part), 26 December 1955.
59 Ed. 46/1000, Eccles to Bray, 16 September 1955.
60 Ed. 46/1001, AAP to Secretary, 6 December 1955.
61 Ed. 46/1000, 22 December 1955.
62 Ed. 46/1002, 23 January 1956.
63 Ed. 46/1002, Eccles to Prime Minister (Eden), 27 February 1956.
64 M. Wiener, *English Culture*, pp. 134–5.
65 G. Ahlstrom, *Engineers and Industrial Growth*, London, 1982, pp. 56–60.
66 *Ibid.*, p. 65, and footnote, p. 160.
67 Gerstl and Hutton, *Engineers*, p. 7.
68 *Ibid.*, p. 46.

69 *Ibid.*, p. 113.
70 Hermann Bayer and Peter Lawrence, 'Engineering education and the Status of Industry', *European Journal of Engineering Education* 2, 1977, pp. 223–7.
71 PRO, Ed. 46/296, HTE 35.
72 IME, Education Committee, 17 December 1945.
73 PRO, Ed. 46/295, Percy Committee 14, 27 April 1945.
74 PRO, Ed. 46/700, 29 May 1949.
75 NACEIC, *Higher Technological Education*, para. 12 (c).
76 ICE 3030/7/3, 23 December 1949.

SEVEN

Higher education and employment: pressures and responses since 1960

Oliver Fulton

Introduction

The development of higher education in Britain in the last three decades provides a particularly interesting case for examining both the relationship between education and employment and the ways in which it is discussed and incorporated in national policy. The main interest lies in the fact that for many years some interest groups and some academic analysts have argued that there is a contradiction between the case for policies designed to 'tighten' the relationship and the realities of current practice; but that these arguments have had very limited success in changing the thrust of national or institutional policy.

In brief, the main arguments heard since 1960 in favour of tightening the relationship have concerned costs and the curriculum. First, the cost to the state of providing higher education is far greater on a *per capita* basis than that of any other sector of education.[1] Indeed, government expenditure on higher education amounted in 1985–6 to over 23 per cent of total government expenditure on education.[2] Expenditure on this scale raises questions about the economic returns to so substantial a national investment. Secondly, the specialised curriculum of most British higher education courses suggests that there ought to be stronger and more direct connections to the labour market than in those countries where undergraduate courses are unashamedly described as 'general' or 'liberal' education. These opinions – mainly (if not consistently, as we shall see) articulated by governments and employers – can be reinforced by students' views. Whatever the motives that lead students to select their subjects for specialisation in the first place, it is clear that relative employment prospects figure

145

largely in their decisions to stay on in school and enter higher education.[3]

In practice, despite these arguments higher education has been provided in the United Kingdom with very little regard for forecast or even assumed employment needs. First, aside from the professional fields of medicine and teaching, in which nearly every OECD country has attempted – with varying degrees of success – to supply places in line with forecast man- and woman-power (herein after manpower) requirements, it would be fair to say that from the early 1960s onward both the overall size of the higher education system and the distribution of places across fields within it have been determined primarily in response to student demand. Throughout this period the commitment to maintaining access for all those qualified (and now, in principle, for all those deemed capable of benefitting)[4] has always, if barely, survived the attacks of those concerned with the danger of 'oversupply'. And although British higher education is in principle a planned system[5] (that is, it is neither market-driven as in the USA, nor does it provide open access to any course for the generally qualified as in most of Western Europe), both governments and system planners have, as we shall see, restricted their influence on the balance of places to a largely ineffective series of 'broad steers' or modest 'switches' of resources towards science and technology and away from social science and the humanities. And secondly, if the quantitative shape of the system has largely been unregulated, external pressures have been no more influential over its qualitative characteristics. The curricula of most courses, even in the professional fields, owe a great deal more to internally-developed academic rationales than to external influences or considerations.

So runs the critique. The result, it has been argued, is an 'inefficient' use of public – and private – resources, and a failure to satisfy the needs of the labour market. What is defensible in the United States, where governments find a smaller proportion of the total costs of the system, or in Western Europe, where there is a constitutional (e.g. West Germany) or legislated (e.g. France) right of *Lernfreiheit*, is unacceptable in Britain where neither of these apply. Arguments like these have been put forward with considerable regularity since the 1960s – and indeed earlier, as the previous chapter suggests – and as frequently abandoned or overruled as supply and demand, and other economic and political pressures, have changed.

In this chapter I shall draw on a number of recent studies both to document and to analyse these changing perspectives on higher education and employment. During the last ten years – or more precisely since the return of the Conservative government in 1979 – there has been a sharply increased output of academic work on higher education and employment, beginning with a large DES-funded project on 'Expectations of Higher Education', and followed by a number of linked projects commissioned by the CNAA in response to the same set of policy concerns. Among these publications are Silver's detailed historical account of the changing expectations of employers;[6] Roizen and Jepson's report of the views of representatives of the more prominent employers of graduates in the early 1980;[7] studies of the responses of higher education institutions and departments to external curricular demands;[8] and studies of graduates' experiences in the labour market.[9] In discussing these I shall make use of an analytical framework developed for a comparative review of work in this area[10] and of an important critique by Teichler et al.[11] of what they call the 'manpower requirements' approach.

Social expectations of higher education and employment

The 'expectations' which society has of higher education can be divided into a number of categories,[12] which are given here as headings for discussion. First, graduates should be adequate in number (presumably neither insufficient nor excessive), both as a whole population and within particular fields. Secondly, they should be supplied at a reasonable cost (to their families, to the state and to their employers). Thirdly, they should receive appropriate training and education to enable them to perform, or learn to perform, their first and future jobs (appropriate, that is, both in content – the curriculum, and in standard – its quality). These three categories of expectation will be addressed directly in what follows. Three more will be referred to in passing at various points in the chapter. They are, fourthly, that graduates should possess other appropriate attributes – both supposedly unlearned qualities such as intelligence, for which higher education is said to merely sort them, and extra-curricular learned attributes such as attitudes and values. Fifthly, it is expected that their training should be provided in ways that are compatible with other functions of higher education – notably research and knowledge creation. And finally, it is thought that graduates should be selected in line with broad social priorities – for example (a) the provision of access to higher education for all who want it; (b) competition and selection by academic 'merit'; and (c) the advancement of previously underrepresented groups –

147

women, ethnic minorities, working-class children and so on. As will become clear, these goals and concerns are neither self-explanatory, self-evident nor necessarily mutually consistent; each of them is socially constructed and politically negotiated and interpreted.

The total supply of graduates

Questions of supply and demand have dominated the discussion of higher education policy for much of the period. Although the supply of demand for graduates has never been far from the agenda, it is the supply of and demand for student places which has taken priority in policy making, as a direct consequence of the commitment to maintaining or increasing access in line with student demand, which was proposed by the Robbins Committee in 1963 and accepted by both the then Conservative government and the Labour Party. As we shall see, this commitment has been sustained from then onwards, despite periodic challenges.

The result has been that over the past quarter century the supply of graduates has increased enormously. Output of first-degree graduates rose from 22,000 in 1962 to 47,600 in 1970, (an increase of well over 100 per cent in eight years); and then, despite the stagnation in the participation rate during the 1970s, demographic growth brought the output up to 70,000 in 1975 (47 per cent in 5 years) and 102,000 in 1980 (46 per cent in 5 years). As demographic growth slowed, then ceased, the participation rate began to rise again, if slowly, and the output reached 127,000 in 1987 (25 per cent in 7 years).[13]

How might we judge whether this total output of graduates is 'right' for our needs? One answer would be to disaggregate the output into specific subject disciplines, match it with the estimated demand or 'need' of particular segments of the labour market, and then sum the results. Indeed, in a centrally planned economy this would be the normal way to do it. I shall turn below to some of the problems with this approach; but if we do not disaggregate we are left with a fairly meaningless level of generalisation. Economists offer the only possible 'technical' (as opposed to political) answer, which is to look at both employment rates and graduate/non-graduate salary differentials – both starting salaries and lifetime rate-of-return calculations.

This approach has a number of difficulties. First, at a conceptual level it involves not only the awkward assumption that the future will be like the past, but also the fundamental claim that the labour market as a whole accurately reflects the 'benefit', in the form of increased productivity, which trained manpower provides to employers and hence to the economy as a whole. To non-economists this may seem plausible only over the long run, if at all. And secondly, there is considerable doubt about the reliability and usefulness of first employment statistics and the reliability of the salary information that is collected. Jason Tarsh[14] has argued strongly that the first destinations statistics, compiled six months after graduation by careers advisers in higher education institutions, provide a good guide to policy-makers which should be used to plan places – both in the system as a whole and in particular subject areas. However, Taylor has claimed that the present method of collecting these statistics is too unreliable for policy purposes;[15] and, even more seriously, Brennan and McGeevor have shown that the unemployment revealed by the first destinations surveys is almost always short-term, so that, even at the trough of the economic downturn of the early 1980s, graduates' employment rates three years after graduation were far better than the national figures for their age group as a whole.[16]

For what they are worth, however, the global first employment figures show that by and large the labour market succeeded in absorbing the massive growth in output described above. The combined unemployment and temporary employment rate for new graduates (as a percentage of all first degree graduates, whether entering employment or not) rose from 1·7 per cent in 1965/6 to 4·9 per cent in 1970/1, 7·9 per cent in 1975/6, and peaked at 13·1 per cent in 1982/3, falling to 11·9 per cent by 1985/6.[17] However politically uncomfortable or personally damaging these rates may be they can hardly be described – except perhaps by economists concerned with marginal changes (below) – as evidence of massive oversupply; in so far as they are comparable, the strict unemployment rates for new graduates as a whole have been consistently lower than those for new entrants to the labour market with fewer or no qualifications.

Tarsh has published the most recent calculations of the other indicators.[18] Both rate of return (based on lifetime earnings) and starting salaries at least have the merit of moving in the same direction as the first employment figures, and confirm that the market for graduates began to weaken in the early 1970s, slipped to a historic low in the early 1980s, and has recovered substantially since then. The reasons are not hard to find. The expansion of the 1960s, huge though it was in relative terms, was absorbed to a substantial degree cannibalistically by growth in employment within the education system itself; and the expansion in the early 1970s was swallowed up by a wide range of other jobs in the expanding public sector. When that avenue was closed, quite abruptly, in the post-1973 expenditure crisis, the private sector found itself faced with a sudden glut of potential recruits. Thus while the first signs of rising graduate unemployment occurred – and were commented on – in the early 1970s, it was not until the sharp recession following 1979 that the problem of total output seemed to demand urgent attention from policy-makers – and only in the context of two other equally demanding policy imperatives, expenditure cuts and demographic decline.

The truth is that, whatever the hopes of the economists, policy responses have always been based mainly on political considerations, not technical indicators. This becomes clear if we examine the changing fashions in rate of return analysis in the context of policies for the total size of the higher education system. In fact, the heyday of rate of return analysis was the 1960s, when the broadly positive figures which were calculated at that time were used – by the Robbins Committee and by educational planning bodies internationally – not to make difficult choices between alternative options, but to justify the expansion of educational opportunities in general. They went hand in hand with a broad acceptance of human capital theory, which suggested that almost any investment in higher education was likely to be worthwhile both for individuals and for governments. If this is true, poor current or past rates of return are not crucial, since human capital theory essentially postulates a latent 'need' in the economy for more graduates, whether or not employers are yet demanding them; according to this, even an apparently 'excessive' output of qualified people will pay for itself in the medium term by improving the performance of the enterprises that employ them. This was certainly a widely-held opinion in the 1960s internationally. The truth is that the massive expansion of educational opportunities, which peaked in almost all the developed countries in that decade, was primarily a response to demand from potential students, indeed to a social demand for the redefinition of citizenship rights, in T. H. Marshall's phrase, to include the right to higher education. But human capital theory, and rate of return analysis, provided an acceptable economic rationale.

During the 1970s the fashion for rate of return analysis was overtaken by events. The high hopes – of social equality as well as economic prosperity – that had been placed in educational expansion were soured, not only by the first signs of graduate unemployment but by the conflicts that broke out: over school reform and restructuring, student unrest, and economic recession, among others. Indeed, by

1971 the age participation rate had stopped rising, and even began to fall among working class males. Forecasts of higher education places which had been moved ever higher – far beyond the Robbins forecasts – were revised sharply downwards in a series of steps from 1971 onwards. By 1976 it was becoming clear that the birth rate was falling, and therefore that the stagnant participation rate was almost certain to lead to declining numbers of students when the smaller age cohorts worked their way through to eighteen. In a series of documents which began with consultation papers and ended with more formal forecasts[19] the DES made it increasingly clear that, without convincing evidence to the contrary, it was planning for a net decline in graduate output roughly in line with the fall in the eighteen-year-old age group. The evidence it was looking for was, first, some sign that demand (whether the eighteen-year-old participation rate, or that of older people) could possibly rise; and secondly, indications to suggest that any such rise would be justified. Viewed in the context of the changing age distribution of the whole population, it was not obvious why resources should not be shifted away from young people's educational needs (whether at school or in post-compulsory education) and towards the needs of the growing numbers of the elderly. Since the age participation rate had been stagnant for some years, and graduate unemployment was on the increase, the evidence was hard to come by; and it hardly needed sophisticated rate of return analysis to make the point.

The nadir of government support for higher education was probably reached in the early 1980s. Higher education has, in fact, always been in a somewhat marginal position in the civil service structure. The Ministry irritation with university autonomy which Davies describes in the previous chapter was not resolved in the 1960s. Robbins had proposed replacing the division between universities under the Treasury, and the rest of advanced further education under the Ministry of Education, with a new Ministry of Higher Education. Although the Ministry succeeded in scotching this idea, and creating the unified DES, this did not deal with the fundamental problems of university autonomy. And the binary system, by creating – for whatever good reasons – the polytechnics and colleges as a new and less autonomous sector of higher education perhaps helped to preserve the universities' unique position for longer. Even the polytechnics and colleges themselves were for a long time much more the creatures of the local authorities than of the DES. Higher education had few good friends at court.

Thus, when a new government took over in 1979 with a determination to cut public expenditure, higher education was in a particularly vulnerable position. For a while, even the Robbins principle of guaranteed access for the qualified seemed to be under threat – perhaps unnecessarily, since it looked likely to do the work of contraction as well as it had helped expansion in the 1960s. Instead of rates of return, the search was on for new tools for planning, and the DES (or its Secretary of State) hit on the notion of 'expectations' – which led in due course to much of the academic work referred to earlier, but failed, perhaps not surprisingly, to come up with a clear set of planning mechanisms which could be used to direct national policy.

During the first few years of the 1980s a series of cuts in expenditure on higher education had considerable consequences, not only in damaging the morale and quite probably the effectiveness of higher education institutions while also improving their efficiency in a technical sense,[20] but also in demonstrating that while demand rates might be stagnant, access could not be reduced without damaging political consequences for the government. Higher education's collective lack of support was not matched, it turned out, by any indifference on the part of individual eighteen year olds (and their parents) as to whether or not they got a degree. Thus by 1985 the government, although still determined not to increase expenditure, was prepared in the Green Paper of that year to accept the proposed revision of the Robbins principle to include all those deemed capable of benefiting from higher education,[21] even if it added, a little churlishly, that 'the benefit must be sufficient to justify the cost'. At this point, rate of return analysis was called in once again, not as the basis for a (grudging) change of heart, but to lend a technical air of justification to it. In an appendix to the Green Paper, various basic calculations were outlined, leading to the conclusion that the rate of return was adequate by the Treasury's standard test for public investment. Unfortunately, although this might be a reasonable defence against further cuts, it gives no hint as to whether more investment is desirable.

And here is the problem. Aside from any doubts about their validity, the various rates recommended by Tarsh are all relative: the difficulty lies in drawing categorical policy conclusions from them. But in any case, as Tarsh himself shows,[22] the calculated rate of return depends drastically on a series of technical – and debatable – assumptions; and if we turn to unemployment the acceptability of any given level is, as we have seen, essentially a matter of political, not economic, judgement.

Are there any other ways in which policy-makers might be guided? In theory, one possible solution would be to rely on market mechanisms. In an entirely private system – that is, one in which the state neither provided nor subsidised higher education – students would make their own investment decisions. Certainly, in the real world it does seem that at the margin some potential students base their decision whether or not to enter higher education on their own estimates of the likely rate of return;[23] and indeed the stagnation in the participation rate of the 1970s seems to have been influenced by young people's perceptions of the state of the labour market.[24] But in Britain – and in practice everywhere – students' decisions are multiply influenced. They are affected by government policies for the availability of places and for the level of subsidy, including student support. So students' decisions can neither be used to provide independent guidance to governments, nor can they be used as market forces to substitute for government policy. (Market forces, and rate of return calculations, may have a stronger case when it comes to relative judgements about balances within the total system: I turn to this in the next section.)

However, employers are not above offering guidance to policy-makers, and not always on the most objective basis: indeed, there is no reason why they should be expected to be disinterested. Teichler *et al.*, writing during the late 1970s from an international perspective, claimed that 'as a general rule, employers in industrialised countries are inclined to believe that there exist oversupplies of highly qualified manpower and general over-qualification in . . . occupations'.[25] If so, British employers' opinions have been less sweeping. Roizen and Jepson, in their interviews with (mostly) larger recruiters of graduates at the depth of the recession in graduate employment in 1981–2, found some confirmation of the critical tone of public statements of employers and their organisations at that time. Complaints included the high cost of education to the taxpayer; declining quality as a result of 'excessive' expansion; low motivation of students who had been 'railroaded' into education; unrealistic expectations of graduates; and expansion in the wrong subject areas. (Each of these is discussed in later sections of this chapter.) But at the same time both these critics and others less critical acknowledged in general terms the need for a 'substantial' investment in higher education, which they mainly justified on grounds of international competitiveness. In other words, the dispute was largely about means, not ends: apart from a few sweeping condemnations ('higher education has expanded too far';

'there are far too many people going to university'), there was little questioning of the Robbins principle or of the overall size of the graduate output.[26] Nor does Silver refer to such complaints in his wide-ranging review.[27]

More recently, British employers' views have become a good deal more positive. Objectively, both graduate employment and starting salaries have improved; and many employers are now publicly worrying about the prospect of a sharp fall in the output of graduates as the age cohort declines – that is, unless participation rates rise substantially. By 1987 unfilled graduate vacancies were a serious concern, and not only in the most obvious specialist fields – and this at a time when graduate output was still rising.[28] This concern led to the formation in 1986 of the Council for Industry and Higher Education, a body consisting of twenty-six heads of large companies and eleven heads of universities, polytechnics and colleges. It was designed unashamedly as a pressure group, whose chief aim was to achieve a very substantial increase in the output of graduates, by increasing the participation rate of both eighteen-year-olds and older people. It was quickly rewarded when – apparently largely in response to its pressure – in the White Paper of 1987, under a new Secretary of State, the government accepted the need to increase participation rates by at least a modest amount in partial compensation for the demographic drop; by 1989 the Secretary of State was talking of doubling participation. Admittedly, rumour had it that the Treasury was much less convinced than the DES – or the Department of Employment's Training Agency, which weighed in heavily on the same side – that increased participation was economically justifiable; and there was, too, throughout the late 1980s considerable uncertainty about who should bear the costs of expansion (see below). But for the time being the case for increased access, and indeed for a considerable net increase in the output of graduates, appeared to be won – but by traditional pressure group and ballot-box politics, rather than by economic argument.

The supply of graduates in specific subjects

When we turn to the supply of manpower trained in specific subjects, the situation becomes instantly more complex. This is not the place for a detailed examination of supply and demand disaggregated by disciplines and occupations, but one or two examples may help to illustrate some contradictory trends. The first problem is the difficulty of forecasting future needs with any reliability. Here the case of teaching is the best example. Employment is almost entirely in government hands, and the 'need' in terms of the demography of the client group is known reasonably far in advance. Nor is the occupation likely to be overtaken by technical change of a kind which would drastically alter demand. Thus, it should be a relatively easy candidate for planning; most countries try to do so, and indeed any British government that did not would be regarded as irresponsible. But in practice, forecasting future needs is quite complicated: rates of first recruitment, retention and return to work after absence (e.g. childrearing) all fluctuate; policies for staffing may change; there are sub-markets (subject disciplines and geographical areas) which require further, quite complex disaggregation: and long lead times are needed for the translation of these forecasts into training course intakes, a process which can – notoriously – leave plans looking hopelessly out of date. Since the apparent fiascos of the early 1970s the general recipe has been greater flexibility, mainly by loosening the connection between course and job (PGCE courses and BAs instead of B. Eds; linking primary and secondary training; and so on). But greater flexibility also gives students more chances to defy expectations. The results of serious and technically quite sophisticated attempts at central planning may well be a considerable improvement over what a completely *laissez-faire* policy would produce; but they cannot be said to have produced an utterly smooth and efficient response to changing needs.

In most other areas the difficulties are magnified. The problem of producing meaningful forecasts is more acute: private sector employers in particular are neither competent nor interested in providing medium- to long-range forecasts of their future needs with enough specificity or reliability to be usable.[29] And secondly, there is the whole issue of 'substitution'. A high proportion of jobs are advertised as requiring 'a degree', without specifying any subject, and for the rest the level of specificity is quite variable. Silver and Brennan[30] have drawn up an elaborate theoretical taxonomy of course-employment relationships on the two dimensions of selection and training. First, the possession of a degree may or may not be used as the 'sole' or 'partial' 'regulator' for recruitment – that is, it may be essential, desirable or irrelevant; and if desirable, the degree subject may or may not be specified. Secondly, the 'training' content of the degree may vary along a continuum from complete occupational preparation (their examples are medicine, education and social work), through part-completion – often combined with part-exemption from on-the-job training (e.g. accountancy, law), a necessary foundation for on-the-job training (e.g. psychology), an optional educational base (e.g. business studies) to the absence of any explicit occupational relevance. By combining these dimensions into a typology, Silver and Brennan are able to make heuristic statements about the consequences of over- or under-supply and the implications for concepts of 'vocational' relevance in eight different types of relationship. The difficulty for policy purposes lies in knowing how rigid the boundaries between these categories are, or need to be. It is clear that particular occupations can move, and have, from one type to another, in response not only to supply and demand, but also to professions' bids for higher status, or to attempts to control the market, by the professions or by employers. What we do not know (unless as an act of faith by educators or by classical economists) are the consequences for the nature and quality of work in an occupation or for the productivity of a firm or industry. There has been very little research to show how much of a set of particular learned skills are used at work, either in the short run or over a working lifetime: indeed such research, which should in theory be able to settle the rather polarised credentialism-versus-human-capital debate which has now gone on for almost two decades, would be almost impossibly hard to carry out convincingly. But if we take Silver and Brennan's taxonomy at its face value, it is clear that only a very small proportion of the jobs which graduates enter fall into their Type A (Sole Regulation and Completed Training) – the 'perfect manpower planning model' in which shortages would be both obvious and consequential. Nor, in fact, did most of Roizen and Jepson's interviewees perceive any serious shortages in these terms, although more recently there has been great concern about the supply of graduates in information technology and a few other technical areas.

The result is that most discussion of specific manpower needs takes a much more diffuse form. The treatment of the science and technology 'problem' provides a good illustration. Essentially, there seem to be four issues. First has been the general human capital/supply-side worry. International comparisons which show that Britain has a lower level of highly qualified scientific and technical manpower in its labour force, or in specific industries, than most of its competitors are used to suggest that a greater supply would help, by prompting employers to use it. Engineering graduates are probably the best example, and the Finniston Report, which used this line of reasoning in 1980, is part of a long tradition which goes back at least to the Barlow Report on Scientific Manpower of 1946. To the counter-argument that the supply is apparently adequate, to judge by starting salaries and employment rates, Finniston replied by reproaching employers for not appreciating the value of engineers, or not being prepared to signal their value by raising salary offers in the face of under-supply. This is obviously a continuation of the engineering associations' dilemma which Davies illustrated in the previous chapter: how can calls for increased numbers 'against the market' be reconciled with their desire to protect or improve their status and maintain intake 'standards'? Indeed, it is a problem which has haunted policy-makers throughout the period, including the Swann and Dainton Committees of 1968[31] as well as Finniston.

Secondly, there is a genuine concern about specific shortages – most frequently in areas of rapid growth and high intra-industry competitiveness where employers want both to expand their intake very quickly and, no doubt, to pass as much as possible of their training costs back to the state. Information technology provides a good example at present, but it is quite hard for a non-specialist to assess whether the consequences of a shortage by employers' definitions will be a marginal increase in training costs or the collapse of whole industries. In any event, it could also be argued that in these cases the state, or higher education, has a responsibility not just to ensure an adequate supply, but to protect institutions and their graduates from the over-supply that is almost bound to occur in a few years' time if short-term needs are used to justify a major expansion in places. The sudden drop in demand for information technology graduates in 1986 was a timely illustration of this.[32] Indeed, some of the highest subject-specific unemployment rates have been in scientific disciplines where the job market had unexpectedly collapsed. There is, it can be argued, no course less vocationally relevant than one that trains solely for a non-existent vocation.

Thirdly, and somewhat differently, there is the curriculum problem: the real issue, it is said, is early or excessive specialisation. The greatest need is not for more scientists, but for non-science specialists to be more numerate and have a better understanding of science. And fourth, there is the 'quality' problem referred to above: what is missing is not scientists but 'good' scientists, requiring special recruitment efforts or incentives. I return to these two latter points below.

Faced with these difficulties, which are fairly well understood, policy-makers have considered two alternative prescriptions. One is to adopt an informed *laissez-faire* approach, essentially relying on the market to do the manpower planning for the society. Evidence from the United States suggests that there at least students are highly responsive to changing job prospects and that enough will follow the market to allow planners to play a very modest part in manipulating the supply of places.[33] West Germany takes much the same view, and sets great store by ensuring a good flow of careers information to high school students to help them respond to these external pressures. There are serious problems if this is not done: access to information is unequally distributed socially, and all students need good forecasts in order to avoid time-lagged over-reaction.[34] But the difficulty for Britain, as has often been pointed out, is that (a) young people make virtually irrevocable decisions at a very young age, when they are less susceptible to careers information, which will in any case be nearly ten years out of date by the time they enter the labour market; and (b) British employers seem until recently to have been unusually unwilling to send appropriate signals about supply and demand by adjusting the starting salaries they offer upwards or downwards. However, this seems to have begun to change: starting salaries in many occupations (not only the financial services sector) have moved up sharply since the mid-1980s.[35]

Thus there has been a constant temptation to adopt the other strategy, namely for the government to step in and attempt to manipulate the supply. Since the 1960s, when the DES first established the right to instruct the UGC not only on total student numbers but on numbers in 'science' and 'non-science' subjects, there have been persistent attempts to steer the system towards science and towards vocational subjects, and away from the humanities and non-applied social sciences. These attempts have recurred, in fact, on an almost predictably regular cycle.[36] In the 1960s they led to the setting up of the Swann and Dainton Committees – which concluded, however, that the need was not so much for a general switch of resources, as for closer links between particular specialisms in higher education and the world of work, which were obviously less amenable to broad-brush planning. In the mid-1970s the DES, under a 'technocratic' Under-Secretary for higher education, undertook a further inquiry; and another was instituted by the incoming Conservative government in 1979, in the political circumstances described above. In each of these cases, however, the conclusion was that it was detailed, not broad-brush manpower planning that was desirable – but that for both technical and political reasons it was simply not feasible.[37]

There is, however, a kind of compromise between the two strategies, and that is the dual-system approach which many northern European countries have adopted since the 1960s. In this, one 'noble' sector, generally the universities, continues to develop its offerings to students, in terms of both the supply of places and curricula, largely in line with the traditional criteria of responses to student demand and academic judgement. The 'less noble' sector, sometimes explicitly named 'vocational', is planned, generally on a local basis, in conjunction with employers and so far as possible in response to their needs. This was certainly part of the rhetoric of the British binary system on its introduction in the 1960s. The difficulty (aside from the ones already discussed) is the multiple set of problems known as 'academic drift' – a combination of academic staff ambition and the market behaviours of both potential students and employers, who tend – in Britain at least – to see the two types of institution as the upper and lower halves of a hierarchy organised on the single dimension of 'quality' (see below). In other words, the dual system, if arranged by institutional sectors, seems to be inherently unstable – at least in a market economy where the choices of staff, students and employers cannot be tightly regulated by the state. Sweden has adopted the alternative strategy of creating a unitary system, divided into disciplinary areas of which some are 'purer' and market-driven, others applied and planned. But this too requires a higher degree of control, and greater confidence in manpower forecasting, than most other Western countries can muster.

Cost

The issue of cost is essentially about how much of the cost of higher education or training for graduates is to be paid by each of three parties – the individual student (or his or her parents), the state and the employer. The debate between the first two, and its implications for student grants or loans, is not our concern here, except in so far as it hinges on graduates' salary expectations. One major argument for loans is that higher education enhances students' individual earnings capacity, out of which they should repay some of its costs to the state. But of course, depending on their market position, graduates may well be able to pass on this cost in the form of increased salary claims to their employers. Thus, a policy intended to reduce the level of wage inequality which state subsidy to higher education reinforces runs the risk of perpetuating the inequality, and simply transferring the burden from the state to employers.

The latter are not above seeing themselves as the major contributors in any case: Roizen and Jepson quote one interviewee as saying: 'The fact remains that the amount we pay as employers into the education kitty is frightening, and it is to benefit others and few will come back

159

into this company. It's socially unfair to make tertiary education freely available . . . [it] should be on a loan basis.'[38] However, employers' willingness to provide financial sponsorship of students, which at the depth of the recession was largely confined to a limited range of subjects, mainly in engineering and related disciplines, has revived substantially as the employers begin to gear up for shortages, both general and specific. Evidently, many employers are not averse to subsidising the cost of higher education for 'good' students (see below) or for those in short supply. In general it seems that there is now a growing acceptance by employers of the use of differential salaries and other subsidies to indicate and respond to a changing market. Indeed, one cannot help suspecting that much of the rhetoric about supply and demand which both Roizen and Jepson and Silver record has been an attempt to avoid doing so by talking down the price of scarce graduates, or by increasing the supply in order to keep salaries low.

As far as government is concerned, the public expenditure squeezes of the last ten years have been motivated by a mixture of educational and non-educational concerns. The former have certainly involved a questioning of the 'true' rate of return to investment in higher education – by implication, adopting a credentialist scepticism, especially about non-science and non-vocational subjects, which have tended to be crudely regarded as self-indulgent consumption rather than investment by the student. But, as we described in the last section, this scepticism has weakened, in response primarily to employers' anxieties, and the policy emphasis has shifted to a concern with 'efficiency'. Cutbacks are now justified on the relative basis of 'value for money', not on the absolute criterion of the undesirability of subsidy. This is not to say that financial efficiency is always the primary concern. At the time of writing, the government's proposals for 'top-up' loans for students are still under discussion, and the outcome is extremely murky. If the critics are right, however, the cost, in administration as well as in interest subsidies, could well exceed the cost of maintaining the present system of grants. It is not entirely clear what principles, other than an ideological commitment, lie behind the proposals.

Education and training

(a) Curriculum
A long-standing suspicion, elaborately documented by Silver,[39] exists that British higher education has consistently failed to 'respond to the needs' of employment – or to put it more precisely, that the universities

in particular have failed to respond to industry. The main accusations (aside from the supply-and-demand and 'quality' issues discussed elsewhere) are of: curricular over-specialisation; university (in particular) staff's alleged suspicion of or contempt for technology and other applied subjects on one hand, and manufacturing on the other; their preference for the 'academic' over the vocational; and their emphasis on prescribed and pre-digested curricula rather than flexible and student-directed learning-to-learn. In his historical account – much of which is echoed in the comments of employers interviewed in 1981–2 by Roizen and Jepson – Silver illustrates these four strands in both their complexity and in some cases, their intellectual confusions. But underlying the complaints (and indeed, the denials and defensiveness of the higher education side) there seems to be a real and basic tension between the inner and outer logics of the education system. It is exemplified in a series of problems, of which the first is perhaps the most intractable.

This tension occurs at all stages of education, but it is more obviously political at the primary and secondary school levels. Here it materialises as a conflict between lay and professional judgements – to what extent should teachers' presumably greater expertise be allowed to override the preferences, and the common sense, of parents, taxpayers, and so on? In higher education, the expertise of academics in their own fields is (virtually) indisputable, and it is sustained by their dual involvement, in the university at least, in research as well as teaching. Staff have a natural interest in training their students at the frontiers of knowledge; while apart from their (usually few) employees in advanced research and development, employers need (or think they need) graduates competent in more mundane skills and capacities. It is inevitable that some graduates' preparation will seem over-specialised, theoretical or remote from the real world. The conflict may be most acute in the professional fields, especially in technology, where academic staff are under greater suspicion from their 'purer' colleagues, and where the imperatives in the external world tend to value thinking less and doing more. Encouraged by recent interpretations of social and cultural history which have emphasised British failings in the worlds of technological innovation and commercial enterprise,[40] British employers tend to see the problem as a uniquely national phenomenon; in fact, however, it is virtually world-wide.[41] It should not be supposed either that all the accusations are true – claims of anti-industry bias among academics have never been satisfactorily documented – nor that higher education is impervious to them. Recent studies have documented a wide range of impressive efforts, mainly but not only in the public sector, to increase course responsiveness to employment needs.[42]

The second issue concerns graduates' general and non-cognitive capacities. For every complaint that graduates are over-specialised or wrongly skilled within their subject area, we find another that they are in fact unskilled in areas that employers most value – namely, the general skills of human co-operation, practicality, adaptability, and the capacity to learn new skills as they are needed. There are also criticisms of the absence of general education over a wide range of disciplines (i.e. of premature rather than over-specialisation), and of the lack of emphasis on general communication skills. Roizen and Jepson particularly highlight (perhaps because they invited them) complaints of illiteracy among scientists or innumeracy among arts graduates – and more broadly, of graduates' inability to make rounded judgements outside their own specialist area.

There are two comments to make about these latter complaints. The first is that the 'truth' of the criticism is probably highly variable, if real enough for some graduates. And secondly, although there is a sense in which these comments also reflect differing values or ideologies emanating from different structural positions, they seem somewhat less intractable than the basic external/internal conflict. Certainly, other higher education systems seem to tackle the problems of general education and of non-cognitive skills with more success than our own; and indeed in Britain from time to time new course options, new courses, and even new ways of teaching and learning have been developed, with mixed success, to try to equip graduates better for demands which most academics probably accept as legitimate.

The latest of these, which in fact tries to deal with both of these curricular issues, is the Training Agency's 'Enterprise in Higher Education' initiative. This offers financial support to institutions which undertake a programme to develop 'Enterprise Skills' in their students and, not incidentally, in their staff. These skills are defined not only as the general transferable skills just described, but also the capacity to respond to 'real world' problems by applying academic knowledge and skills to them. The main thrust of the programme is to provide students with opportunities to work on projects of concern to outside 'clients' as part of their courses, and to provide staff with training in enterprise skills and in particular, in teaching methods which can build on such project-based learning.

(b) 'Quality'

It will already be apparent that the issue of the 'quality' of higher education or of its graduates has become one of the key terms of the policy debate of the 1980s. Quality is a hydra-headed slogan, and many of the issues are better discussed under other and more meaningful headings – for example, cost effectiveness; the responsiveness of the curriculum to external pressures; or political accountability (below). Nevertheless there are a number of issues that seem appropriately labelled as 'quality' problems – notably those of entry, process, and exit standards. There has, it is true, been little criticism of higher education graduates to rival that frequently levelled by employers at secondary education and the 16+ examinations; but such complaints seem to be a persistent underlying theme in the Roizen and Jepson study. Again, one cannot help suspecting an attempt by some employers to talk down the salary expectations of graduates by explaining how little they are worth; but we should perhaps suspend scepticism for the time being and take the criticism at its face value.

There seems to be a long-standing and uniquely British concern about entry standards.[43] Despite the clear evidence from the Robbins Report onwards that A level standards have not fallen, and that entry to higher education is as competitive as it ever was, many employers, politicians and even academics are reluctant to accept that an increase in the participation rate for eighteen-year-olds from 4·5 per cent in 1958 to 14 per cent today can have been accomplished without some drop in entry requirements. In a sense, the conviction that intelligence, or the capacity to learn, is both fixed and quite limited seems to override any empirical evidence to the contrary. Roizen and Jepson's interviewees repeatedly harked back to their own higher education (at a time when participation was very low), or to Oxford and Cambridge, as the true models of selectivity, compared with which all other institutions were self-evidently of a lower standard. There are also hints that those interviewees who were not graduates had complex and mixed feelings about 'standards' which had excluded them, but might not do so now – and took some pleasure in decrying the accomplishments of modern graduates.

But, aside from a general scepticism about the exclusiveness of entry standards in the 1980s, Roizen and Jepson also illustrate how strongly these employers tended to rely on entry standards as a proxy for exit standards, not only of individuals but even of whole institutions or sectors. As far as individuals are concerned, this is understandable, if unfortunate: when students are recruited before graduation in institutions with a heavy reliance on end-of-course assessment, the only hard evidence available for selection between them, apart from personal references, will be their A level scores. But what is more disturbing is the way in which many employers selected the institutions in which to concentrate their recruitment on the basis of their average A level intake, preferring the more selective universities to the less, and universities as a whole to polytechnics. (Colleges of higher education were virtually invisible in this study.) By implication, they were totally discounting the claim that university external examiners and the CNAA's validation of public sector courses ensure a 'gold standard' for final degree results. This was justified occasionally by the need to concentrate recruitment where it would yield the biggest pay-off, but more often by the implicit confidence that 'intelligence' is innate, and nothing that education does can change it. Any notion of differential 'value added' (by institutions with lower intakes and equal or higher results) seemed entirely foreign to them – to the chagrin of the public sector. It should be added that the Roizen and Jepson sample was a highly skewed one – focusing mainly as it turned out, on major firms recruiting largely for management positions. Although polytechnic graduates' unemployment rates are marginally worse than universities', the first destinations figures clearly show that many employers, if largely unrecorded by Roizen and Jepson, rate their capacities sufficiently highly to consider them worth employing at noticeably higher wages than non-graduates. In employers' public statements as well, one sometimes gets the impression that most of the discussion is based on a very small number of élite graduates.

The same phenomenon provides another intriguing footnote. For many years, and largely because of successive governments' efforts to switch or steer resources and student places away from the humanities and social sciences and towards science and technology, the A level entry scores needed for a place in the latter subjects have been lower on average than for the former. Employers, in their pursuit of 'bright' employees, have tended, at least at the margin, to recruit able arts graduates in place of less able scientists or engineers, so defying the purpose of government policy, which was to increase the employment of the latter in management positions, and sending messages to the next cohort of students through the labour market which perpetuates the cycle.

In other words, employers, government and the professions, along with academics themselves, are caught in the trap which Davies outlined in the previous chapter, of pursuing simultaneously the incompatible goals of increased supply, increased status and higher entry qualifications. As a recent study documents, it is precisely the applied sciences which feel the conflict most acutely, and resolve it by refusing to change their entry 'standards' even in the face of extreme difficulties in filling places on their courses.[44]

Conclusions

Two kinds of conclusion may be drawn from this review. The first is technical, and has to do with the substantive relationships of supply and demand in complex and vertically, as well as horizontally, segmented labour markets; the second is political, and has to do with relationships – social and economic as well as purely political – between the main actors on the scene.

On the technical side, I do not propose to repeat conclusions drawn earlier in the chapter – indeed, the chapter itself provides only a superficial glance at the changing labour market for graduates and at higher education's effects on and responses to it. A few general points may be worth making, however. With a participation rate of 14 per cent of eighteen-year-olds, Britain stands, by one reckoning, on the verge of 'mass' higher education[45] (and, if current government plans come to pass, may shortly finally attain it). One of the most important consequences of the widening of access since the late 1950s is that participation in higher education has gradually shifted from being a privilege for an élite few to a fairly normal expectation for children of a certain social class and ability level: we can see this in the unprecedented political resistance to proposals to restrict access after 1981. The difficulties and confusions of the last twenty years may in part be ascribed to the gradual adjustment of employers' expectations: the realization – to which some major employers have come only very recently – that the kind of employee that they hope to recruit for certain positions is simply not to be persuaded out of higher education, however attractive an offer they may make at eighteen or younger. Whether or not these employers want any of the skills that graduates possess, they are essentially stuck with them.

Secondly, the balance of supply of, and demand for, graduates seems to be settling down after a period of uncertainty. Arguably, it is only in the mid-1980s that employers have learned how to recruit and how to value graduates in ways that other countries have become accustomed to for some time – just at a time when the level of graduate output is likely to fall. Current changes in the whole economic basis of British industry are unlikely (one hopes) to lessen the demand for highly qualified manpower. The prospect of an economy of relative scarcity is already provoking very different views and expectations among employers from those recorded by Roizen and Jepson.

If these generalisations provide a kind of economic backdrop to the subject of this chapter, there is nevertheless another way of looking at the discussion that has taken place over the past twenty-five years. It is arguable that public and social 'expectations' – an attractively passive and unthreatening phrase – conceal a rather more uninhibited struggle for control and influence over the higher education system. If we follow Burton Clark's terminology, there are four (ideal) ways in which higher education can be co-ordinated or controlled: the 'guild' model in which decisions are made by academics themselves; the 'bureaucratic' model, in which a state administration formulates rules and procedures by which broad instructions from political authorities can be carried out; the 'political' model, in which higher education is at the mercy of direct political influence from a wide variety of external interest groups; and 'the market', in which it responds autonomously to supply and demand on the input and output sides. Real life systems, of course, incorporate elements of all of these in a kind of dynamic compromise.

Since the 1960s, we have seen movement in all four spheres. The market – for students and for graduates – has had obvious effects on higher education, many discussed earlier in the chapter, and has perhaps served, as markets are said to do, as the arena in which some value conflicts are resolved by the arbitration of the price mechanism. Certainly, many of the actions and statements of employers, and from within higher education, have been intended in one way or another to 'fix' or influence the market. There have been direct political conflicts as well, with interest groups ranging from political parties to schools, parents, and so on, attempting to exert pressure both on government and on higher education directly. The academic guild, which still holds some crucial cards (notably its technical expertise) has been on the defensive, but has retained considerable capacity to influence the size, shape and content of higher education.

The politics of British higher education, however, are not purely market driven, nor are they conflictual or self-governing. The size of the state subsidy makes bureaucratic intervention inevitable – increasingly so as public expenditure tightens – and this limits the capacity of the other models or methods of decision-making to resolve autonomously the conflicts that arise. The active intervention of the state in education arguably reached a new plateau under the Callaghan government, which tries to advance the interests of education consumers and taxpayers more forcefully against the power of the guild. But bureaucratic interest climbed to a higher level again after 1979. Essentially, the DES (on behalf of Ministers) was looking for a new planning rationale to replace the Robbins principle, and it turned to public expectations – and especially employers' expectations – as its first choice. The difficulties and pitfalls of manpower planning, or even of rate of return analysis, were well known; expectations seemed the next best alternative. Unfortunately, if not surprisingly, the research commissioned by the DES turned out, aside from inevitable methodological problems, to elicit a collection of inconsistent, sometimes ill-informed and even half-baked opinions which were obviously inadequate to steer the system in a rational way.

Since then, although the Robbins principle has been reaffirmed, it is clear that government is unwilling to leave its interpretations to higher education itself, and simply sign the cheques for the result. The replacement of the UGC and NAB with the new Funding Councils under the 1988 Education Reform Act, and the public debate over their funding criteria which has followed, are a sign that the struggle for the appropriate model(s) of control is not over. Recent developments, such as the pressure on institutions to respond to increased student fees, and the use of 'categorical funding' for the Enterprise in Higher Education initiative, suggests a greater reliance on the market, and a hope that it can be reconciled with a degree of guild autonomy. But neither civil servants nor politicians (and the interests which they represent) find it easy to relinquish their own control; and in any case, as long as higher education is subsidised, hard decisions have to be made about where and how the subsidies are to be distributed. We – and the DES – must surely agree with Peter Scott's conclusion: 'In the end, a country needs as many graduates as it feels it needs.'[46] But the question still remains, who is to articulate its feelings?

Notes

1 'Expenditure per FTE student' (a set of vexed concepts) in universities was (provisionally) £5,170 in 1985–6; in polytechnics £3,150 and voluntary/direct grant colleges £2,950. In maintained schools 'net recurrent institutional expenditure per pupil' was £1,040. Department of Education and Science (DES), *Education Expenditure 1981–82 to 1985–86: Statistical Bulletin 14/87*, London, DES, 1987, Tables 4 and 5.

2 *Ibid.*, Table 3.

3 G. L. Williams and A. G. Gordon, 'Perceived earnings functions and ex ante rates of return to higher education in England', *Higher Education*, Vol. 10, No. 2, 1981.

4 This revision of the 'Robbins principle', which referred to all those 'qualified to enter', to include all those 'able to benefit' will be discussed later in the chapter. It was first proposed by the National Advisory Board for Local Authority Higher Education (NAB) in its document, *A Strategy for Higher Education for the late 1980s and Beyond* (National Advisory Board, London, 1984), and endorsed by the University Grants Committee (UGC) in its strategy document published at the same time, *A Strategy for Higher Education in the 1990s*, UGC, London, 1984. It was half-heartedly endorsed by government in the Green Paper of 1985 (DES, *The Development of Higher Education into the 1990s*, Cmnd. 9524, HMSO, London, 1985), and became government policy as a result of the 1987 White Paper (DES, *Higher Education: Meeting the Challenge*, Cm. 114, HMSO, London, 1987).

5 Up to the time of writing, at least. But in mid-1989 government plans for somewhat greater 'market responsiveness' through increased fees and other rewards for increased student recruitment were out for consultation, and press speculation talked of more radical changes in funding principles in the future under the newly-constituted Universities Funding Council (UFC) and Polytechnics and Colleges Funding Council (PCFC).

6 Harold Silver, *Education as History*, Methuen, London, 1983, chapter 8.

7 Judith Roizen and Mark Jepson, *Degrees for Jobs: Employer Expectations of Higher Education*, SRHE & NFER – Nelson, Guildford, 1985.

8 Harold Silver and John Brennan, *A Liberal Vocationalism*, Methuen, London, 1988; Chris J. Boys *et al.*, *Higher Education and the Preparation for Work*, Jessica Kingsley, London, 1988.

9 Chris J. Boys and John Kirkland, *Degrees of Success*, Jessica Kingsley, London, 1988; John Brennan and Philip McGeevor, *Graduates at Work*, Jessica Kingsley, London, 1988.

10 See Oliver Fulton, 'Needs, expectations and responses: new pressures on higher education', *Higher Education*, Vol. 13, No. 2, 1984.

11 U. Teichler, D. Hartung and R. Nuthmann, *Higher Education and the Needs of Society*, NFER, Windsor, 1980.

12 See Fulton, 'Needs, expectations and responses'.

13 Sources: 1962, 1970: University Grants Committee (UGC), *First Destinations of University Graduates 1962, 1970*, UGC, London, 1963, 1971; 1975, 1980, 1987: DES, *Student Numbers in Higher Education – Great Britain 1975–1987* (Statistical Bulletin 4/89), DES, London, 1989. 1962 and 1970 figures are for UK and for universities only; 1962 figures exclude medicine and dentistry. 1975, 1980 and 1987 figures are for Great Britain only and include universities, polytechnics and colleges, including the Open University.

14 J. Tarsh, 'Higher education and the labour market: a view of the debate' in Hywel Thomas (ed.), *Economics and the Management of Education: Emerging Themes*, Falmer Press, London, 1987.

15 J. Taylor, 'The employability of graduates: differences between universities',

Studies in Higher Education, Vol. 11, No. 1, 1986.
16 See Brennan and McGeevor, *Graduates at Work*, and also Boys and Kirkland, *Degrees of Success*, for a more guarded view.
17 DES, *Education Statistics 1986, 1988.*
18 J. Tarsh, 'What happens to new graduates?' and A. Clark and J. Tarsh, 'How much is a degree worth?' in A. Harrison and J. Gretton (eds.), *Education and Training UK 1987*, Policy Journals, Newbury, 1987.
19 DES and the Scottish Education Department (SED), *Higher Education into the 1990s: A Discussion Document*, DES, London, 1978; DES, *Future Trends in Higher Education*, DES, London, 1979; DES, *Future Demand for Higher Education in Great Britain (DES Report on Education no. 99)*, DES, London, 1983; DES, *Demand for Higher Education in Great Britain 1984–2000 (DES Report on Education no. 100)*, DES, London, 1984; DES, *Development of Higher Education into the 1990s* (see note 4); DES, *Higher Education: Meeting the Challenge* (see note 4).
20 The cost per graduate was substantially reduced, especially in the public sector: DES, *Statistical Bulletin*, 14/87. This was achieved mainly by increasing the output of graduates without proportionate increases – indeed in many institutions by net decreases – in staff numbers.
21 See note 4.
22 Clark and Tarsh, 'How much is a degree worth?'
23 See Williams and Gordon, 'Perceived earnings functions'.
24 C. Pissarides, 'From school to university: the demand for post-compulsory education in Britain', *Economic Journal*, Vol. 92, no. 3, 1982.
25 Teichler *et al.*, *Higher Education and the Needs of Society*, p. 43.
36 Roizen and Jepson, *Degrees for Jobs.*
27 Silver, *Education as History*, chapter 8.
28 Richard Pearson and Geoff Pike, *Graduate Supply and Demand into the 1990s*, IMS Report No. 150, Institute of Manpower Studies, Brighton, 1988.
29 See O. Fulton, A. Gordon and G. Williams, *Higher Education and Manpower Planning: A Comparative Study of Planned and Market Economies*, International Labour Office, Geneva, 1982; and Teichler *et al.*, *Higher Education and the Needs of Society*.
30 Silver and Brennan, *A Liberal Vocationalism.*
31 Council for Scientific Policy, *Enquiry into the Flow of Candidates in Science and Technology into Higher Education* (Dainton Report), HMSO, London, 1968; and Committee on Manpower Resources for Science and Technology, *The Flow into Employment of Scientists*, Engineers and Technologists: Report of the Working Group on Manpower for Scientific Growth (Swann Report), HMSO, London, 1968.
32 See Pearson and Pike, *Graduate Supply and Demand.*
33 R. B. Freeman 'Response to change in the United States' in R. Lindley (ed.), *Higher Education and the Labour Market*, Society for Research into Higher Education, Guildford, 1981.
34 In 1984 the DES tried to improve the availability of such information by publishing a booklet entitled *Graduates and Jobs: Some Guidance for Young People Considering a Degree* (HMSO, London), which spelled out current

employment and unemployment rates and tried to some extent to talk up the prospects both of admission to higher education and of subsequent employment in science and technology; in part it seemed designed to counter, if that is not too strong a word, the regular publication from the Association of Graduate Careers Advisory Services (AGCAS) of *What Do Graduates Do?* (Hobsons Press, Cambridge, annual), which has generally taken a rather more bullish line about career prospects both in general and for those with non-technical degrees, encouraging potential students to follow their own academic interests first.

35 See Pearson and Pike, *Graduate Supply and Demand*.
36 See G. Williams and O. Fulton, 'Higher education and manpower planning': memorandum submitted to the House of Commons Education, Science and Arts Committee. *The Funding and Organisation of Higher Education*: Fifth Report from the Education, Science and Arts Committee, 1979–80, Vol. II, HMSO, London, 1980.
37 See House of Commons, *The Funding and Organisation* (*ibid.*).
38 Roizen and Jepson, *Degrees for Jobs*, p. 129.
39 Silver, *Education as History*.
40 E.g. M. Wiener, *English Culture and the Decline of the Industrial Spirit 1850–1980*, Cambridge, Cambridge University Press, 1981.
41 Fulton, 'Needs, expectations and responses'.
42 See Silver and Brennan, *A Liberal Vocationalism*, and Boys et al., *Higher Education and the Preparation for Work*.
43 O. Fulton, 'Elite survivals?: entry 'standards' and procedures for higher education admissions', *Studies in Higher Education*, Vol. 13, No. 1, 1988.
44 O. Fulton and S. Ellwood, *Admissions to Higher Education: Policy and Practice*, Department of Employment Training Agency, Sheffield, 1989.
45 Fulton, 'Elite survivals'
46 P. Scott, *The Crisis of the University*, Croom Helm, London, 1984, p. 103.

EIGHT

Control and influence: recent government policy on technical and vocational education in British schools

Murray Saunders

Introduction

The argument that schooling has become increasingly 'irrelevant' both to society (in particular the industrial sector) and individual student's lives is a hardy if confusing perennial. However, the central position in public debate of the two issues of apparent decline in British industrial competitiveness and, during the early and mid-1980s, the steep rise in unemployment has sharpened the re-emerging discussion concerning the connection between education (particularly compulsory schooling) and other areas of social life (particularly 'work'). At the same time the function of technology and technological change has featured strongly in the plethora of analyses as a causal factor in both processes. These connections, made in official debate, have provided a fertile seed-bed for the growth and cultivation of a more interventionist stance by national government on the school curriculum and teacher effectiveness.

In a nutshell, the issue of educational effectiveness, however defined, became important enough in the public and political mind for an attempt, by government, to readjust the traditional autonomy of schooling characterising British education and to move toward more direct forms of influence. It is clear that part of the problem was identified by government as a 'deficiency' in the school system, in what and how students learn.

The recent initiatives of TVEI (Technical and Vocational Education Initiative) and TRIST (TVEI Related In-Service Training) are government responses to the argument outlined above. For a theoretical examination of the functionalist analysis which this response embodies, the reader should see Saunders, Helsby and Fulton's forthcoming book, *Changing the curriculum: the TVEI experience*. In brief, the initiatives arose from the ascendancy in the British Cabinet of the 'training lobby' headed by David Young in the early 1980s, against the background of a slump in productivity, high levels of youth unemployment, and inner-city riots. The reorientation of education to embrace a larger element of training and hence a tighter fit with the supposed industrial demand for school leavers was urged as the solution to these problems. Technical and vocational education was understood, initially, as specific curricular content, but increasingly over time it became seen as a curricular orientation or influence. It thus differs markedly in respect to its ultimate emphasis in the process of learning from the technical and vocational education provided in response to popular demand by school boards in the 1880s and 1890s and to the low grade, under-resourced forms of technical and vocational education permitted by central government to develop in higher elementary, central and junior technical schools after 1900.

In this chapter I intend to address, not the content of technical and vocational education under TVEI, but the mechanisms by which the government, via the Training Agency (formerly the Manpower Services Commission) set about stepping up its capacity to shape the priorities, intentions and practices of schools. Government intervention on technical and vocational education in the early twentieth century was restrictive in character. It was concerned with drawing up regulations which stated what secondary schools might not do with regard to technical and vocational education, and limiting what other schools might do, on pain of losing their grants. TVEI represents a reverse strategy. It aims to influence schools to adopt a vocationally oriented curriculum by a system of financial and other rewards, through the mechanism of 'categorical funding', i.e. inviting bids for funds according to well-defined guidelines. There are several important features of this strategy which constitute an unprecedented break with the tradition of government attempts to change the way in which compulsory schooling and further education does its work. It is to this strategy that this chapter is addressed.

Government policy is not, however, one-dimensional or consistent. While TVEI aims to achieve its objectives by 'influence', the government has simultaneously developed a separate strategy to legislate curriculum content through 'complicity'. The shift mirrors the process depicted in an earlier chapter of relegating to lower status vocational and more locally-oriented curricular reforms, in deference to centrally directed developments based on the assumed superiority of a liberal–academic curriculum. As I shall argue, although it is an effective means of achieving complicity or even consensus, categorical funding is a relatively weak form of control in comparison to legislation.

Dale notes that TVEI represents an obvious and deliberate schism with the essentially incremental, apparently haphazard, pattern which has typified post-war educational change.[1] The pattern, more or less, falls into four categories:-

Embodiments of curriculum	The Schools Council or curricular project model
Prescriptive/advisory	The Advisory Committee of interested and informed parties structuring and making recommendations
Legislative	The Butler Act of 1944, the raising of the School leaving age in 1974
Inspectorial	Department of Education and Science and Her Majesty's Inspectorate reports based on surveys of current practice.

Clearly, these categories are not mutually exclusive, but they refer to the emphasis given to a particular case. The strategy adopted with TVEI has posed some interesting questions about the balance in our structure of educational provision between the influence and control of education by central government.

As TVEI has, through its pilot and extension phases, been in existence since 1983, the context of its development has changed rapidly. Perhaps the most important changes have been the development of a new common exam at 16+ (the GCSE) for all pupils, first taken by students in 1988, and the development of the National Curriculum through the Educational Reform Act of 1988. Both these changes have affected the way in which TVEI has been perceived and implemented. Both these changes, unlike TVEI, fall into Dale's 'legislative' category and differ markedly from TVEI as a centralised change strategy. While they rely on the full weight of the law to shape and prioritise practice in schools, TVEI involved a more oblique form of consensus management. I will suggest later the likely outcome of any inconsistencies there may be between the practices 'encouraged' by these different strategies.

173

What is TVEI?

While the government may have considered there to be sufficient consensus on their diagnosis of the 'education problem' they were left with the difficulty of establishing the most effective mechanism for pushing through their remedial action. Previous models (see above) were not immediately viable for the timescales the government had in mind, for the control it wished to exercise, or for the potential resistance of the target group (LEAs).

A consideration of these strategic problems underscored the decision to adopt a certain strategy and a particular style of communication of the adoption of the policy to other involved and interested parties.

Mrs Thatcher announced the TVEI in a brief statement on 12 November 1982:

. . . in response to growing concern about existing arrangements for technical and vocational education for young people expressed over many years, not least by the NEDC, I have asked the chairman of the MSC together with the Secretaries of State for Education and Science, for Employment, and for Wales, to develop a pilot scheme to start by September, 1983, for new institutional arrangements for Technical and Vocational Education for 14 to 18 year olds in existing financial resources, and where possible, in association with local authorities.[2]

According to the *Times Educational Supplement* (*TES*) report one week after the Prime Minister's announcement, it had 'stunned the local authorities, who had received no indication of what was afoot: not only had they not been consulted, but DES officials had been left in the dark too'.[3] The decision to adopt then, was, to use the jargon, very much top–down, if the TES information was accurate. Owen points out that there was no indication that the DES had been involved in discussions.[4] Later in the day on which the announcement was made, in a press conference given by both Mr Young (Head of Manpower Services Commission) and Sir Keith Joseph (Secretary of State for Education and Science), Mr Young, in answering a question on consultation or the lack of it, said there had been no time to consult, but advance talks had taken place with the CBI and TUC.[5] The decision to launch TVEI was non-consultative, non-participative, and presidential. In by-passing the DES it had a provocatively confrontational style to it.

The government made no attempt to dilute the messages it was sending out to the educational service. The first press conference on TVEI, just hours after Mrs Thatcher's Commons announcement, was held by the Secretary of State for Employment Mr Tebbitt, rather than

Sir Keith Joseph, Secretary of State for Education and Science. (First message: the needs of industry rather than educational criteria were at work; TVEI represented a narrow vocationalism.) Mr Tebbitt said that there was a 'growing recognition that technical and vocational education needed to be given a higher priority if Britain was to match its competitors'.[6] TVEI was a 'nourishing technical diet for those who did not fancy a rich academic diet'. (Second message: TVEI was a covert form of dual curriculum; it was anti-comprehensive.) Mr Tebbitt also reaffirmed Mrs Thatcher's telling point that TVEI would be run with LEAs 'where possible'.[7] (Third message: the government may set schools up outside the existing LEA framework to deliver TVEI.) David Young confirmed this message during interviews with TES in the following week, saying: 'Anybody who says we have no legal power to do this is wrong. We have, and if we have to, we will, because the job needs to be done.'[8] Both Gorbutt and Dale give useful accounts of why the MSC was 'invited by the PM' to set up the pilot scheme.[9] They emphasise and expand on David Young's observation that both the governmental style of Margaret Thatcher and the speed with which changes were envisaged ruled out the DES as the 'agency' for TVEI implementation. As Gorbutt points out, it is likely that 'Mrs Thatcher, as a former Secretary of State for Education, knew precisely the length and breadth of the red tape which she was ignoring'. The 'interventionist' style required to push TVEI through and the link with training may explain why the DES was bypassed and the invitation went to the MSC, which was a 'different kind of bureaucracy – unhampered by the trappings of democratic control and accountability [which] can act with speed and decisiveness to get things done'.[10]

The guidelines for TVEI which were sent to authorities in the spring of 1983 can be summarised in the following way.

TVEI policy description

Sponsors	HM Government
Agency	Manpower Services Commission
Managers/designers	Local Education Authorities
Users	Teachers/students
Purposes	To explore and test methods of organising, delivering, managing and resourcing replicable programmes of technical/vocational education.

Stated aims
To widen and enrich the curriculum.
To prepare students for the world of work.

To help students lead a fuller life.
To enable students to contribute to the life of the community.
To enable students to adapt to a changing occupational environment.
To help students to 'learn how to learn'.

Agency operational principles
LEAs should be direct line managers, designers and responsible parties of schemes, following centrally devised general criteria with specific design features developed locally.
Funding of *all* extra costs incurred in educating the cohort within a scheme will be met by the agency under strict financial account procedures.
Participants should be consulted during the development of project proposals.
The agency will accept a variety of approaches in order to meet the 'purposes' and 'aims' above.

Features of the 'designated' programme: agency guidelines
Target group
A scheme should include 1,000 students during its life.
Two cohorts of students should complete the course in the 14–18 age range.
Participation by students in the scheme should be voluntary.
Students should be attracted from the full ability range.
Both sexes should be equally represented.
Mixed sex classes should be the norm.
Some provision for students with special educational needs should be provided.
Curricular features
Curricular designs should be for four years in the 14–18 age range:
Designs should state specific objectives, including attitudinal objectives.
Designs should link to subsequent training or vocational opportunities.
Designs should include a 'work experience' component.
Designs should be responsive to local and national shifts in 'employment opportunities'.
Designs should consist of both general and technical/vocational education (i.e. the provision of courses which lead to students' acquisition of generic or specific skills with a view to employment).
Assessment
Courses should lead to nationally recognised qualifications. Negotiation of assessment of performance should take place continuously and on completion, with records of achievement or 'profiles' which should express student achievements not readily deducible from formal qualifications.
Management and staffing
Each LEA scheme should appoint a co-ordinator.
Each participating institution should appoint a co-ordinator.
Local management should be by a 'support arrangement', i.e. a committee of interested persons.[11]

The furore created by the initial pronouncement left the government with the political problem of how to co-opt the educational service and develop a more compliant stance.

The offer of extra resources (without any acknowledged withdrawal of resources from the DES/DoE system) at a time when the educational service considered there to be a massive contraction in spending was clearly a trump card. The eventual soft pedal on control and 'alternative schools' apparent in earlier, more aggressive government utterances was also a strategic response to the political opposition which was gaining considerable momentum. However, there was another strategic response which set the seal on the LEA's complicity; this was the 'promise' that TVEI was actually a misnomer. From the schools' point of view, the educational mileage to be derived from participation in the initiative, as opposed to any technical and vocational preparation for work, began to emerge as a justification for the submission of proposals. The National Steering Group were in place to vet proposals by January 1983, and were free to exert some influence on criteria. The membership of the National Steering Group had a good representation from the 'educational lobby'.[12] In the adoption process of TVEI, a progressive ideology began to emerge as an ascendant force. Particular kinds of assessment, review and recording practices were singled out suggesting a much higher involvement by students in discussion and reflection. Particular kinds of teaching and learning methodologies were also stressed which were described by a 'born again' progressive vocabulary; indeed, a new orthodoxy arose which stressed 'active learning'.

The adoption of TVEI by the authorities in the first instance was characterised by its speed, its lack of consultation, but most significantly by its responsiveness and flexibility. Fulton describes how a centrally devised and managed innovation shifted in the space of a few weeks to an operationally decentralised, categorically funded method of reform.[13] He argues that this shift illustrates the tension between an aggressive governmental drive for change and political expediency and accommodation. The educational service was introduced for the first time to 'restrospective policy definition' by TVEI's 'agile superiors' the MSC, as a method of accommodating emerging interests and circumstances. Essentially, under these new rules of engagement the policy never quite emerged until changes started to happen. The adoption, by every LEA in the country of some form of TVEI experiment in their schools, is a testament to the degree to which the MSC strategy co-opted the educational service and has successfully accommodated an enormous divergence of interests.

177

Style of intervention

The characteristics of the style of intervention have had a profound effect on the way the TVEI pilot has been implemented in schools and colleges. Two characteristics are particularly significant. The first concerns the implications of categorical funding which has now been adopted for funding educational development in general (in particular Grant Related In-Service Training), and the second concerns the effects of the attempt by government to use TVEI as a pilot to test methods of delivery. Janet Harland has provided an excellent summary of the mechanism used by government to control and influence the curriculum via an agency which has no authority or mandatory power to do so.[14] We have outlined above why the MSC was invited to push through TVEI. However, alongside the advantages were also disadvantages. Having once chosen the MSC, the government could not engage in compulsion. Despite the initial disquiet from the educational service, it is quite clear that complicity, on a massive scale, has occurred. For an operational definition of the mechanism of categorical funding we can turn to Harland's work, where it is described as:

a strategy which can be used to facilitate a policy where the policy makers or their initiating agency, under existing conditions, have neither the statutory right nor the means to implement remedial changes without the co-operation of those who have both. They do, however, have the resources and proceed to use the normal processes of contract to implement their policies.[15]

TVEI was not, of course, coercive. However, the newly available resources it provided proved an enormous temptation for many authorities. The practical outcome of the categorical funding mechanism involves the following stages, as Harland demonstrates:

1 A policy is developed (TVEI guidelines).
2 Funds, generous enough to attract those who can and may deliver (local authorities) are made available.
3 Voluntary co-operation is initiated in exchange for the resources.
4 Acceptance of resources is equated with the acceptance of the policy and also with the ability to deliver.[16]

Arising from these stages are a number of processes which have given TVEI its particular flavour. While post-compulsory education had considerable experience of this mechanism through a train of initiatives (funding of work-related non-advanced further education, Youth Training Scheme policy, etc.), it was schools' first encounter with categorical funding. It has transformed resource procurement

and nurtured an entrepreneurial culture on the part of LEA official-
dom right down to the classroom teacher. The compulsory school
sector has been colonised by a new hegemony, a competitive market
place ideology with the functioning of a market place, in which
effective competitors are massively rewarded. This has been achieved
by the down-draught created by the bidding system. LEA competes
against LEA for nationally distributed funds. LEAs may invite proposals or bids from individual schools. Within schools, headteachers may
invite proposals or bids from departments or individuals. This process
has a number of unintended effects which we examine, in detail,
below.

Harland outlines the process which constitutes categorical funding
as it applies to TVEI. In the first instance, the policy initiative includes
published criteria which provide the broad framework or principles to
which proposals have to adhere. In the case of TVEI, they include both
operational scope (total cohort size, age range of pupils, time scales)
and prescriptive characteristics (mixed ability, non-gender-specific,
links to industry, etc.) These criteria are non-specific and provide for a
wide range of embodiments at LEA level. Neither curricular context
was specified, nor teaching methodologies, nor numbers of schools.
What is interesting is the way this lack of specificity passed to the LEAs
the operational responsibility and made them the source of the actual
character of individual projects. The sponsoring agency (MSC) could
thus claim responsibility in general but deflect any responsibility for
individual failures. At the same time the local projects could legiti-
mately lay claim to 'ownership'.

As we have noted above, the process of bidding itself is a complex
affair. Several methods of constructing bids were used by LEAs. For
example, some local authorities passed on the invitation to bid to
schools, and teams of advisers attempted to synthesise a federation of
bids from schools on any number of criteria, including political expediency, attempting to serve different districts, give fair representation to
secular and religious schools, etc. On the other hand, some local
authorities constructed their bids centrally and then instructed certain
schools to participate. In either case, negotiation was allowed both
within LEA and between LEA and the MSC. In most cases original
proposals changed substantially in the process. With the extension of
TVEI from pilot to mass initiative in 1986 (see below), this process of
negotiation has hardened, with many LEAs having to make explicit
changes to original ideas or being rejected outright.

The contract itself, which constitutes the deal struck between the

LEA and MSC, forms the basis on which a project may proceed. However, as first- and second-round projects bring the pilot phase of TVEI to a close during 1988 and 1989, it may be that 'contract' is a misnomer for the kinds of deal struck between LEAs and the MSC. Despite a good deal of bluster on some occasions, no project has had to give up any funds on the basis of not having kept to original proposals. Indeed, no project has kept to original plans, and even more so, no school has kept to the deal. Despite elaborate and extensive monitoring, the control that 'contract compliance' may imply has been a sheep in wolf's clothing. Writers (for example, Harland)[17] were mistaken in assuming that control might be achieved through the mechanism of a contract. TVEI has colonised schools, there is no doubt, but not because of any monitoring procedures. Its influence has more probably derived from the attractiveness of several other factors – funds, progressive educational ideology and speed of delivery, and the resultant complicity of the teachers themselves. This is most graphically illustrated by the enthusiasm with which schools and local authorities, which had until recently opted out, are presently engaged in pursuing TVEI developments.

In the first years of TVEI, the impact of categorical funding was thought to be lasting and significant. However, it may not be the monitoring (the direct, observable mechanism of control that attracted most vitriol) which will have the most lasting effect. Of far more significance is the competitive bidding for development funds which typifies the 'enterprise culture' promoted by the Thatcher government. This culture of educational entrepreneuralism has permeated most parts of the service and has its own emasculated managerial vocabulary. Those who are able to master and manipulate it have thrived while those who either have not, or who adopt an oppositional stance to it, have found themselves outside this ascendant culture and increasingly marginalised.

The second feature of the implementation process is that of the piloting and testing theme which was a strong characteristic of original guidelines. The requirement that LEAs piloted TVEI (i.e. were asked to identify the specific effects of TVEI funding in comparison with the 'normal' case) had a series of quite unintended effects. The responses of schools were such that the MSC was forced to abandon a strong adherence to this central and original policy characteristic. The parallel system within schools which the TVEI generated, and the culture which went with it in order to service the piloting discreteness, were gradually eroded as projects proceeded.

The original conception was of TVEI as a mechanism of quasi-experimental character in which the particular impact of resources channelled into practices within specific guidelines would be clearly identified; this conception broke down. It was possible to discern impacts on whole schools but rarely on specific groups within schools, although this was not exclusively the case. Where impacts could be discerned on specific groups, it was normally the case that they were experiencing TVEI-supported experiences which were not easily replicable. Examples include bands of students in CGL1 365 courses (in which the whole curriculum was designed as pre-vocational preparation for middle- to low-achieving students) or other specially designed discrete areas of practice which attracted mainly middle- to lower-ability students.

When practices were considered by the school to have more generally beneficial potential they quickly spread from within the TVEI sponsored 'enclave' to a wider group. The concept of an enclave is of key importance here. It is to this feature of the early years of TVEI that we will now turn. Because the effects of these characteristics have been described elsewhere,[18] we will reproduce the argument in summary here. The piloting rationale which underpinned TVEI initially gave rise to what may be called an 'innovation enclave'. This is defined as a set of actions, expressed in a policy text, inserted into an established or developing set of practices, from which it may be both clearly and self-consciously distinguished, and which it may, in some cases, even subvert.

A corollary of the characteristics outlined above is that an innovation enclave may produce a 'vigorous rhetoric' (used literally to refer to a set of 'rallying' or 'mobilising' concepts and ideas) which draws participants together and, by mutual identification with the 'enclave' culture, distinguishes adherents from non-adherents. This rhetorical practice should, however, be distinguished from the policy realisation mentioned above. Indeed, it may be that the stronger the rhetoric is, the greater the gap between rhetoric and policy realisation.

If we characterise TVEI implementation as having some of the characteristics of an innovation enclave, then how is it manifested and what are its effects? TVEI has developed a strong administrative identity with its line management of central teams, regional advisers, LEA project co-ordinators and School co-ordinators/liaison officers. It has a strong and broadly identifiable curriculum orientation, developed through the process of adoption and implementation rather than pre-set. Typically, while forms of curricular organisation varied

181

enormously, curricular content fell into a broad pattern. Most projects experimented in forms of 'beyond classroom' learning experiences. The most common were work experience, in which students spent from one to three weeks in a place of work, and residential projects in which students spent some time away from home together in unfamiliar surroundings and engaged in outdoor pursuits, problem-solving activities and other broadening activities.

More formally, options appeared in the range of possible courses students could take at the end of the third year which were designated 'TVEI'. Usually these were in the area of Information Technology and Computing, more general technology courses including CDT (Craft, Design and Technology), Electronics, Control Technology or Engineering, and vocationally oriented courses like Business Education, Food Technology, Community Care and Horticulture. There were also a number of examples of courses in Media, History and Art. The unifying feature in these courses was that they experimented in the use of a particular technology to enrich the curricular experience of the students and/or had an explicit connection with a vocational area. They proposed a set of teaching and learning practices as characteristic of TVEI orthodoxy (student centredness, enquiry, problem-solving, group and co-operative work, less teacher direction, less literary or text-based activity, experimental rather than symbolic approaches, unspecified links between theory and practice, new, more egalitarian relations between students and teachers) which may counter conceptions of conventional practice. Finally, and most importantly, in terms of enclave effects, TVEI is separately and lavishly funded and staffed in comparison with current real and perceived spending.

In summary, TVEI had a strong tendency toward the development of enclaves in terms of its administrative, curricular and resource characteristics. It should be noted, however, that enclave development was usually unintended and, indeed, expressly opposed by school managements. What is of interest is the way in which different schools responded to or counteracted this tendency.

If it is the case that TVEI implementation strategy has, embedded within it, a tendency to create enclaves, how have managers of schools responded? The dilemma for headteachers suggests that teachers outside TVEI create a strong pressure to pre-emptively replicate TVEI enclave practices and thus dismantle its claim as a pilot innovation, at least internally to the school. The question is, if the notion of pilot breaks down in the best school exponents of TVEI, does this put any strain on the overall innovation strategy? However, headteachers have responded quite differently. In shorthand, three (ideal) responses might be distinguished:

1 *Extension:* replication of TVEI practices throughout the school; TVEI as a springboard for internal school change.

2 *Accommodation:* replication of selective elements of TVEI practice, particularly, informal assessment procedures; TVEI as a lever for internal school change.

3 *Containment:* non-replication of TVEI practices outside cohort group; TVEI as a palliative to problem areas of school organisation.

To some extent the lessons from enclave creation, as a phenomenon associated with pilot implementation strategy, informed government thinking early on in TVEI development. TVEI has been in operation in British schools since September 1983. It involved fourteen local education authorities in its first year, a further forty-eight in 1984, twelve in 1985 and twenty-nine in 1986.

In June 1986 the government announced that the TVEI was to be extended and opened to every LEA in the country.[19] The idea of the extension is to allow authorities, which had been running a pilot for at least three years, to submit proposals for the replication of their TVEI experience across the whole authority. It has been estimated that the funds to be made available will amount to an average of £30,000 per school per annum over the ten years of the extension (1986–96). The average annual expenditure over the ten years will be about £90m. In the event these sums are likely to be unevenly distributed during the extension period.

What is clear is that the government's attempt to use the pilot as an experiment was rapidly undermined as pilot enclaves became either extended or contained. Either way, the pilot structure itself was in danger of shaping many of the developing practices, thus distracting from its stated intention of developing replicable programmes of technical and vocational education. However, the variety of evaluation procedures established by the MSC were not in a position to make any recommendations at the time of the announcement of TVEI extension. The national evaluations had only been in place for a year and the longest running projects still had a year to go. Most were either just beginning or half way through. Extension demonstrated the victory of a political rather than an educational battle to move the curriculum towards industrially relevant forms.

TVEI and the National Curriculum

The early choice of the MSC as the agency for pushing through the TVEI rested on the Commission's quasi-ministerial status, and its relative flexibility and autonomy. These characteristics, however, have led to its demise. The Manpower Services Commission was dismantled in 1988 and its functions, through the Training Agency (TA), were placed squarely in the Department of Employment. There is now no official voice from the trade unions on training policy development as there had been through their membership of the Manpower Services Commission. The relative autonomy of the MSC and the attempts to manage consensus on industrial relevance through categorical funding have been superseded by the apparently contradictory messages of the National Curriculum. TVEI created alliances between elements in the progressive educational lobby and the industrial relevance protagonists in their support for active learning and technological competence, and thus created a growing consensus on professional priorities in teaching and learning styles. The influence of the National Curriculum will undermine these developments and reinstate a traditional curriculum. In terms of governmental control and influence on educational practice, the comparison between legislative and categorical funding mechanisms embodied in the Education Reform Act and TVEI respectively is instructive. While TVEI was generally prescriptive, locally defined (thus flexible) and unified broad interests around some common themes, the National Curriculum is specifically prescriptive (through a high proportion of time allocated to core and foundation subjects, specified programmes of study and, most importantly, attainment targets in each curricular area at the ages of seven, eleven, fourteen and sixteen). Two questions arise here: firstly, are the National Curriculum and TVEI compatible; secondly, if they are not, what is likely to happen to the 'influence' of TVEI on the curriculum?

Although the initial reception of the *Consultation Document* on the National Curriculum[20] by those involved in TVEI was a widespread fear that the structures suggested in the document would smother transformations due to TVEI participation, National Curriculum advocates have argued that consistency or, at least, non-contradiction exists between the Act and the TVEI. Essentially the arguments rest on a distinction between content and process. Put another way, the differences between what is taught and the way it is taught (and learned) are such that one can specify the former without any particular implication for the latter.

In the *Consultation Document*, for example, in the section on Programmes of Study this distinction is sustained: 'They [the programmes of study] should also specify in more detail a minimum of common content, which all pupils should be taught and set out any areas of learning in other subjects or themes that should be covered in each stage.'[21] However, the document goes on to stress that 'within the programmes of study teachers will be free to determine the detail of what should be taught . . . How teaching is organised and the teaching approaches used will be also for schools to determine'. Legislation will allow schools full scope for professional judgements on delivery, allowing 'curriculum development programmes such as the Technical and Vocational Education Initiative to build on the framework offered by the National Curriculum'.[22] This aside is the only reference to TVEI offered in the document and connects it firmly to the level of delivery. Does this distinction stand up in practice? If it does not, the confusion on the part of those interested in making sense of the government's growing and various direct influences on the institutional shape of educational practice is understandable.

One of the gains made by TVEI has been the growth in sophistication of participants' thinking about the teaching and learning process. These gains have not been translated into radically different practices, but there has been a discernible shift in the way many teachers think and talk about the core of their work. Appreciation of the relationships between the development of conceptual understanding, motivation and more active participation by students in learning has increased with the boost of TVEI funding and discussion. Involving the mass of students in effective conceptual development in any discipline suggests longer timescales and quite different resource use and use of space (particularly out-of-school contexts for learning) than the conventional note-taking or reading used in solely symbolic modes. GCSE project or enquiry-based coursework has demonstrated this quite effectively. Alongside this there may also be gains on the students' part in ways of going about learning which active enquiry has encouraged. If all this is so, and certainly most teachers involved in TVEI perceive it to be so, specifying National Curriculum *content* which uses up the vast proportion of curriculum time (reinforced by attainment targets) and allowing apparently little time for active learning strategies amounts to an about-turn in government curricular priorities. Anne Jones (Director of Education Programmes, Training Agency (formerly Manpower Services Commission)) suggests that 'while the national curriculum has a set of important knowledge, . . . the process of learning offered by TVEI was also important. Knowledge + Process = Capability [is the] new equation.'[23] One can only assume this rhetoric was a result of the urgent political need to reconcile quite different emphases emanating from government departments. Anne Jones has attempted to reassure those teachers who might have been 'confused' about the relationship between the National Curriculum and TVEI with the following:

So what about integrated subjects or cross curricular approaches to learning? Much teacher anxiety focuses on these. Yet the National Curriculum guidelines stress the concept of 'framework' rather than a strait-jacket, emphasise the importance of giving teachers space to accommodate their enterprise, and room for creativity and flexibility. As long as subject specific criteria are met across the curriculum, there is no reason to suppose that 'combined' subject courses will be ruled out of court.[24]

Conclusions

It is true that the Education Reform Act specifications on the curriculum do not lay down requirements that particular periods of time should be allocated to particular subjects and specifies that schools are solely responsible for the curriculum. Ostensibly schools have the power to organise the curriculum and develop such teaching and learning strategies as they see fit. However, the significance of the proposals is that knowledge is presented as formal, theoretical, segregated and clearly defined. In the present and future lives of the students, however, knowledge must be marshalled and integrated around issues and problems in order to have any real value. TVEI had begun to develop strategies and plan learning experiences which reflected this reality.

However logically possible it may be to develop programmes of study and achieve attainment targets using issues or problems as a unifying mechanism within the National Curriculum, the likelihood is that the systemic constraints imposed by the assessment of subject-based attainment targets will shape the expectation of both parents and teachers, given the market forces generated by Local School Management and open enrolment. Teachers will return to a segregated, rather than integrated curriculum.

At the same time, unless the specification of the programmes of study allow sufficient time to engage in active learning methods, the delivery systems associated with TVEI will also be placed under considerable retrogressive pressure. The National Curriculum is likely to affect the delicate balance teachers have to reach between educational ideas and professionalism on the one hand and systematic pressure arising from assessment systems on the other. It is quite clear that under the Education Reform Act, the accountability of both teachers and schools will depend upon their ability to achieve competitive attainment targets.

If this prognosis is correct, then it is likely that the ascendancy of themes like relevance, active learning and student centredness under the influence of TVEI will prove to have had a relatively short life. In comparison with legislation, categorical funding is a weak form of control. We can speculate therefore that the outcome of the two forms of intervention is the product of a battle of ideas, within government, on the way education should best serve the interests of society. The traditional advocates of the curriculum have won the battle, leaving the role of technical and vocational education (embodied in TVEI), within the compulsory school sector, uncertain. It emerged as a government priority in the early eighties as a response to the convergence of a number of pressures. By the end of the 1980s things had changed. TVEI became a general influence on the curriculum in the direction of the world of work. Technology is in the National Curriculum but its content has yet to emerge. We might say these are real gains for technical education. However, in the light of the priorities of the National Curriculum it is in danger of relegation to the inferior status it has had since the Board of Education took the decision to curtail the development of higher grade schools in 1900. Thus industrial relevance, allowing as it did the entry of progressive ideas on teaching, learning and curricula through the back door, has now lost its appeal for the conservative ideologues. The original aim of the need for a more direct connection between curricula and the world of work is not likely to be achieved under the Education Reform Act. We might now retreat to an essentially decontextualised, abstract curriculum, success in which will be high in exchange value, but will have reduced use value for most students.

Notes

1 R. Dale, 'The background and inception of the TVEI' in R. Dale (ed.), *Education, Training and Employment: Towards a New Vocationalism*, Pergamon, Oxford, 1985, p. 44.
2 *Hansard*, 12 November 1982, columns 269–70.
3 *Times Educational Supplement*, 19 November 1982, p. 1.
4 J. Owen, 'TVEI: future-control' in 'TVEI', *Perspectives*, 14 School of

Education, University of Exeter, 1984.
5 *TES*, 19 November 1982, p. 6.
6 *Ibid.*
7 *Ibid.*
8 *TES*, 26 November 1982, p. 4.
9 D. Gorbutt, 'The new vocationalism: a critical note' in 'TVEI', *Perspectives*, 14, p. 50; Dale, 'Background and inception of the TVEI', p. 51.
10 Gorbutt, 'The new vocationlism', p. 53.
11 J. Lauglo and K. Lillis (ed.), *Vocationalizing Education*, Pergamon, Oxford, 1988, pp. 158–9.
12 MSC, *TVEI: Operating Manual*, MSC, Sheffield, 1985.
13 O. Fulton, 'Categorical funding and its limitations: the experience of TVEI' in H. Thomas and T. Simkins (eds.), *Economics and the Management of Education: Emerging Themes*, Falmer Press, London, 1987, p. 220.
14 J. Harland, 'The TVEI experience: issues of control, response and the professional role of teachers' in D. Gleeson (ed.), *TVEI and Secondary Education: a Critical Appraisal*, Open University Press, Milton Keynes, 1987.
15 *Ibid.*, pp. 39–40.
16 *Ibid.*, p. 46.
17 *Ibid.*
18 M. Saunders, 'The Technical and Vocational Education Initiative: enclaves in British schools' in Lauglo and Lillis, *Vocationalizing Education*.
19 Department of Employment/Department of Education and Science, *Working Together: Education and Training*, Cmnd. 9823, HMSO, London, 1986.
20 DES, *The National Curriculum 5–16: A Consultation Document*, HMSO, London, 1987.
21 *ibid.*, pp. 10–11.
22 *Ibid.*, p. 11.
23 *Education*, 16 December 1988, p. 570: 'Mrs Jones sees scheme "Thriving in Chaos" '.
24 *Guardian*, 24 May 1988.

NINE

Learning lessons from abroad

Ian Bliss and Jim Garbett

Introduction

'Bring us your questions and we will complicate them for you' is reported to have been the sign affixed to a department of education in a British university. The humour points to a truism that most educational debate rapidly becomes complex, and often confused, perhaps nowhere more so than when such debate draws on practices to be found in foreign systems. This inherent tendency to complexity is seen as a nuisance by those who want clear, simple answers to problems that they inescapably face as they plan educational provision; and it can function as a defence-system behind which academics retreat when they are called upon to defend or advise on matters of policy. Yet if the complexity is inherent in the nature of the case (and not simply in a professional desire to avoid commitment) then the related difficulties need to be faced, rather than avoided.

Why then should a chapter with this title appear in a collection of essays on technical education and its relation to the state, particularly if an effect of its inclusion is to make a complicated matter more so? One answer is that in 1978 Max Wilkinson produced a polemic published by the Centre for Policy Studies and entitled 'Lessons from Europe'. Iconoclastic, it arguably set an agenda for the revision and remodelling of the education system in the decade that followed. It did so by suggesting that the kinds of lessons that were taught in Europe, the curriculum content, the teaching styles and the patterns of curriculum organisation could profitably be imported into the education system of England and Wales. The argument of this chapter is that there are indeed lessons to be learned from a consideration of education in other countries in Europe and beyond, but that the processes of learning these lessons are not at all straightforward. Indeed, it is a commonplace of comparative educational study that systems are rooted in varied historical traditions. Anglocentric assumptions about such apparently simple matters as the division of schooling into age phases, or into different sectors (such as technical or general) can quickly cause difficulty if transferred too precipitately.

The concept of technical education has in England and Wales a range of meanings which native English speakers familiar with our system will take for granted. However, one of the lessons which might be learned from abroad is that the concept of technical education is not always, and not necessarily, to be interpreted in the same way in the context of other systems. It will also be suggested that in some ways the very notion of technical education as a clearly definable sector is one that needs challenge. The feeling that there is a need to bolt on such a sector may indicate that we have an educational system which in its entirety is properly geared to meet neither the needs of industry nor more generally the needs of individuals in society.

Problems of interpreting data, of learning lessons from abroad, are thus not simply technical, statistical ones, but take us to central definitional problems about what are to count as legitimate usages of terms such as 'education' and 'technical education'. The notion of 'education' is one that has been much debated, but even the apparently more precise notion of 'technical education' is by no means transparent in meaning. A look at the history of European provision suggests that there are at least four ways in which a 'technical' aspect of an educational system might be identified.

The first and most obvious is the provision of separate, 'technical' institutions providing vocational training for specific needs in the world of adult work, whether at a fairly sophisticated degree level, or whether at less intellectually demanding technician level. Such institutions cater overwhelmingly for those beyond the period of compulsory schooling. The second possibility is for such institutions to have no separate existence but to be formally a part of integrated institutions of further and higher education. The third possibility refers to the provision, within the years of compulsory schooling, of specific vocational schools or curricula (such as the 'Rhine barge' programmes found in the Netherlands for boys of thirteen and over). And the fourth possibility refers to the provision of curricular elements in general education schools on which students' future technical success is likely to depend. An obvious example is mathematics. Not surprisingly, it is on levels of success abroad in general school mathematics that some recent government advocacy has been based.

This simple four-fold categorisation merely begins the quest for distinctions that make comparative discussion possible. Further questions – about the ages at which provision is directed, who controls and funds such provision, what are judged to be appropriate schemes of study – quickly present themselves. If technical education is taken to mean 'educational processes designed to develop the attitudes and the skills required by the world of adult work' then there is room for debate both about the nature of those educational processes and the assumptions concerning the ways in which industry should be organised and therefore about the skills and attitudes it might need. Crudely, it is possible to think of technical education as involving the teaching of specific manual skills required by low-level operatives or of prescriptions about management skills required by higher operatives, such as managers. Alternatively, it is possible to think of technical education as initiating people into thinking critically and creatively about the whole of an industrial process and its place within the economic structure of the company and the country. Clearly these ways of thinking about technical education are based on radically different assumptions about the needs of industry and will lead to radically different approaches to the organisation of teaching and learning. It will be suggested in the account to be given of Japan, Sweden, and West Germany that there are differing value systems and differing assumptions which make the simple transfer of a practice from one country to another something that would be uncertain in its consequences.

Current concern with technical education appears to be rooted in the dilemmas of those responsible for economic policy in the Britain of the 1980s and 1990s. It is useful to start from the commonplace point that Britain has experienced, at least since 1945, a comparative and sometimes absolute decline in economic performance – and this in spite of increased expenditure as a proportion of gross national product on the maintained sector of schooling and on further and higher education. Indeed, in recent years, the received wisdom has come to be that the formal education system has actually contributed to our decline through its commitment to values which are hostile to our 'industrial spirit'.[1] Although a variety of explanations is available for this decline, the assumption – or at least the possibility – of a causal connection between formal education and economic weakness is one which has led to a search for better models of practice from other countries of comparable size, particularly ones with strong and powerful economies such as West Germany or Japan. The growing economic and political ties with the European Community (EC) has strengthened the urge to look at continental systems, at least at those parts of the EC where the economies are strong. Other non-EC countries with a recent history of outstanding economic growth, such as Sweden, have likewise attracted interest. Thus we have seen, in addition to Wiener's study refered to above, enquiries into aspects of continental practice in curriculum structure, control and assessment by H. M. Inspectorate, such as that into education in the Federal Republic of Germany[2] and, yet more recently, references to continental practice in the curriculum recommendations made by the Task Groups set up by the Secretary of State for the purposes of preparing schemes of study for the National Curriculum. Appendix 4 of 'Mathematics for Ages 5–16' is a good example.[3] Government concern has been accompanied by a wider interest in such matters both in the press, and on radio and television.

This interest in overseas educational provision has not focused on separate technical sectors as such, even though the concern has been economic, but rather on broader questions of structure, curriculum and attainment. This is particularly so where comparisons have been drawn about the period of compulsory education, the *scolarité obligatoire*, the *Schulpflicht*. Throughout this age-range, typically six to sixteen, it is problematic to decide what is or is not to be counted as technical education.

Comparative study: some problems and approaches

Learning lessons from abroad requires some exploration of the complexity of relationships that connect a school system to a nation's economy, and of some aspects of the idea of development (a notion that has directed interest – and funding – towards public education during the post-World War Two decades) and of insights comparativists can give into these complexities. This last problem will require at least rudimentary treatment of the scope and methods of comparative studies in education. The focus will be mainly on education during the compulsory years of schooling, and there is an attempt to tease out the part played in this by what is conventionally labelled 'technical'.

Although the wish to look abroad is, arguably, stronger at the present time than has been normal in Britain, it should not be thought to be new. There is a considerable history of comparative enquiries, particularly into continental Europe (often with an economic concern). It may therefore be useful at this point to look at the way in which comparative studies have grown. The evolution of comparative studies is seen as having several phases. The first stage is often described as 'travellers' tales', observations brought back by travellers about practices in other states, but not necessarily related to any particular theories about social, economic or political development, or about education provision.[4]

A second stage becomes discernible in the nineteenth century, the stage of 'educational borrowing'. Such an interest is entirely proper, and a broad ameliorative thrust indicates much comparative enquiry. Britain was much interested during the later nineteenth century in the schools of Prussia, and as the German Empire was formed, in the perceived excellence of technical provision throughout the new Reich. Indeed, some prophecies of gloom rooted in such perceptions are to be found in well-known reports such as the 'Report Relative to Technical Education' (1867) which received its impetus at least in part from the lessons from Europe which Lyon Playfair sought to publicise, the Taunton Report of 1868, the Devonshire Report of 1875, and the Samuelson Report of 1884.[5]

Interest in foreign practices can usefully be seen as related to a domestic concern, the relationship between British schools and the British world of work. As Reeder has shown, this concern has risen and fallen over the last century; the rise and fall mirrors the interest in foreign systems; both arise when a problem of economic performance is perceived to exist.[6] However, the enthusiasm for borrowing from abroad, at least on the simple transference model *tout court*, from one system to another, has to be set against the views of comparativists that such policies were likely to be inefficacious, not least because school systems could be understood only in relation to the highly specific cultural environments in which they grew. A *locus classicus* of such warnings is to be found in the Michael Sadler Guildford Lecture of 1900, made when he was Director of the British Office of Special Inquiries and Reports.[7] Sadler argues that comparative study can lead us to a better understanding of our domestic situation, but cannot of itself tell us what to do, a point the force of which is still not fully grasped.

The first half of the twentieth century might, however, be seen by those valuing free and pluralist democracy as a phase of alarm rather than of borrowing. It was a period in which totalitarian governments acted on the assumption that schooling was of importance not simply for the industrial development of a state but also for its ideological transformation. Three societies, Fascist Italy, Nazi Germany and

193

Leninist–Stalinist USSR, have provided us with decisive case studies of the way in which state educational provision can be taken over and subverted. Few would deny that, in one measure or other, educational developments in these states did in fact support industrial development during this period, but the concomitant political message give the liberal West much cause for alarm. So comparativists writing about this period, such as Hans and Kandel, stressed the importance of the values embedded in educational provision.[8]

The period since World War Two has been in the developed countries one largely of expansion, not simply to cater for the increases of population that followed the war, but expansion based on a consensus of beliefs: that increased formal education could overcome the inheritance of social injustice; that increased provision was economically productive as well as ethically proper, since schooling would pick out and foster talent, which would be available for the economy; and that schooling was a form of human investment, i.e. it would, however indirectly, promote economic development.

Underlying this are a number of hypotheses about the relationship between education and industrial effectiveness that are open to empirical enquiry, though the scale of the enquiry is such as to put them outside the range of individual comparativists. Enquiries into policy, into educational attainment, into the links between forms of schooling and outcomes and student aspirations have become the concern of organisations such as OECD (CERI), and UNESCO (the International Bureau of Education). It is these large-scale comparative investigations that characterised comparativist ambitions during the late fifties and sixties. Of particular interest has been the 'International Study of Achievement in Mathematics: a Comparative Study of Twelve Countries' (a report of the International Association for the Evaluation of Educational Achievement). Data generated might give answers to questions about optimum forms of organisation, types of curriculum and styles of teaching. Evidence of this sort, together with a widespread belief in the immediate post-war period that planning was vital for social and economic reconstruction, created a climate which predisposed governments to see education as a major element in optimistic aspirations for a 'better world'. Such a world, as well as guaranteeing social justice, would develop human skills in a broad programme of modernisation. Modernisation would in turn ensure an increased flow of goods and services to populations, and also require much greater and more sophisticated inputs from national education systems.

Fagerlind and Saha amongst others, have traced the rise of optimistic assumptions of this kind, and of a climate in which governments were prepared to spend massively increasing amounts of money on public education, assuming that there would be a 'return' in the form of an enhanced economic performance.[9] This return would then provide funds for sustaining and further enhancing provision. Education supports development; development supports education. Cause might be difficult to distinguish from effect, but the symbiosis was evident enough. Such views appeared to be backed by international agencies, who would *inter alia* be able to adduce evidence to support these policy assumptions.

Indeed, during the 1960s one can see significant shifts in the interests of comparative studies, away from the historical–explanatory analyses of the generation of Hans and Kandel, and into social scientific approaches of framing and testing hypotheses about the likely results of particular educational policies. Noah and Eckstein describe this phase succinctly.[10]

However, as the data generated has grown, comparativists have been quick to point out the complexities of data interpretation. Brian Holmes has produced a cautionary analysis of the complex relationships between data, political policies, educational aims, and the debates that underlie methods in comparative education.[11] Given such difficulties, it is not surprising that evidence of clear links between any one sort of provision and general levels of economic performance in a nation is difficult to find. Nevertheless, governments continue to show interest in the elusive relation between educational provision and economic success. One explanation for such an interest is the sheer cost of public provision. To spend something of the order of 15 per cent of gross national product on public education is common in societies such as the UK, the USA or Sweden. Government departments responsible for such expenditure are clearly likely to be interested in 'value for money'. However, any hopes that hypotheses could be simple, or that data collected could provide straightforward signals for policy, whether about technical education or school provision generally, have not been met.

How comparative education is being used in current debates

In an attempt to explore these issues further it is suggested that in much current debate there has been a misuse of comparative materials. Diagnoses have been made and prescriptions been written on the assumption of simple causal relationships between education systems and national economies, and believing that it is possible to transfer practices with ease from one system to another.

Interest in such diagnoses and prescriptions commonly start from the claim that Britain is performing below expectations in some aspects of the economy, and an assumption that the fault is to be found in the publicly provided education system – though Wiener's analysis might suggest that it is the culture associated with the independent schools and ancient universities which is to blame.[12]

A straightforward statement of such a case is made by Twining: 'Because of the consistent failure to invest in vocational education from the 19th Century through to the 1950s, there are few countries in the world where dissatisfaction with industrial performance has been so great as in the United Kingdom.'[13] This can be taken together with the assumption that the industrial, and more generally economic, performance in the UK can be improved by importing aspects of the educational system of more successful countries. Edmund King appeared to be making this point in 1966: 'On the continent of Europe a high regard has always been felt for direct and businesslike vocational education of adolescents . . . *Through the instrumentality of* vocationally linked education after the end of compulsory schooling all these countries have a very high standard not only of material but of civic and cultural life.'[14] [Our emphasis.]

Anne Sofer refered to the 'skills gap' between Britain and other European countries and the need for as many young people as possible to have 'something worthwhile to carry with them into employment anywhere in Europe, a sort of skill passport for 1992 and beyond'. She suggests that France and Germany offer two possible courses of action to remedy that gap. From Germany she picks out the approach through partnership between industry and what she calls further education colleges. From France she notes the 'positive drive to increase post-16 full time education'.[15]

S. J. Prais is currently influential in this country, and his ideas can be seen to have influenced the response by the Secretary of State to the Mathematics National Curriculum Report.[16] He sees France and, to an even greater extent, West Germany and Japan as providing models to be followed. They are more successful economies when success is measured in terms of 'income per head' and 'output per employee'; therefore presumably it must follow that they have more successful educational systems.[17] He selects features of the educational systems of those countries which he sees as being causally related to that

196

economic success. For Japan, he asserts that it would be wrong to ask employers to provide the range of technical training provided by Japanese employers until and unless those features were introduced into English schools. Traditional mathematics is taught, calculators are not used, and Japanese pupils do better than English pupils on traditional tests of traditional mathematics. Teachers follow text books and work longer hours than do teachers outside the independent sector in England; he rhetorically and somewhat sneeringly asks: 'Could anything be done to persuade teachers [in maintained schools in England] to give lessons after school hours to those pupils in need of them?'[18]

At both upper secondary and lower secondary levels in Japan the system is overtly comprehensive but Prais notes that some schools have a better reputation than others. Consequently there is intense competition for entry to those schools which have the better reputation. This leads to 'processes of successive creaming'. 'Firms know the quality of the schools in the area and recruit accordingly.' Moreover, the intensity of the competition provides for pupils 'an incentive to do a little bit better which might make all the difference'. Finally, private supplementary schools provide additional tuition for those whose parents are able and willing to pay the fees in the hope that their children can be enabled to enter one of the more prestigious educational institutions from which employers prefer to recruit. Prais concludes that the results are 'not attained by mixed ability teaching in comprehensive schools during normal school hours'. A competitive environment and attitude, as well as the standards in Mathematics it produces among average and below-average pupils, are, according to Prais, the key to Japanese economic success.

Defining success

Underlying such uses of comparative education have been three different kinds of assumption. The first is that the notion of a 'successful economy' is one that requires no argument, is beyond analysis or dispute, and is to be defined, as Prais defines it, in terms of increasing output per employee and increasing income per capita; the second is that the successful economy so defined is an intrinsic and absolute good to be valued in itself and for itself, and is a major defining characteristic of a good society; the third is that there is a causal relationship between the education system and the national economy so that a successful education system is to be defined as one which 'causes' a successful

197

economy in this sense.

The assumptions appear to be related to a 'human capital theory', according to which education is both seen and justified as a capital investment to improve the quality of the workforce: 'for politicians and decision makers efforts to promote investment in human capital were seen to result in rapid economic growth for society'.[19] It is implied that educational systems can be defined in terms of simple input–process–output models. The role for the comparativist is confined to seeking out systems which have desirable outputs, in this case high income per head and output per employee, and to identifying the processes which turn the raw material of the uneducated child into the appropriate product.

Within this paradigm of comparative study value assumptions are not questioned. However, it is possible to envisage alternative models in which an important function is to take explicit models such as the input–process–output model of education, and also to make explicit the values underlying them. Comparative education in this sense seeks to expose, and explore the implications of, a range of views 'about the characteristics a society ought to have, how people ought to be classified and treated, and how knowledge ought to be acquired and what status it ought to have'.[20]

A common-sense account of the values underlying much current thinking would suggest that a successful economy is defined as one in which there is: 'a widely diffused wish to own goods and use services; generation of the wealth to do this; [and] a willingness to accept efficient methods of working and the life- demands that these impose.' The educational system would then serve these ends by means of some or all of: teaching the basic skills of reading, writing and arithmetic; teaching vocational craft and mechanical skills; providing the combination of applied training and scientific principles that is required by engineers; advancing scientific knowledge, and particularly applied science, and inculcating the view that this is what success means.'[21] Curtis would add to that list the importance of appropriate attitudes to marketing.[22]

Ideas of success, like notions such as development, modernisation, and progress depend on assumptions about aims and values. Underlying any statement about economic success and the means of achieving that success are assumptions about the kind of society that is desirable. And there is the possibility of alternative values, alternative criteria of success both for an economy and also for a society. Two examples, one from West Germany one from Catalonia, may make this point.

Wilkinson appears to define economic success in terms of economic output. He refers to the competitive pressures of the German educational system:

These pressures undoubtedly produce casualties, a considerable amount of stress and unhappiness with even a sprinkling of child suicides. Nevertheless the Germans have achieved a truly amazing increase in prosperity since the devastation of war and it is more than probable that their primary schools have contributed to the atmosphere of hard work, discipline, and respect for excellence . . .[23]

The difficulty of deciding on the precise weight of the word 'nevertheless' in that passage produces a difficulty in identifying the social values which Wilkinson is adopting. The passage does however clearly open up the possibility of conflicting sets of values. On the one hand, the possibility exists that there might for some be a price which is too high to pay for a 'truly amazing increase in prosperity'; on the other hand, what for some appears to be a truly amazing price in terms of human suffering may be worth paying to achieve economic development.

It is instructive to compare this with the current situation in Catalonia. The Generalitat de Catalunya, Department d'Ensenyament, certainly points to the need for technical education and sees contact between the 'education system' and the 'productive system' as essential. However, the values stressed are 'the full development of the human personality', 'democratic principles', and 'the collective participation of all sectors' involved in the planning of education. It argues that: 'after the Civil War and the establishment of the dictatorship . . . the use of the Catalan language and co-education were prohibited, liberal, secular, and autonomist ideas were censored, and efforts to make quality education generally available were abandoned.'[24] Clearly the definition of quality education adopted here goes beyond mere economic prosperity, and sees as its underlying values the contributions it can make 'to dialogue, to expression and creativity both personal and collective, and to a critical vision of the world'. In that respect, there are clear similarities between Catalonia and Spain.[25]

The argument is, first, that economic success needs to be defined widely enough to accommodate the discussion of appropriate aims and values, and secondly that, as Kostecki points out, educational systems have 'multiple functions' and multiple value possibilities underlying those functions.[26]

The notion that the education system is in some simple way to be seen as the cause of economic success or failure is equally problematic.

Lowe's well-known remark about the need for 'our future masters to learn their letters' is not to be taken at face value; part of the purpose of the elementary school, it has been argued, was to ensure that the privileges of the English class system should be retained for as long as possible for Lowe and his class. However it does point to the fact that educational change often follows, and is therefore an unlikely cause of, social and economic changes.

This suggests a somewhat different hypothesis from that implied by human capital theory – *viz.* that after every significant shift in social and economic structures an attempt is made to reshape the educational system to confirm to the new ideologies. By implication the old educational system is rejected as being a part of, and even sometimes presented as being a cause of, the system which is to be replaced. In England the industrial revolution was not caused by changes in the educational system; changes in the educational system followed the wider social and economic changes in both the nineteenth and twentieth centuries. There has also been, between the 1870s and 1970s in England, a gradual process of change towards an opening up of general education (as opposed to technical education or skill training), including general education at degree level. This has followed increasing wealth, and decreasing inequalities in the spread of wealth. This same process has been apparent throughout Western Europe. It can be argued that the West German 'economic miracle' in the 1950s and 1960s developed when the school system was highly traditional, even backward. Pressure for significant change came only after the 'miracle' had generated enough wealth to make the country a contender for the first position in the European economic league table. The process has been halted in part by the oil crisis – and the consequent shift of resources away from Europe towards the major oil-producing countries. In England in the 1980s, demands for radical changes in educational policy have followed the Thatcher revolution, which has radically altered the shape of the country's institutions and its economic and social structures.

This alternative hypothesis – that educational systems do not cause, but merely respond to economic change – is no doubt an oversimplification, and it seems likely that the interaction between the education system and the development of a country's economy is more complex than it would suggest. It is, however, no more of an oversimplification than is the human-capital theory. Comparative perspectives at least warn of the danger of taking oversimplifications at face value. The purpose of comparative studies should not be to effect a simple transfer of practices from one system to another. It is to identify the functions which educational systems might serve, and to seek to understand these functions and the relationships between them. In particular, it should be concerned with the ways in which economic prosperity is to be defined, the means used to establish that prosperity, and the purposes which it is seen to serve. To illustrate this, aspects of developments in Sweden, West Germany and Japan are examined.

Sweden

Sweden offers one example of the complex relationship between definitions of vocational education and the social values which underpin them. The values underlying Swedish society, and the education which it provides, are those of social democracy. In particular there is a willingness to confront the dilemmas and contradictions implicit in the attempt to promote both freedom and equality.

Sweden in the eighties may not, as Boucher suggests, have the same degree of affluence and self-confidence as Sweden in the sixties.[27] It remains, however, an affluent country, technologically advanced and possessing political stability founded on notions of social justice, of equity, and of democracy. The fundamental values which underpin the system are significantly different from those found in Britain in the eighties.

The nine years of compulsory schooling between seven and sixteen are years of general education rather than specific vocational training. However, general education necessarily involves developing an understanding of the values on which Swedish society is based – and the notion of understanding may be deemed to include an acceptance of those values. The intention is to ensure that all pupils are equally well equipped for citizenship and for working life – *as those notions are perceived and defined in Sweden.*

During the final phase of compulsory schooling there are periods of work experience. The purpose of this is not vocational training, but a way of encouraging among pupils the ability to make informed choices, which is the characteristic of free people in a democratic society. There are two weeks in the autumn and spring terms of grade eight, and two weeks in the autumn term of grade nine. Pupils are expected to gain experience of work in the three sectors of industry, trade and office work, and education and service, and are specifically encouraged to ignore traditional gender stereotypes in their experience of work. Structurally this process is supported by the

SYO-konsulent in school, whose function is to help with the process of decision-making, and by the network of committees and parent organisations which aim to link home, school and work.

Within the overt curriculum there has in the 1980s been an increased stress on the 'basic knowledge and skills' which 'give all pupils a good start'.[28] However this, in intention at least, does not imply an acceptance of the 'back to basics movement' as it has often been interpreted in Britain and USA. The notions of equality, and choice, social justice and freedom remain crucial in the selection of curriculum content as well as in decisions about teaching method. Lgr 80 – the curriculum document which marked the transition from the romantic idealism of the sixties and seventies – in some ways offers even greater freedom of choice in the devising of 'project studies and free activities'. In one school in 1987/8 this involved teachers and pupils planning work together on: computers, drama, driving mopeds, immigration, patchwork, peace, physical education (including food and how to look after your health), tourism, traffic, typing and welding. The same emphasis on democratic values of informed choice clearly underpins the following sample of compulsory topics taken from Lgr 80: child care, communication by images, consumer economics, nature and people, people's activities – a societal perspective, people's questions about life and existence, creative activity, producing and consumption, environment and culture; all of them, including child care, metalwork and textiles, for both boys and girls.

And these values are reinforced by the hidden curriculum in which 'teachers and pupils are expected to talk to each other about what is right and wrong and to agree on the rules they are to go by. They plan their work together and they make certain decisions together. The purpose of all this is to train pupils in co-operating, deciding things together, and shouldering responsibility.'[29] Certainly that includes punctuality, reliability, and a conscientious approach to work – attitudes which are valued by all employers – but it goes far beyond any narrow view of training for a world of work which might see initiative and debate as insubordination and obstruction.

In the years after compulsory schooling, the Upper Secondary School is attended by 90 per cent of those leaving the compulsory school, not least because of the lack of employment possibilities at the age of sixteen. The Upper Secondary school was defined in terms of preparation for a range of occupations through a range of study routes. Boucher says: 'while the content was still expressed in terms of subjects, the framework was expressed in terms of occupational fields.'[30]

This is reinforced by statutory provision for the participation of employers in the work of the Upper Secondary School, at the level of planning and also at the level of providing on-the-job experience and training during the courses. These study routes are to be chosen, partly on the basis of work experience, and partly on the understanding of the structure of Swedish society which had been acquired during the years of compulsory schooling.

The element of choice leads inevitably to competition for limited places on the more popular lines, but this element of competition seems more often to be presented as an unfortunate necessity than as something valued for itself. There seems to be a much greater readiness to affirm the ideological position that the Upper Secondary School represents an attempt to assert the social equality of all occupations. This includes those occupations for which an academic preparation of this level, followed by a University course, is seen as being appropriate, and those which are seen as requiring more specialised preparation in the Upper Secondary School, such as hairdressing (a course for which there is currently intense competition) or vehicle engineering.

Clear tension exists within the Upper Secondary School system. There has been a perception of the Upper Secondary School as being predominantly vocational in its orientation. However, the practical problem of forecasting the future needs of the labour market in an advanced economy and the ideological desire to preserve as much individual freedom as possible for as long as possible both point to the need for a system which is as flexible as possible.

Two approaches to this problem are to be found in Sweden. First, there is increasingly an emphasis on the broader educational aspects of the Upper Secondary School. It is stressed that for most students a broad general education only gradually narrows down to particular occupations or particular study routes. Secondly, there is the stress on adult education, and the need to open up courses to adults, whether for professional retraining and updating or for broader educational purposes. Educational institutions, unlike most in Britain even at university level, are concerned to meet the needs of mature students, and there is a much more general recognition that it is normal to seek education throughout one's career. Adult education is treated as central, not peripheral. And Sweden remains a comparatively affluent country, willing and able to provide the money and the time without which systematic adult education is impossible.

It is not suggested that the intentions of the educational planners in

Sweden are always achieved in practice. The Swedish system, like every other, demonstrates both the inevitable gap between intention and realisation, and the ease with which it is possible to write curriculum documents and change structures, compared with the difficulty of effecting changes in the attitudes and beliefs which determine classroom practice. A teacher commented to one of the present authors: 'The main thing I know about the latest curriculum document is the colour of its cover.' There are worries that boys and girls continue to choose stereotyped sex roles, worries about differential achievements based on ethnicity, gender and class, worries about drop-outs, worries about the welfare state, worries about the level of taxation and of debt, and so on. What Sweden does offer is a clearly defined set of values and a systematic, and often surprisingly successful, attempt to follow through the practical implications of those values for the organisation and structure of the educational system; even the reservations and worries which are expressed about the system can be helpful in illustrating what these values are. There is a broad definition of technical and vocational education; there is broadly-based, democratic, control of the system involving the state and the employers; and there is an attempt to integrate the theoretical and the practical, to address both the need for immediate skills and the need for future flexibility.

Japan

The problems of deriving lessons from abroad can be further illustrated by means of a consideration of Japanese education. This provides a valuable test case since the system was quite deliberately established to help with the modernisation and development of the country's industry, a perfect illustration of human-capital theory. This was explicitly the case in the late nineteenth century, and again after the Second World War. It is equally true that the Japanese economy has been enormously successful, and its industry has been profitable and innovative (despite the implication drawn from some racist Western stereotypes).

For Prais, as has already been suggested, the competitive environment, and the attitudes and the standards in mathematics which this competition produces among average and below-average pupils, provide the basis for the later development of technical skills and the key to Japanese economic success. However, there are also opportunities for technical education at Upper Secondary level; these are seen by

Prais as important, and lead to between ten and twenty times as many people holding Japanese diplomas equivalent to the BTEC National Diplomas as there are holding those diplomas in England. The vocational upper secondary schools offer general subjects for up to half the day and specific vocational education for the rest of the time. Central for Prais's analysis is the competition between schools and the competition for entry. The result is that, even though on average those of higher ability go to general secondary schools rather than vocational secondary schools, some brighter pupils prefer a high-status vocational school to a low-status general school – hence the 'dividing lines between the two are not rigid in terms of ability'.[31]

Prais offers one explanation of economic success, but it is not the only possible explanation of what is happening in Japan. Takahashi Ohta sees one aspect of modern Japan as 'home violence, school violence, and the rejection of schooling', complains that 'a calculating and heartless society has developed among people where all must pay for getting others' help', and refers to the pressures of a 'vast restless hierarchy'. The point is also made that the Japanese system is less than totally effective in developing the resources to be found among women and ethnic minority communities.[32]

Others make less of the disadvantages of Japanese society but offer quite different explanations of its strengths. Where Prais stresses competition within the school system, Shimahara suggests that: 'The Japanese belief is culturally rooted in group orientation characterised by homogeneity and inclusiveness. It contributes to their perception that they are equal members of the group.' Shimahara links this with Holloway's finding that 'both Japanese mothers and children attributed performance largely to effort, though American mothers and children explained ability as the central factors determining performance', and with the point that in Japanese schools each pupil has a teacher whose responsibility it is to see that pupil as a whole person, and to see her/his school career as a whole.[33]

Ford argues that, for an understanding of Japan's industrial success, we should look to the organisation of industry rather than to the curriculum of schools: concepts such as 'teaching', 'training', 'curriculum' and the like do not provide the key to such an understanding. He suggests that Japan has prospered because the whole workforce of an industry is encouraged to be a part of a learning community, and again there is to be found here the stress on inclusiveness and equality, on the wholeness of the individual, rather than on exclusion and demarcation: 'Learning, like research and development, is not seen as a discrete function in Japanese organisations but as part of an integrated and human and organisational development plan.' This plan involves the whole work force: 'People are encouraged to contribute at all levels of the organisation to improving production processes. Regular incremental and participative change is an important characteristic of individual and organisational learning in Japan.'[34]

The problem with Prais, and with others who assert a simple input–process–product model, is that they take one interpretation of the system, and attempt to pre-empt any further argument by suggesting that it is the only possible explanation. However, their approach is complicated first by the difficulties of describing a system and its workings. It is difficult to see the processes as they are. This is in part because the perceptions of those seeking to describe the processes which make up the system are inevitably influenced by their own cultural preconceptions. As Ford suggests, this means that 'what people see depends on what they want to see or what they have been conditioned to see'. That can first involve misdescribing or omitting aspects of a school system. It can seriously involve assuming that schools are producing results which are arguably the result of factors outside the system of education.

One problem with mechanistic models is the problem of describing the system. The cultural preconceptions of those outsiders seeking to do so are likely to influence what they see. A related source of difficulty is that they take little account of the perceptions of those within the system. Pupils and teachers both bring a culture with them to school. This culture filters their perceptions of the processes of teaching and learning, and it is these perceptions which make the system work for them. Even the definition of the role of the teacher in school is culturally determined. In Japan the patterns of understanding which teachers, pupils, and for that matter parents and the community at large, bring to bear on making sense of what is happening in classroom, and hence on making decisions about their own responses to it, stem from a cultural tradition in which 'school is worshipped as a shrine'. Here teachers, 'regarded as saints',[35] seemingly have a higher status than in England.

It is a culture in which the notions of equality and inclusiveness which are stressed by both Ford and Shimahara are seen and reinforced by the visual contexts within which people live: 'The buildings [i.e. of the Edo period and style] discourage analysis by being at once standardised in their general characteristic and infinitely varied in details. Except under special circumstances they are all built from the same narrow repertory of materials and equipped in the same general way. The difference between the lord's house and the commoners' houses is incomparably less than it was in England. The Japanese equivalent for marble and giant Palladian order is usually a better quality of standard house materials and better workmanship.'[36] This may be contrasted with the rigid separation of architectural cultures of the Isle of Dogs in which the post-modernist technology of the centre and its 'yuppy' inhabitants is separated by a literal as well as a metaphorical wall from the decaying Victorian housing of the old working class on the periphery, and it may be compared with the often-noticed overalls worn by senior management in Japanese industry.

The result of these various factors is that even if the possibility of differences of opinion about aims and purposes is left out of account it is:

(i) Impossible to provide a description of a system which is not filtered through the preconceptions of the person who is describing it;

(ii) Impossible to be sure how the system is perceived by those within it;

(iii) Impossible to be sure about what causes what in such a complex system of interactions, and

(iv) Impossible to know how one element from one cultural context would function when transposed from the context which defines its meaning to participants to another context, in which it would be likely to be perceived in quite different ways.

It follows that much of the use to which comparative education has been put in the debate about technical education in England and Wales is misconceived and methodologically dubious.

Federal Republic of Germany

To administrators concerned with the task of developing educational provision that will best support an economy, and to researchers concerned with analysing the possible links between the two, the case of West Germany looks, at least *prima facie*, an interesting one. Certainly one of the desiderata is present, namely a successful economy exemplified by high-quality goods, high productivity, a good export record, low inflation and good labour relations. Surely here one might imagine it would be possible to set out some lessons we should learn.

Given that the economic strength of Germany has been a matter for comment and envy for more than a century (even though since World

War Two the territory denoted by common English usage of the term Germany has changed), it is however a matter of surprise that so little that is distinctively German has taken root in England. Armytage has shown that Germany has over a long period been the source of many ideas and practices which have aroused interest and favourable comment, but it is not easy to go further and demonstrate that provision of schools has been significantly or permanently altered, even in the matter of technical provision. 'Look at Germany' may have been a 'ritual incantation' in the 1860s, as Armytage points out, but the fruits of such looking were small-scale innovations in individual universities or schools.[37] The question why influence was so limited can be addressed usefully after observations have been made about the contemporary scene.

Whether or not lessons have been learned in the past, the value has been urged of looking at West Germany in the 1970s and 1980s and of learning lessons about practices to be found there. The commendation of West Germany has been made in simple terms (with the assumption that any lessons can be learned and acted on equally simply?). Two examples can illustrate the problem: one from the period of compulsory schooling, the *Schulpflicht*, and the other from the post-sixteen phase. The argument runs thus. A successful economy depends on the availability of appropriately trained manpower; the technical or vocational sector is the crucial means by which this is achieved; good achievement in such schools depends on the wide acquisition of certain skills during the period of the *Schulpflicht*, particularly in areas of the curriculum such as mathematics. A system which can deliver a widely-diffused skill in mathematics is to be commended. The claim that West Germany has superior attainment of low-ability pupils in mathematics at age thirteen has been the subject of discussion and ministerial comment in Great Britain.[38] Like most educational issues, this one is easily politicised. The schools concerned stress vocational orientation as part of the compulsory curriculum (*Arbeitslehre*), a feature the absence of which from many British schools has been much criticised. Commendation of these curricular features has been associated with commendation of the type of school, the 'Hauptschule' (ages ten to fifteen), where the majority of low-ability children obtain their schooling between the ages of ten and fifteen. Perhaps surprisingly, there has been comparatively little interest in the *Realschule* (ages ten to sixteen) even though these schools represent an area of significant dedication to technical orientation during the *Schulpflicht*. They have become increasingly popular with West German parents and, not insignificantly, represent the technical curricular thrust missing from both the former so-called tripartite system in England, and the existing comprehensive system.

If we take one of this collection of issues – superior attainment in mathematics by lower-ability pupils – we see a range of problems typical of the business of learning lessons from abroad. The analysis made by Prais and Wagner is clear enough. They draw on the data gathered by the twelve-country International Educational Attainment Survey of the 1960s (which examined the attainment of thirteen-year-olds), and on their own enquiries into the achievements of some 5,000 *Hauptschule* pupils in 1984 compared with the APU material based on representative samples of all British fifteen-to-sixteen-year-olds. Prais and Wagner conclude that there are significant differences, to the advantage of German schools, between the mathematical attainments of pupils who fall broadly into the lower half of the performance range. That mathematical attainment is a crucial prerequisite of much technical–vocational education few would wish to deny. Nor has it been denied that lower-ability German pupils demonstrate superior mathematical skills to those of their English counterparts.

Commentators are tempted to put forward unhelpful hypotheses to explain the differences in performance. It is not enough simply to assert that 'we must do better', or to imply that teachers in England do not work hard enough, or are fools, are inadequately trained, or are culturally or politically motivated to undervalue maths teaching. To attempt an analysis of levels of significance in the differing patterns of achievement, or to attempt to advance hypotheses accounting for these differences is to be reminded of the caveats made by comparativists from Sadler through Hans to such differing figures as King and Holmes: that school systems are interpretable only in terms of the culture, the conventions and legal arrangements within which they operate. Hypotheses are impossible without an intimate knowledge of such matters as forms of assessment, (e.g. that the school-leaving certificate in the Federal Republic is a group examination, unlike the English GCE/CSE – now GCSE – and that success across a range of core subjects therefore becomes very important), the ways in which young people move from school into the work place (in West Germany the possession of a school-leaving certificate is crucial for entry into many trades).

The existence of the *Hauptschule* itself is also important. Although when the IEA work was undertaken in the 1960s the majority of low-ability children in both countries were in separated schools, the

209

situation was very different in Prais and Wagner's later survey when over 80 per cent of British children were in comprehensive schools at fifteen to sixteen years old, whereas in West German little more than 3 per cent were so located. Does the culture of the relatively small, more academically homogeneous, *Hauptschule* offer a stimulus to performance, compared with the culture of many comprehensives as they have come to be organised? Does the knowledge of the demands of the post-sixteen vocational cycle, significantly different in the two systems, have any bearing? Does the significantly higher usage of class learning as distinct from individualised or group learning to be found in the German primary school (*Grundschule*, ages six to ten) offer a fruitful field for investigation? Does it matter that German children, unlike English children (at least up to 1989), follow a state-directed curriculum? How significant is the fact that all German children in *Hauptschulen* and *Realschulen* follow courses during school years nine and ten (ages fourteen to sixteen) with adult-employment-related emphasis, and including a *Praktikum*, i.e. a period in employment which is prepared for and followed up by the school course?[39] (This scheme of study parallels those of other Länder; it sets out aims for the development of self-understanding in each pupil, related to the political and economic situation of the Bundesrepublik.)

These questions necessitate a critical appraisal of any prescription for action which might be urged. But in turn they lead us to others. Even if the school structures and pedagogical styles found in West Germany were to be translated to Britain, there are no strong grounds for imagining that a specific result would follow. Again, as in the illustrations made of Sweden and Japan, we are driven to consider wider perspectives of culture, of ways in which the worlds of formal schooling and of the workplace are commonly perceived.

The questions raised above recur in the post-school German vocational system. It is easy to make contrasts between the jungle of provision in England charted by the Macfarlane Report (1981) and the reputed functionality of the German vocational system. Yet the German system is a dual one, financed, located, and controlled in and through both the public education system and private industry. It is a system of considerable complexity, deriving both from theories of technical instruction influential in the nineteenth century, and also from *ad hoc* responses to current needs. It is successfully incorporated into the apprenticeship system the 'main path of vocational education for about 60 per cent of West German youth',[40] a path which has given its followers considerable legal protection over wages and conditions, and full-time work prospects.

The complexity, the close connection with German industry, the inability of many in Britain to read material in German, and – until the remit of BTEC – the extraordinary level of divergence of practice in Britain has made it exceptionally difficult to undertake comparative work.

Towards a comparative analysis of technical and vocational education

It should be clear from the previous sections that the conditions for learning lessons from abroad need to be carefully scrutinised. It does not follow that comparative studies are valueless. They are useful first because they remind us of what King calls the unpredictability of much education policy.[41] Uncertainty might be a better term than unpredictability, since the latter term might imply a randomness in human affairs which would make it impossible ever to learn from any past experience. The notion of uncertainty calls into question input–output models of education, which suggest a mechanical relationship between certain kinds of educational policy and certain kinds of educational, or for that matter economic, outcome. Moreover, if uncertainty of this kind is a reasonable conclusion, then the claims about the supposed benefits of borrowing practices from abroad need to be studied with some scepticism. It follows also that changes of policy need constantly to be monitored so that any adjustments can be made in the light of evidence acquired about the effects of implementation. The greater the change, the greater the need for constant vigilance in monitoring them.

Secondly, a study of other educational systems can sharpen understanding of issues in our own system, if only because those systems are different and based on different assumptions and different patterns of understanding. To look at systems which make different assumptions can help to make explicit things which within our own system we take for granted.

Finally, comparative study in education draws attention to a range of policy options which might extend the debate in this country, though it necessarily adds a warning to its description of these options that they carry no guarantee of success. All the evidence is that they will have drawbacks and problems and are likely to be uncertain in their consequences in other systems.

The reasons for studying comparative education, now accepted in relation to education in general, can be seen to apply to technical and vocational education also. A series of interrelated questions about technical and vocational education can be posed to ensure that comparative enquiry exposes an appropriate range of issues:

(a) What are the aims of technical and vocational education? How do they relate to broader socio-political aims?
(b) To whom is it directed and at what stages during their career?
(c) Who controls it and funds it?
(d) Where does it happen (for example, within the mainstream of educational provision or in a separate sector) and who does the teaching?

It may be suggested that technical education aims to meet the needs of industry. True enough, but aims expressed at a high level of generality invite agreement, though implying very little in the way of content. Even a brief look, however, at the arrangements in these three countries alerts us to a number of difficulties.

West Germany, for example, appears to offer examples of good practice which might be borrowed. Yet a consideration of the arrangements which have grown up in Germany which are both culture-specific and the subject of intense debate in Germany itself, makes such an operation seem almost impossible. Nevertheless, a comparative perspective can help us to form useful hypotheses about technical education and how it relates to education in general.

If we start by defining technical education as that which provides the skills required by industry, it is clear that the content of 'technical education' will vary according to the perceptions within industry of what those skills might be. Within West Germany there are disagreements about this, and these disagreements can suggest how it might be helpful to think about educational policy in Britain. They also provide hypotheses for testing, rather than the panaceas which politicians often seek.

Braun, following Lutz, argues that there are clear differences between what he defines as firms with a professional structure and firms with a bureaucratic structure, and they perceive their training needs differently.[42] In firms with a professional structure there is flexible division of labour and minimal differentiation of status and wage. Such a firm requires in its employees a broad and adaptable understanding of principles. Such a system is like that which Ford perceives in Japan.[43] It requires a willingness to continue to learn while working, and it requires an understanding of theoretical perspectives. Such an aim for technical education implies that there will be very weak boundaries between technical education and general education.

It suggests too that the educational system should concentrate, not on inculcating skills which are likely to be out of date by the time they are taught, let alone used, but should aim instead at helping pupils to develop their abilities to think critically, with adaptability, and with self-confidence.

Experience in other systems further suggests that this model carries with it certain kinds of difficulty. The products of such a system have a wide and flexible range of skills which would be of value to many employers. Industry may fear that, if such education and training is based on a single undertaking, they may invest money in training people only to find them moving elsewhere, and their investment benefiting a competitor. The Japanese solution to protecting investment by industry in the development of flexible and professional skills in the workforce is the well-known one of lifelong loyalty of employer to employee and of employee to employer. It is suggested in Germany, therefore, that such an aim for technical education carries with it implications for financing and control, that technical education cannot be seen as merely the responsibility of a particular company, but needs to be seen as a part of the overall system of education.

The alternative model is that which is characterised as bureaucratic. Here, firms are characterised by inequalities and by 'strictly controlled pre-planned tasks'.[44] The skills required are of a low level, the training enables them to employ people to do these jobs at a relatively low rate of pay. The skills may not be easily transferred and periods of retraining – as opposed to the continuous process of learning required by the first model – may be necessary. However, since they are low-level there is likely to be little difficulty in learning new skills. The important thing is the disciplined and accurate performance of routines (something which is well trained in schools by the endless repetition of problems in traditional maths?). Training by outside agencies is barely necessary, though it may be seen by some firms as a useful way of cutting expenditure by relying on others to provide skills. Certainly any kind of theoretical understanding is seen as an unnecessary frill. These perceptions of the needs of industry provide for schools and for the education system a definition of technical education, of the ways in which it might be offered, and to whom.

The problem inherent in this model is that it does not offer the flexibility and sensitivity to the changing demands of tasks or to the changing demands of people which is needed if industry is to remain flexible. The specificity of training means that skills are quickly outdated, a fate that can befall the trainers themselves. Flexibility, and the

213

ability to innovate, are seen within this model to come only from the top. Braun suggests that it is only the 'possession of a University degree which can protect one from being tied to a job which is subordinate, badly paid and under constant disciplinary control'.

The case of Sweden is interesting, not least because it has declined over the past decade as a source of practices to be commended in England and Wales. Yet Sweden shows us an economy which has enjoyed massive growth, linked to a social-democratic philosophy. This economy is fed by talent developed in a state-led, comprehensive, educational system which promotes values of non-competitiveness and social equality. Both the nine-year comprehensive school and the post-sixteen institutions appear to promote choice, understanding and social cohesiveness – values which appear to relate well to the professional model expounded by Braun. The very existence and success of such a system reminds us of the range of choices open to us as a nation, and that there are alternatives worth examining.

In the task of attempting to see how Britain might learn lessons from, say, Germany and Japan, it is possible to take a less than despairing stance. Provided that an awareness exists of the historical and cultural features that make systems unique, it is possible to examine features and postulate their likely usefulness in Britain. An example is the question of skill training. If Ford's analysis of skill training in Japan is accepted, and set alongside that made by Braun of the professional model in Germany, then the structures and attitudes that lead to continued learning in such professionally orientated firms becomes worth study. They lead us towards answers to questions (b), (c), and (d) above: the answers to the questions 'When?', 'To whom?' and 'Where?' appear to be 'always', 'to everyone', and 'institutions where there is the least possible demarcation between firm and training establishment, and the least possible demarcation between general education and technical education'. Those answers carry with them clear implications for financing and control. It is this professional definition of skill training, in Ford's view of Japan, and in Braun's view of Germany, which affects the whole system and which produces the ability to innovate and adapt. Prais suggested that there was no point in asking industry in Britain to change until English schools became more like the picture of the Japanese educational system which he presents.[45] Perhaps the opposite is the case. There is no point in asking the English educational system to change unless and until attitudes in industry move towards a more professional model of training. Education will, once again, respond to, rather than initiate, change.

Notes

1 M. Wiener, *English Culture and the Decline of the Industrial Spirit*, Cambridge University Press, Cambridge, 1981.
2 Department of Education and Science (DES), *Education in the Federal Republic of Germany: Aspects of Curriculum and Assessment*, HMSO, 1986.
3 DES, *Mathematics for Ages 5–16*, HMSO, 1989.
4 H. J. Noah and M. A. Eckstein, *Towards a Science of Comparative Education*, Macmillan, London, 1969, ch. 1.
5 M. Argles, *South Kensington to Robbins: An Account of English Technical and Scientific Education since 1951*, Longman, London, 1964.
6 D. Reeder, 'A recurring debate: education and industry', in G. Bernbaum (ed.), *Schooling in Decline*, Macmillan, London, 1979.
7 J. H. Higginson, 'The centenary of an English pioneer in comparative education: Sir Michael Sadler, 1861–1943', *International Review of Education*, 7, 1961–2, pp. 291–2.
8 N. Hans, *Comparative Education*, Routledge & Kegan Paul, London, 1949.
9 I. Fagerlind and L. Saha, *Education and National Development: A Comparative Perspective*, Pergamon, London, 1983.
10 Noah and Eckstein, *Towards a Science*, ch. 5.
11 B. Holmes, *Comparative Education: Some Considerations of Method*, Allen & Unwin, London, 1981.
12 Wiener, *English Culture*.
13 J. Twining *et al.*, (eds.), *World Yearbook of Education, 1987: Vocational Education*, Kogan Page, London, 1987, p. 15.
14 E. J. King, *Education and Social Change*, Pergamon, London, 1966, p. 132.
15 *Guardian*, 11 August 1988.
16 *Times Educational Supplement*, 25 December 1987 and 8 January 1988.
17 S. J. Prais, 'Education for productivity: comparisons of Japanese and English schooling and vocational preparation', *Compare*, 16, No. 2, 1986, p. 121.
18 *Ibid.*, p. 131.
19 Fagerlind and Saha, *Education and National Development*, p. 18.
20 Holmes, *Comparative Education*, p. 134.
21 Adapted from D. S. Landes, *The Unbound Prometheus: Technological Change and Industrial Development in Western Europe from 1750 to the Present*, Cambridge University Press, Cambridge, 1969, p. 340.
22 J. Twining *et al.* (eds.), *World Yearbook of Education 1987*, pp. 196–7.
23 M. Wilkinson, *Lessons from Europe*, Centre for Policy Studies, London, 1978, p. 33.
24 Generalitat de Catalunya Department d'Enseyament, *Education in Catalonia*, Generalitat de Catalunya, 1987, pp. 14, 4.
25 J. M. Jauma, 'To teach what culture?', *El Desenvolupament Professional del Enseyants en una Societat encanyi*, 13th Conference of Association for Teacher Education in Europe, 1988.
26 M. Kostecki, 'The economic functions of schooling', *Compare,* 15, No. 1, 1985, pp. 16–17.
27 L. Boucher, *Tradition and Change in Swedish Education*, Pergamon, London,

1982, pp. 194–5.

28 Swedish Board of Education, *Curriculum Outlines for Comprehensive Schools (Lgr)*, Stockholm, 1980, p. 15.

29 Swedish Immigration Board, *Sweden: A General Introduction for Immigrants*, 1987, p. 87.

30 Boucher, *Tradition and Change*, p. 105.

31 Prais, *Schooling Standards*, p. 133.

32 T. Ohta, 'Problems and perspectives in Japanese education', *Comparative Education*, 22, No. 1, 1986, pp. 27–8.

33 N. K. Shimahara, 'The cultural basis of student achievement in Japan', *Comparative Education*, 22, No. 1, 1986, pp. 22–3.

34 J. Twining *et al.*, *World Yearbook of Education*, 1987, pp. 265–71.

35 T. Ohta, 'Problems and perspectives', p. 28.

36 R. T. Paine and A. Soper, *The Art and Architecture of Japan*, Penguin, London, 1955, p. 265.

37 W. H. G. Armytage, *The German Influence on English Education*, Routledge & Kegan Paul, 1969.

38 S. J. Prais and K. Wagner, *Schooling Standards in Britain and Germany: Some Summary Comparisons on Economic Efficiency*, National Institute of Economic and Social Research, London, 1983, and *Compare*, 16, No. 1, 1986.

39 Schleswig-Holstein, Kultuministerium, *Lehrplan fur Wirtschaft-Politik (Realschule)*, 1981.

40 K. Schober, 'The educational system, vocational training and youth unemployment in West Germany', *Compare*, 14, No. 2, 1984, p. 141.

41 E. J. King, 'Notes and comments', *Comparative Education*, 23, No. 2, 1987, pp. 119–22.

42 F. Braun, 'Vocational training as a link between schools and the labour market: the dual system in the Federal Republic of Germany', *Comparative Education*, 23, No. 2, 1987, pp. 130–2.

43 B. Ford, 'A learning society: Japan through Australian eyes', in J. Twining *et al.*, *World Yearbook of Education, 1987*.

44 Braun, 'Vocational training', p. 132.

45 Prais, 'Education for productivity', p. 140.

Index

employers, 13–16, 153–67
employment, 145–67
  statistics for graduates, 149
endowed schools, 55–6, 62, 65–6
engineering, 1, 19–33
  armaments, 20, 30
  in Coventry, 37–53
  education in, 124–7
  graduates, 156–7
  institutions, 129–32, 134–5, 138, 141
  locomotive, 20
  marine, 20
  status of, 138–9
enterprise culture, 180
Enterprise in Higher Education scheme, 12, 162, 167
Erickson, Charlotte, 121
European Community, 192
Evans, Eric, 1–18
evening classes, 46, 57, 111
expansion of education, 194, 200
expectations of higher education, 147–8, 152, 166–7
expenditure, 195
  on higher education, 152

Fagerlind, I., 195
Fairfield Road School, Bristol, 67, 68
Federation of British Industries, 122, 132, 139, 141
Finniston Report, 139, 156–7
Fisher, H. A. L., 106
Ford, B., 205, 206, 214
France, 11, 31, 68, 104, 112, 138, 146, 196
Friedman, A., 43
Fulton, Oliver, 145–67, 171, 177
funding
  of education, 8–9, 72–3, 114–15, 116
  of higher education, 145, 159–60, 167
  of TVEI, 172–3, 178–80, 182, 183
further education, 12, 56, 89–90, 102, 116
  see also higher education;

polytechnics, technical colleges; universities

Garbett, Jim, 189–214
Gateway School, Leicester, 109
GCSE, 173, 185
GEC, 38, 44
George Dixon School, Birmingham, 67, 68
Germany, 1, 7, 11, 13, 16, 28, 31, 68, 104, 105, 112, 122, 138, 146, 158, 191, 193, 196, 198, 200, 207–11, 212, 213
Gorbatt, D., 175
government policy and influence, 171–87 see also Conservative Party
graduate inadequacy, 162
graduate supply, 148–60
grammar schools, 63, 66 see also endowed schools
Grant Related In-Service Training, 178
'Great Depression', 6–7, 28
Greenwich Park Central School, 85
'Guide to Employment for Boys and Girls', 86, 91

Hadow Report, 84, 89, 91, 108, 109
Hankey Committee, 121
Hanley Technical Secondary School, 70–1
Hans, N., 194, 195, 209
Harland, Janet, 178–9, 180
Harrod, Frank, 42
Herbert, Alfred (company), 38, 40, 41, 49, 52
higher education, 145–67
  expectations of, 147–8, 152, 166–7
  expenditure on, 152
  and politics, 166–7
  quality of, 163–5
  see also further education; universities
Higher Elementary School Minute, 1900, 10
higher grade schools, 57–64, 78, 98,